The Operations of Chinese Infrastructure Multinationals in Africa

Yuxuan Tang

The Operations of Chinese Infrastructure Multinationals in Africa

Mediating Two Development Processes

palgrave
macmillan

projects.Secondly, the analysis argues that in the operations of these firms, Africa can be seen as mediating between important facets of two differently-phased development processes. Thus the study provides two key groups of findings from its empirical study on the determinants and motivations of location choice of two representative ICT firms in Africa, and case studies to overview the whole process of China's infrastructure investment in Africa and how Chinese IMNEs involve themselves in. The case study is based on semi-structured interviews of the companies (both ICT and construction) and other participants of infrastructure provision in two differentiated countries—South Africa and Mozambique.

Contents

Abbreviations

BOT	Build-Operate-Transfer
CADF	China–Africa Development Fund
CDB	China Development Bank
CSA-D	Developmental Country Specific Advantages
CSA-I	Institutional Country Specific Advantages
EXIM Bank	Export-Import Bank
FDI	Foreign Direct Investment
FOCAC	Forum on China–Africa Cooperation
FSA-A	Asset Firm Specific Advantages
FSA-R	Relational Firm Specific Advantages
IMF	International Monetary Fund
IMNE	Infrastructure Multinational Enterprises
IMNEsp	Sponsor IMNE
IMNEsu	Subcontractor IMNE
IP	Infrastructure Project
LOF	Liability of Foreignness
MNE	Multinational Enterprise
MOFCOM/MoC	Ministry of Commerce
NDRC	National Development and Reform Commission
ODA	Official Development Assistance
OECD	Office of Economic Co-operation and Development
OFDI	Outward Foreign Direct Investment
PBC	People's Bank of China

SAFE	State Administration for Foreign Exchange
SASAC	State Asset Supervision and Administration Commission
SOE	State-Owned Enterprise
UN	United Nations

List of Figures

List of Tables

1

Introduction of Study

1.1 Introduction

A notable phenomenon leading to a number of discussions in both international business and political economy is the crucial rising role of the People's Republic of China in the economic development of Africa. Three factors underpin this exponential growth between Chinese/African development tie: (1) the abundance of resources across Africa meets the requirement of supportive resources in China; (2) the market opportunities for Chinese firm global expansion; and (3) the need for infrastructure development across all African regions.

Africa has risen as one of the important destinations of Chinese enterprises' overseas investment since the establishment of the China Africa Cooperation Forum in 2000, China's OFDI in Africa investment stock has grown dozens of times, from less than US$ 500 million in 2003 to over US$ 46 billion by the end of 2018, while the flows of China's investment in African countries have maintained an upward trend with slight fluctuation. Under the negative environment of de-globalisation, the diversification of increasing needs of Africa widens another path for China to achieve its global investment improvement. From the

Y. Tang, *The Operations of Chinese Infrastructure Multinationals in Africa*,
https://doi.org/10.1007/978-981-16-2562-6_1

perspective of China's OFDI, quality improvement of investment in Africa becomes the goal in concert with domestic requirement of high quality development. From the side of Africa, the key to Africa's development is industrialisation, which is based on the continuous completion of infrastructure. It is also a key and priority area for China's cooperation with Africa. The latest Beijing summit of China Africa Cooperation forum (2018) pointed out that the China-African cooperation needs to focus on improvement of long term sustainability and net value of investment.

Infrastructure construction is not only an urgent need for Africa's economic take-off and structural transformation, but also the strength and experience of China. China's participation in Africa's infrastructure construction began with assistance to Africa. At present, it mainly focuses on project contracting, at US$ 56 billion new contract in 2019. China's funds, equipment and technology have effectively reduced the construction costs of African countries, and gradually improved the current situation of weak infrastructure in Africa, which restricts development. However, it also faces the problems of small proportion of direct investment and low project sustainability.

In 2012, the African Union adopted the African infrastructure development plan (PIDA), which proposed a series of livelihood infrastructure projects covering four major areas of transportation, power, ICT and cross-border water resources, with a total investment of US$ 360 billion. The latest statistics of the African Development Bank (AfDB) shows the annual capital demand for infrastructure construction in Africa is approximately US$130 billion to US$ 170 billion, the actual investment is only about US$ 93 billion, and there is a funding gap of US$ 68 billion to US$ 108 billion. African countries attach great importance to infrastructure construction, which makes the field present a strong demand for funds and huge investment space. Consequently, African countries have widely introduced private sector investment in the field of infrastructure. Such investment will also become an important way for Chinese firms to participate in and support infrastructure construction more commercially in Africa.

As one of the most important players, Chinese infrastructure multinational corporations are generally considered as emerging investors, which to some extent is disregarding China's early engagement in the infrastructure sector of Africa. The booming of China's infrastructure investment in Africa has constantly accounted for the larger part of China's involvement in Africa. Infrastructure forms a fundamental part of development, so that increasing investment in this field is considered to be the priority for developing countries (WIR, 2008). With the evolution of policies, changing roles of actors and approaches of financing, infrastructure investment has been diversified from predominantly being politically tied to natural resources to being increasingly motivated commercially. Infrastructure multinationals have become the one of the major players involved in the investment in infrastructure creation and provision in host countries, e.g. contracting in infrastructure projects, building up and/or maintaining infrastructure facilities and networks, etc. Differently from firms in other industries, infrastructure multinationals are seldom involved in operating of infrastructure.

According to World Bank's definition,[1] infrastructure includes activities in the energy (e.g. electricity, power plant), information and communication technologies (ICT), water, and transport sectors. Infrastructure is not only a simple sum of individual sectors; it also involves multi-functions to address modern developmental challenges. In the long-term international concern with responsibilities for infrastructure provision, those sectors are now provided through the involvement of private participants, with agreement on shared objectives for delivery and implementation of public infrastructure and its services. In the context of this study, energy, water and transport are defined in general as *Construction sectors*, due to the its provision of basic necessities of the development functions, while *ICT* as an individual sector acts as a driving force of modernisation and acceleration of economic growth (UNCTAD, 2011).

Under the encouragement of the 'going abroad' policy, Chinese infrastructure firms are highly motivated to conduct investments that benefit both economic and political objectives. Therefore, there are two strategic drivers of Chinese infrastructure firms in Africa. They are pursuing country-level political objectives through official development assistance

[1] Foster, Vivien; Briceno-Garmendia, Cecilia (2010). Africa's Infrastructure: A Time for Transformation: A Time for Transformation. Africa Development Forum. World Bank. Available from http://hdl.handle.net/10986/2692.

involved in economic development and often controlled by bilateral governments, which adds new perspectives in analysing the contexts in which this type of new MNE operates.

1.2 Why Focus on Infrastructure Investment and Infrastructure Multinationals?

China's OFDI in Africa is mainly driven in two vital directions—infrastructure and natural resource exploitation, which are normally dominated by SOEs or collective enterprises. The investment in infrastructure sectors in Africa has traditionally been dominated by European companies and normally based on ODA. Nowadays, Chinese companies have become active in almost every infrastructure sector. To examine the factors driving China's infrastructure investment and motivation, the competitiveness and strategies of these infrastructure related companies, and the Chinese government's efforts to build and nurture political relationships with Africa, all need to be addressed.

On the national-level perspective, China's role in infrastructure investment in the region can be understood by looking at the evident economic complementarities. Africa counts among its development challenges a major infrastructure deficit. China has developed one of the world's largest and most competitive construction industries, with particular expertise in the civil works critical for infrastructure development. China's fast-growing manufacturing economy is generating demand for oil and mineral inputs that has rapidly outstripped domestic resources. Africa is already a major natural resource exporter, and with enhanced infrastructure it could develop this potential even further, accelerating economic development in the region.

On the strategic firm-level context, in terms of sectors that can feed positively into early stages of development more widely, we can see that such enterprise-level competences can be significant elements of China's African involvement, from construction of very basic transport infrastructure through to creation of ICT networks which then lay the foundation of future expansion in ICT markets. With complicated aims on investment, Chinese infrastructure MNEs would have multidimensional strategies on dealing with host markets.

The key issue of the study is to understand and evaluate such Chinese infrastructure enterprises, the research will focus on studying the firms that do it; i.e. emergent Infrastructure Multinational Enterprises (IMNEs) from China. Three important issues can be discerned: To what extent do they pursue 'national-policy' aims and do so with Government support, and when do they seek normal competitive objectives with their own capabilities? Is there a generalised framework to explain the strategic combination of Chinese IMNEs toward African markets?

1.2.1 Strategic Nexus of China's Operation in Africa

What are the correlations of two major potentially policy-driven sectors of natural resource 'exploitation' and infrastructure creation, and with the more technology-driven sector of ICT (where firm-level strengths may be more decisive)? To what extent are Chinese infrastructure MNEs in Africa part of a wider political implication for African-Chinese Alliances?

1.2.2 Framework of Infrastructure MNEs' Strategies in Developing Markets

How do Chinese infrastructure MNEs organise their strategies through the steps of infrastructure investment? How do they achieve their objectives through taking advantages of home- and host- countries institutions?

1.3 Theoretical Contributions

The book is devoted to make various contributions to the existing literatures. Under mainstream theories and the expanding literatures on OFDI from emerging markets, the internationalisation of Chinese MNEs will involve strong institutions and an evolving purpose of both country- and firm- level considerations. Different from traditional multinationals and FDI, infrastructure MNEs derive from the infrastructure projects which are generated by host countries' governments. Infrastructure itself is a key element for potential investment and development processes. Many

Africa and Mozambique, and both governments' institutions. Within the qualitative analysis, Chap. 6 also applies the quantitative data collection and analysis focused on two Chinese telecommunication companies' location-decision timing in 40 African countries and their macro-level data over eight years. The limitation of the data is the criteria of entering time. The data is coming from the local newspaper or reports and companies' websites' reports. Thus, the data will be used for the panel probit model in order to find out what factors of host countries determine the companies' location decision.

Chapter 5 begins with an attempt to formalise the broad concept of infrastructure MNEs based on the modes of IB analysis and applies aspects, of this to the discussion of Chinese FDI in the construction and ICT sectors in Africa. Chinese infrastructure MNEs expanding into Africa are serving to mediate between the needs and potentials of two differently-based and differently-phased processes of economic development. At the macro-level Chinese economic growth has generated notable surpluses of capital and foreign exchange, which are being leveraged to support, inter alia, the internationalisation of Chinese business. But aspects of this international expansion target policy objectives that have specific roots in the sustainability of China's own growth and development. A very significant and familiar component of this is shortages of the energy and raw materials needed to secure continued industrial growth as a core of China's development.

Chapter 6 analyses the determinants and motivations of investment in ICT sectors in terms of two Chinese MNEs. Using the Panel Probit model, the analysis relies on correlates of the digging firm-level data from relative data resources and then country-level factors and institutional indicators on determinants of investments. This chapter evaluates the influences on location choices by general country-level factors as the objective determinants and sectoral conditions as the subjective motivations in specific sectors. It thus provides a fundamental and complementary analysis for the latter case-study chapter.

Chapter 7 draws a comprehensive wide-range picture of performance of Chinese MNEs in infrastructure-related investment. It provides exploratory work based on propositions regarding the internationalisation processes of Chinese infrastructure MNEs and their developmental implications. The first part is country-level view: bilateral needs started the motivation of investment; bargaining process between countries will enhance the future investment; how home and host countries (host countries location-advantage differences) influence the focusing firms. The second part is firm-level view. It compares firms from two perspectives: the comparison of telecommunication and construction (sectors) in different countries, and the influences of ownership structures on the investment of these firms.

Chapter 8 draws together the key concepts and arguments. It concludes that the central theme will be to demonstrate how careful and case-specific application of extensions of existing frameworks and analytical constructs can secure important understandings of vital real-world issues. Thus it applies the comprehensive understanding of IB theories with an overview of how and why Chinese IMNEs have asserted a significant participation in African development to allow for an informed evaluation of the implications of this interface.

Appendix: Example of Involvement of Chinese Firms in African Infrastructure

Sector		Main activities	Participating Chinese MNEs
Construction	Energy (power)	Power plant, the electrification of rural areas, National Electricity transfer line, hydroelectric dam	CWE,[a] CMEC,[b] CWHE[c]
	Water	Water supply system, water treatment plant, water distribution system	CAMC,[d] Beijing Construction Engineering Group, CGC,[e] CCECC
	Transport	Construction of railway, ports, bridges	Shanghai Construction Group, China Railway Group Co., Ltd, JIETDC,[f] CREGC,[g] CCECC,[h] CRBC[i]
ICT		Internet broadband, telephone lines, mobile and fixed networks, GSM mobile system	Huawei, ZTE, ASB[j]

Source: FOCAC, Foster et al. (2008), reorganised by author
[a]China International Water & Electric Corp.
[b]China National Machinery & Equipment Import & Export Corp.
[c]China National Water Resources and Hydro power Engineering Corp.
[d]China National Construction & Agricultural Machinery Imp./Exp. Corporation
[e]China Geo-Engineering Corporation
[f]Jilin Province International Economy & Trade Development Corporation
[g]China Railway Engineering Group Co. Ltd
[h]China Civil Engineering Construction Company
[i]China Road and Bridge Corporation
[j]Alcatel Shanghai Bell

Bibliography

Alden, C., & Davies, M. (2006, Summer/Autumn). A profile of the operations of Chinese Multinationals in Africa. *South African Journal of International Affairs, 13*(1). (original version: Chinese Multinational Corporations in Africa, Offshore Oil, Issue: 3–4, 1–11, Africa Institute of South Africa).

Boisot, M. (2004). Notes on the internationalization of Chinese firms. Unpublished paper, Open University of Catalonia, Barcelona, Spain.

Buckley, P., Clegg, J., Cross, A., Liu, X., Voss, H., & Zheng, P. (2007). The determinants of Chinese outward foreign direct investment. *Journal of International Business Studies, 38*(4), 499–518.

Child, J., & Rodrigues, S. B. (2005). The internationalization of Chinese firms: A case for theoretical extension? *Management and Organization Review, 1*(3), 381–410.

Deng, P. (2004, May–June). Outward investment by Chinese MNCs: Motivations and implications. *Business Horizons, 47*(3), 8–16.

Foster, V., Butterfield, W., Chen, C., & Pushak, N. (2008). *Building bridges: China's growing role as infrastructure financier in Africa*. Public Private Infrastructure Advisory Facility, Trends and Policy Options, No. 5. World Bank, Washington.

Hong, E., & Sun, L. (2006). Dynamics of internationalization and outward investment: Chinese corporations' strategies. *The China Quarterly, 187*, 610–633.
Ramamurti, R., & Doh, J. P. (2004). Rethinking foreign infrastructure investment in developing countries. *Journal of World Business., 39*(2), 151–167.
Rugman, A., & Li, J. (2007). Will China's multinationals succeed globally or regionally? *European Management Journal, 25*(5), 333–343.
UNCTAD (2008). Measuring the Impacts of ICT for Development, avalible from https://unctad.org/system/files/official-document/dtlstict2011d1_en.pdf

2

Background of Chinese Outward FDI and Chinese MNEs in African Countries

2.1 Introduction

Wide attention on expansion of China's footprint in Africa has been attracted from both academic and policy research. The intensity of the debate has not always been proportional to the actual extent of China's activities on the continent. Besides trade, investment and aid make up three main components of China's economic involvement in Africa. Relying on the official data, a considerable positive trend has been shown in Chinese outward investment to Africa over recent decades, although it still represents a small portion of China's total FDI stock. Reviews of the last decades suggest, however, that China's investments in Africa have increasingly diversified into different fields with immense and long-term profitability ambitions. It is accompanied by a clear governmental policy support of commercial ventures, abundant financing and tax benefits and robust diplomacy. This chapter reviews general perspectives on China's involvement in Africa from policy-, total FDI, firm structure- and development- levels.

Y. Tang, *The Operations of Chinese Infrastructure Multinationals in Africa*,
https://doi.org/10.1007/978-981-16-2562-6_2

2.2 Overview of Chinese Outward FDI in Africa

China's outward investment flow in Africa grew by 71% and reached $4.1 billion by 2017. Meanwhile, it involved not only expanding in traditional industries but also into agriculture, manufacturing and tourism. The number of Chinese enterprises operating or being registered to do business, in Africa has increased to approximately 3700, involving sectors of manufacturing, natural resource development, transportation, agriculture and agricultural production.[1] The increasing involvement of private enterprises has diversified China's FDI in Africa. In reference to the annual data of the Ministry of Commerce (www.fdi.gov.cn), China's investments in Africa have grown significantly since 2000 when the Forum of China-Africa Cooperation (FOCAC) was set up. A rapid increase of China's FDI outflows to Africa as a whole from 2003 to 2008 meant that there was a greater potential market for further involvement of Chinese Multinationals. Although the flows started to drop considerably in 2009 owing to global economic recession and recovered afterwards, the FDI stock in Africa kept significant increasing and reached over US$ 46.1 billion by the end of 2018 (Fig. 2.1).[2] This accounted for 4.6% of China's total outward FDI stock and 3.8% of total outflows in 2018 (MOFCOM, 2019). It is worth emphasising that China's FDI in Africa grows at a high speed with small percentage of occupation of China total outward FDI are a result of the low level of investments and simplification of motivation in Africa in the early years.

Bilateral trade between China and Africa has risen dramatically since 2000 and reached total volume of USD 204.2 billion in 2018, that keeps as the largest trading partner for a decade. With long-term expansion in Africa's permanent capacity, in parallel with the deepening trade relationship supported by preferential policies of the Chinese government, has led to foreign investment by Chinese companies in Africa has increasing substantially. By the end of 2018, Chinese

[1] The Ministry of Commerce of China established a data system for outward FDI (OFDI). Therefore, reliable and comparable data on Chinese OFDI statistics are available from 2003 onwards.

[2] 2019 Bulletin of Chinese outward FDI is a comprehensive and annual report on statistical data of Chinese outward FDI.

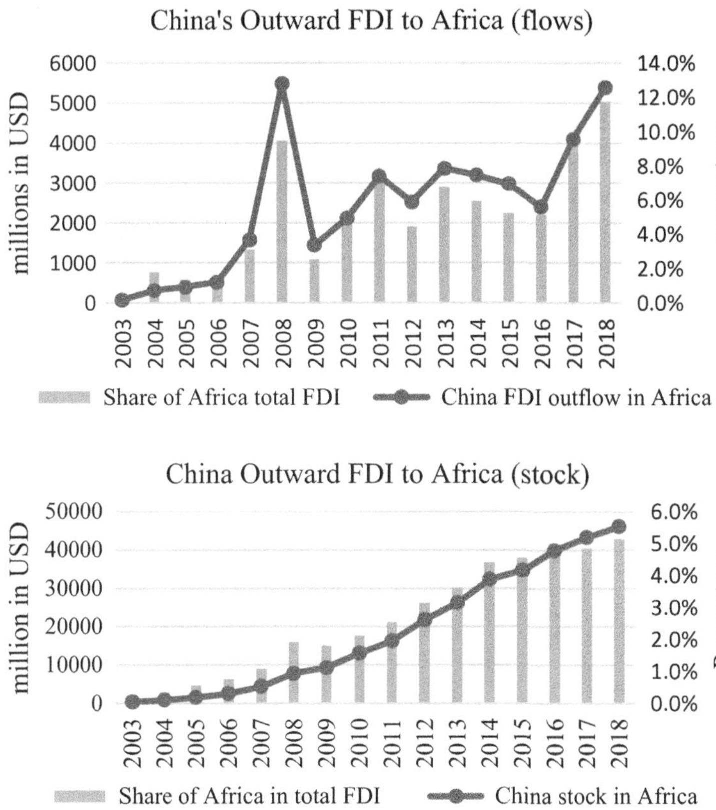

Fig. 2.1 China's outward FDI in Africa. (Source: 2019 bulletin of Chinese outward FDI; UNCTAD statistic)

companies have covered 52 African countries with 86.7% area of the continent (FOCAC, 2018) and becomes a new popular destination of Chinese multinationals (MOFCOM, 2018).

In terms of the industry composition, China's FDI in Africa is mainly accounted for by these major industries—natural resources, traditional infrastructure and gradually rising telecommunication. Accordingly, available information indicates a high share of FDI in oil industries, driven by the resources-seeking target of Chinese oil and mining companies. However, it would be a mistake to simply conclude that Africa is merely a host to FDI in the oil and natural resources sectors. Increasingly, projects in other industries including telecom, electricity, physical

(Brautigam, 2011). Thirdly, drawing from its own experience, China has invested US$250 million in infrastructure in six industrial parks as planned in Zambia, Mauritius, Nigeria, Egypt and Ethiopia. It is reported that the industrial park in Zambia, as the first such one invested in by China overseas, has utilised US$600 million and created over 6000 local jobs.

2.3.2 The Demand-Side

Fulfilling the Requirements of China on Natural Resources

By 2018, China's imports from Africa reached USD 203.9 billion. Most of them came from Sub-Saharan Africa and more than 80% are accounted for by oil and other natural resources. Thus 30% of China's oil imports depended on Africa (Foster et al., 2008). With the intensified economic dependence on infrastructure, Chinese oil companies have obtained exploration rights to those cooperating countries, including Angola, the Republic of Congo, Côte d'Ivoire, Ethiopia, Gabon, Kenya, Mali, Mauritania, Nigeria, Sudan, etc. (Foster et al., 2008).

Accelerating Optimisation of Industrial Structure

Due to the goals of industrial restructuring makes a series of industrial transformation strategies. The cooperation with Africa speed up the optimisation of China's economic structure through industry sector transfer. China's resource intensive industries and labour-intensive industries have relatively lost the previous advantages for China's development. However, the African continent has become an important choice for those industries. In various ways, China's direct investment in Africa is also more advantageous than direct material and financial assistance.

Meeting the Development Needs of Africa on Infrastructure

Booming Chinese investment in Africa is not just one-way thinking from the Chinese side. From the demand-side perspective, the level of infrastructure determines the absorptive capacity of Africa. Africa retains low level of absorptive capacity that impedes the effective FDI inflows, on the one hand. Hence, first, as a programme of foreign assistance, China's infrastructure investment promotes absorptive capacity of African countries. Second, since Africa is a vital source of natural resources for China, infrastructure investment improves the availability of access to natural resources exploitation. On the other hand, the gap of local infrastructure provision gives these countries opportunities to attract infrastructure FDI. The general features are impacting on Chinese business. In construction and ICT services sectors, normally offering low-cost technology and bringing skilled workers who are willing to work in difficult environments; most companies are able to provide end-to-end solutions combining transportation, energy generation, resources extraction and refining; Chinese investors have access to long term capital owing to Chinese government supportive policy.

2.3.3 Bilateral Investment Treaties

Investors in most African countries are facing risks that go beyond ordinary market risk. In poor, high-risk environments FDI is likely to be a major source of investment funds. Thus, host country governments work to attract FDI. They offer incentives to MNEs designed to attract FDI from competing countries and seek to offset potential risk factors that might deter investment. China also promotes its economic interest in Africa by concluding bilateral investment treaties. By 2010, China had concluded bilateral investment treaties (BITs) with 33 African countries (see Fig. 2.4) and double taxation treaties with four African countries to protect and promote FDI to Africa, and to create a more secure investment climate for Chinese investors in the continent. In this way, the Chinese government offers Chinese enterprises an opportunity to pull themselves up through participation in projects in Africa.

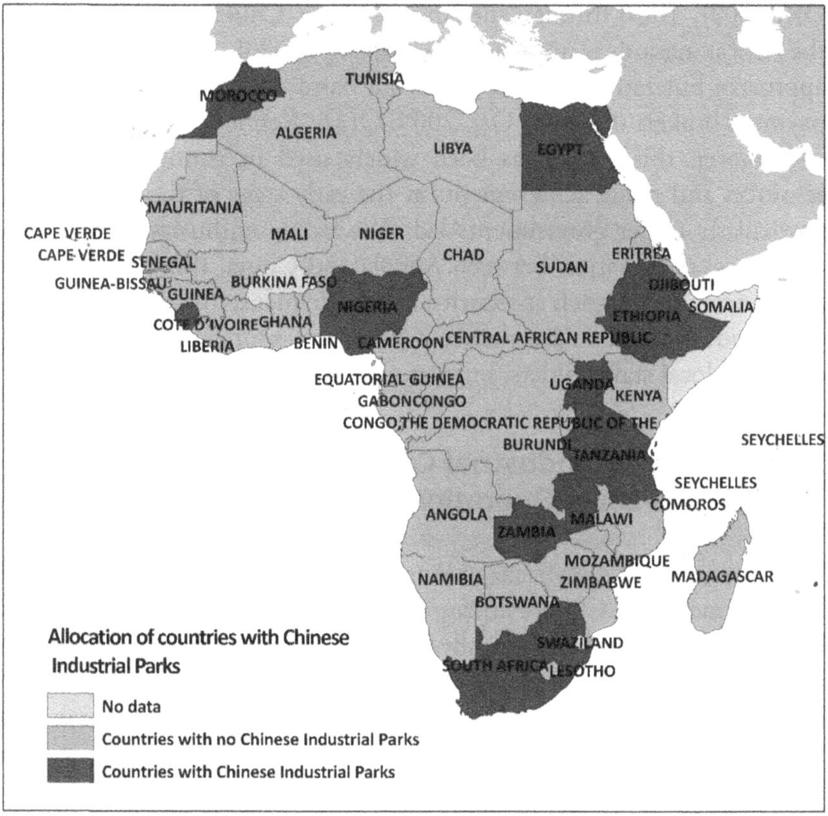

Fig. 2.6 The allocation of Chinese Industrial Parks in Africa

developing and the industrial cooperation zone itself is 'spillover' infrastructure investment. Involving the construction of the park provides a guarantee of infrastructure for enterprises to form supporting capacity for local production, and creates production and operation chain with local market for the rapid improvement of the international competitiveness of the relevant industries in the host country. As an investment mode of 'Going global' of Chinese enterprises cluster, the overseas economic and trade cooperation zone itself is developing constantly to offset the risks of the external environment and strengthen the comparative advantages of firms. The existing industrial cooperation zone mainly has three formats. The first is to exploit the local capacity of the host country to develop and utilise resources. The second is to transfer the production of Chinese traditional advantageous industries, which forms complementary advantages with relatively low local labour resources, in order to internalise the different advantages of Chinese firms within the industrial parks. The third is to form coordination and explore new industrial fields. Both sides use the platform of the cooperation zone to gather capital, talents, technology and other production factors to promote industrial development (Table 2.1).

2.4.4 Aid-Based Cooperation (Project-Government)

The most traditional financial flows with Chinese firm participations into infrastructure sector is through aid-based cooperation projects, which targets to individual contracting project in recipient countries. By the end of 2015, China has carried out engineering contracting projects in 53 countries or regions in Africa, with an investment coverage rate of 88%. The contracts of projects are signed as inclusive part of bilateral government aid documents. On behalf of the government, Chinese construction companies undertake all or most part of the survey, design and construction process of the project. The equipment and building materials are provided by the Chinese suppliers, and the engineering technicians are dispatched by the Chinese government or guided by Chinese organisation. The project is handed over to the recipient country after completion.

To ensure the quality of the construction of projects, the selections of Chinese construction enterprises are according to the 'Measures for the qualification of enterprises implementing foreign aid projects' designed by the Ministry of Commerce.[5] The ability of overseas operation qualification of firms is investigated through the audit process, the construction

---

[5] Ministry of Commerce. Measures for the qualification of enterprises implementing foreign aid projects (for Trial Implementation). EB/01. www.mofcom.gov.cn/article/b/c/201510/20151001151458.shtml, 2015-10-29.

Table 2.1 List of overseas economic cooperation zones in Africa

Name	Country	Founded year	Number of companies	Industries covered
China-Egypt TEDA Sues ETCZ	Egypt	2008	77	Building materials, petroleum equipment, manufacturing
Ethiopian Eastern Industrial Park	Ethiopia	2007	100	Automotive assembly, textile, metal processing
Zambia-China ETCZ	Zambia	2007	62	Mining, metal processing, trade logistics, free trade
Lekki free zone	Nigeria	2006	141	Trade logistics product processing manufacturing
Djibouti FTZ	Djibouti	2018	60	Logistics, commerce, electronic appliance, equipment manufacturing
China-Uganda Agriculture ETCZ	Uganda	2014	6	Industrial chain
Mautitius Jinfei ETCZ	Mauritius	2006	40	Tourism, financial business
Sierra Leone TZ	Sierra Leone	2003	17	Processing manufacturing, production commodity exhibition
Hisense SA Industrial Park	South Africa	2013	7	Home appliance
	Tanzania	2014	4	Scientific research, mining and mineral processing, mechanical equipment processing, logistics trade
Jiangsu-shinyanaga agricultural industrial zone	Tanzania	2013	4	Cotton industry chain
China National Building material Zambia industrial Park	Zambia	2015	1	Water hear power generation, high-tech materials
Morocco Mohammed VI tangier Tech City	Morocco	2019		Logistics trade, financial centre, industries covered

Source: Data collected and sorted from MOFCOM by author

capacity, environmental management, enterprise reputation. The Chinese side conduct the strict dynamic management on the qualification of enterprises participating in aid-based projects.

2.5 The Emergence of Chinese MNEs in Africa

2.5.1 Competitive Advantages of Chinese MNEs

Chinese firms have been investing in Africa for several decades. At a certain time, Chinese firms invested in Africa only for ODA reasons and were absolutely controlled by Chinese government. After a significant growth of trade between China and Africa and a rapid internal growing need for resources, large and mostly state-owned enterprises (SOEs) entered SSA as proper investors and as 'contractors to Chinese-aid-funded projects in infrastructure and public buildings (Kaplinsky & Morris, 2009) in order to gain more natural resources exploration opportunities. Acting as international tenders defines the most features in building investment relationship between Chinese multinational enterprises and local institutions in developing African countries. Morck et al. (2008) believes that greatly profitable SOEs are listed as the largest contributors of China's FDI in Africa and 'officially sanction monopoly' in major industries. Chinese MNEs investing in Africa were still with strongly political links. Within recent 10 years, Chinese MNEs' interaction with SSA was diversifying. Many large non-SOEs are now involved as major players in significant amounts of big projects. For Chinese firms, particularly SOEs, on the one hand, the purposes of their initial roles in Africa strongly related to mandated ways of feeding back into China's own development. This may not immediately endow the firms with ordinary profits. The governmental level agreements and institutes on infrastructure projects also financed the Chinese SOEs to obtain the investment opportunities. They enjoyed the low rate loans, subsidies in designated projects at the first stage. On the other hand, Chinese SOEs possess certain competitiveness of investment due to their advantages of getting access to the home country resources. The dynamic process of investing in Africa turns Chinese firms into a new stage, i.e. more traditional MNEs. Under the OLI view of OA/ FSA and LA/CSA can operate in traditional eclectic framework terms. All the operations of MNEs can be seen as in some way targeting profits (current MS/ES or future KS). Thus, at the later stage of investment, the purposes of Chinese SOEs diversified into not only the national agency but also commercial-driven MNEs.

There are two main classifications for identifying the competitive advantages of Chinese MNEs: first, firm-specific ownership advantages, which include the advantages in areas of technology, managerial skill, finance, business development, work-quality issues, etc. (Jiang, 2005), possessed by the firm that influence the firm's competence in international competition. Chinese MNEs have competitive advantages in low production cost operations based both on access to materials and labour force. Many Chinese firms have now also invested in technology research programmes in local university or in other developed countries, so that large Chinese investors to some degree have obtained the advanced technologies. Kroeber (2005) pointed out that China is a 'unique combination of first world infrastructure and third world labour costs'. Second, national-specific competitive advantages that are mostly derived from by home country have affected Chinese MNEs as a whole. The crucial resources originating from home countries are considered to be the availability of capital and financial support, the relationships between governments of home and host countries and the governmental special assistance for MNEs to invest overseas (Jiang, 2005). From successful domestic economic development, more financial support could be provided by both governments, such as China ExIm bank, and by more commercial institutions which strengthen the competence of Chinese companies to operate against the risks burden, on investing in Africa. For another thing, the political relationship between Chinese and African governments reduces the cost of bargaining on investment projects between firms and host countries. Most SOEs access government subsidy for their low-profit return projects in Africa. China, as a developing country, can often provide more suitable experience and products to meet the needs of African society better than those offered by industrialised countries (Bosshard, 2007). Chinese firms had suffered from similar economic circumstances in the past as often does Africa today. The home-specific ownership advantages of Chinese firms are more affordable and competitive to support investment in Africa. Therefore, Chinese MNEs have the advantages of running their business in Africa on the back of growth of a home market which provides advantages in terms of economics and political factors (Alden & Davies, 2006). It is generally accepted that foreign direct investment contributes to economic growth over the long term, especially for its spillover effects on knowledge and technology, productivity and poverty reduction through economic development. However, simply attracting a quantity of investment has less directly positive effect on development. China's multinationals are then emerging as potentially proactive players in Africa. Chinese firms are at the moment interested in their internationalising into the global economy. With the strong link with government, Chinese MNEs are encouraged in many specific areas of traditional industries in Africa. China's MNEs possess their own firm-specific advantages both from firm-level competences and beneficial government policy. The 'foreign entry' activities of Chinese Multinationals in Africa are based on both historic and political linkages and on business relationships. Most distinctive achievements of China's FDI in Africa are concentrated in following fields: infrastructure, natural resources exploration (oil and mining industry) and new investors (telecommunication), that define the agendas of research. However, Chinese SOEs are not the only investors of FDI from China; many private firms are now engaged in FDI in Africa. China's FDI is no longer limited to the several traditional industries which have strong connection with government strategies. Moreover, some of Chinese SOEs themselves gradually transit into a profit-driven investment. While the government funding used to be the subsidy of FDI, it now turns to the focuses of complete ODA and government cooperation.

2.5.2 Structure of Chinese Multinationals Corporations in Africa

Within recent years, Chinese MNEs' interaction with SSA has been diversifying. For instance, in the ICT area, Chinese telecommunication groups are taking major projects of ICT infrastructure. Chinese SOEs possess competitive advantages that are more likely attribute to country specific advantages rather than their own created firm specific advantages. At the same time, small and medium sized Chinese firms start to occupy private-sectors. Table 2.2 is compiled by Kaplinsky and Morris (2009) to compare the features of Chinese MNEs in SSA. Central government regulated SOEs usually take high level projects, similar to provincial government SOEs. In other words, they engage in the big projects within host countries, such as mining, oil and gas exploration, and the cross-country infrastructure construction which needs high responsibility to the missions. Resource-seeking and strategic asset-seeking are the main motivations of those MNEs. Most of time, these projects are agreed between bilateral governments and SOEs are the executants.

Three typically majors of international-oriented national oil companies from China are examples—Chinese National Offshore Oil Corporation (CNOOC), China National Petroleum Corporation (CNPC) and Sinopec. They differ in their corporate missions, market position and relationship with government (Hodel, 2008). They participate in African oil scrambles for China's energy in extraction, offshore exploration and downstream processor, respectively. Wuhan Iron and Steel (group) Corporation, Nanjing Iron & Steel United Co. Ltd. are provincial supported large MNEs. ZTE Corporation and Huawei Technologies—two well-known telecommunication MNEs in Africa participating in large ICT infrastructure construction and also doing manufacturing—motivated by efficiency and market seeking, are non-SOEs but partly supported by provincial governments. The projects within MNEs are overlapped in some cases and motivations vary. Newly appeared private enterprises are entering in Africa driven by commercial benefits based on market-seeking externally, and also to enhance their domestic competition and trading motivations. They are running business and funded by themselves, but are also able to obtain assistance from government.

2.5.3 Political Implications: Three Main Relationships of Chinese Multinationals in Africa

Chinese government encourages firms investing in Africa by financial and policy supports related to China's 'development strategies'. To what

Table 2.2 Features of Chinese enterprises in different level

	Central Government SOEs	Provincial SOEs	Incorporated in China	Incorporated in SSA only
Types of ownerships	accounted by State	Controlled by Provincial rather than Central Government objectives	Act independently from central government but associate with provincial government	Act independently
Source of finance	project taker for Central Government funded EXIM Bank financing	project taker for Central Government funded EXIM Bank financing	Largely self-financed Easy access to EXIM Bank loans	Self-financed
Main industries	resource sector, infrastructure projects and construction	resource sector infrastructure projects and construction	Manufacturing and services	Trading and services
Level of policy support	Involves formal government cooperation projects and political economic agreements	Generally some form of twinning between China provinces and governments	May be supported by Chinese provincial government (domestic support)	Familial contacts

Source: Adapted from Kaplinsky and Morris (2009)

extent MNEs are supported and regulated depend on their 'strategic' function. As an affordable location for developing oil and mining which are needed for domestic economic development, Chinese 'strategic' SOEs are driven to take on this responsibility of national demand and accept being administered. Meanwhile, owing to their large-scale production, they also pursue profit by their competitive capabilities. Government is less interfering with firms pursuing market-seeking and asset-seeking but are 'cooperating' with firms. From this point of view, Child and Rodrigues (2005) indicated that Chinese governments (central and regional) own some stock in the companies and provide international-domestic competitive advantages. This can be also explained as government provides country specific advantages to supplement firm's ownership advantages.

MNEs' projects, especially in infrastructure, are substantially related to African government development demands. These firms act as a partner with local governments in helping them to achieve economic development. However, whether MNEs' help can really meet development needs depend on how much spillover and linkage is secured from MNEs and the attractive policy from local government. Indeed, relationship between Chinese MNEs and local authorities is a bargaining process. First, infrastructure assistance can be the condition for permit of oil, and mining exploitation. Second, will local attractive policy be a risk of 'obsolescing bargain' in the second tier of MNE-host government bargaining? (see Chap. 7). Mutual government relationships have been frequently discussed as a crucial level of cooperation between China and Africa. An internal formulation of China's African policy found institutional expression in the subsequent meetings of China and Africa—FOCAC which provides the integrated governing structured of Chinese-African relations. It refers to mutual agreement of development, and national-level cooperation. To meet global strategy and mutual benefits are China's interests in Africa. Based on political relations, African governments are trying to rearrange their way of seeking economic support.

2.5.4 A Heterogeneous Continent: Africa in China's Eyes

Chinese OFDI has covered 50 countries which is a heterogeneous group with different sizes of economies, populations and geographic environment. Differentials in levels of development and ability of attracting FDI are fragmented geographically. Inconsistent and costly transportation compromises the prospective role of global investment. However, abundance of natural resources leads to dependency on resources in many African economies. Over the past decade, this Continent shows a more persistent and sustainable growth rate. Africa provides a great commercial opportunity for Chinese business. In spite of this, Africa is, certainly, a difficult place to do business—underdeveloped market institutions, poorly developed infrastructure and political instability (Table 2.3).

Table 2.3 Heterogeneity of selected African countries

Countries	Risks	GDP growth rate%	Doing business ranking	Oil producer	Land locked	Export diversification
South Africa	58.73	-2	10			
Egypt	39.93	5	74			
Nigeria	41.35	6	59	√		1.3
Algeria	39.29	2	74			
Morocco	49.42	5	154			
Angola	38.31	1	59	√		1.1
Libya	32.33	2				
Sudan	29.23	5	154	√		1.6
Tunisia	46.15	3	74			
Kenya	38.04	3	93			16
Ethiopia	33.7	9	120		√	4
Ghana	45.33	5	44			4
Cote d'Ivoire	26.35	4	154			4
Cameroon	31.21	2	120			4.4
Tanzania	38.41	6	93		√	21.7
Uganda	38.39	7	132			7.3
Senegal	30.84	2	167			12.2
Zambia	35.65	6	74		√	5
Botswana	57.91	-4	44		√	
Mozambique	35.62	6	44			2
Namibia	48.27	-1			√	

(continued)

Table 2.3 (continued)

Countries	Risks	GDP growth rate%	Doing business ranking	Oil producer	Land locked	Export diversification
Mali		4	147			1.3
Madagascar	30.45	-4	59			8.1
Mauritius		2	12			11.7
Chad	13.72	-2	154	√	√	2.6
Benin		4	154			2.1
Zimbabwe	18.88	6	120		√	8.1
Malawi	33.21	8	74		√	3
Mauritania	10.25	-1	147			3.8
Sierra Leone		4				3.8
Eritrea	5.13	4				5.2

Source: Data from World Bank and Harry Broadman, Africa's silk road (Washington, DC, 2007)

The heterogeneity of the continent is seen especially in its economic growth. Some are partly as a result of resource-dependence. With the heterogeneity of developmental levels and resource-endowments, Chinese investors diversify investment into more sectors. Many African countries are now more competitive in attracting FDI. Chinese investments are no longer merely looking at natural resources but being viewed by policy makers, business persons and workers as becoming potential markets in many industries.

Bibliography

Alden, C., & Davies, M. (2006, Summer/Autumn). A profile of the operations of Chinese Multinationals in Africa. *South African Journal of International Affairs, 13*(1). (original version: Chinese Multinational Corporations in Africa, Offshore Oil, Issue: 3–4, 1–11, Africa Institute of South Africa).

Bosshard, P. (2007). China and the West in Africa: Shared interests? *The China Monitor, 19*, 8–10.

Brautigam, D. (2011). *The Dragon's gift: The real story of China in Africa*. Oxford University Press.

Broadman, H. G. (2007). Chinese-African trade and investment: The vanguard of south-south commerce in the twenty-first century. In R. I. Rotberg (Ed.), *China into Africa—Trade, aid and influence*. Brookings Institution Press.

Centre for Chinese Studies. (2006). *China's interest and activity in Africa's construction and infrastructure sectors*. Stellenbosch University.

Chen, C., & Orr, R. J. (2009). Chinese contractors in Africa: Home government support, coordination mechanisms, and market entry strategies. *Journal of Construction Engineering and Management, ASCE/Nov, 2009*, 1201–1210.

Cheng, S., & Liang, G. (2011). Social responsibility of Chinese investment in Africa: What does it mean for EU-China Cooperation on development policy towards Africa? *Trade Negotiations Insights, 10*(3), Access from International Centre for Trade and Sustainable Development (ICTSD).

Child, J., & Rodrigues, S. B. (2005). The internationalization of Chinese firms: A case for theoretical extension? *Management and Organization Review, 1*(3), 381–410.

FOCAC. (2018). http://www.focac.org/

Foster, V., Butterfield, W., Chen, C., & Pushak, N. (2008). *Building bridges: China's growing role as infrastructure financier in Africa*. Public Private Infrastructure Advisory Facility, Trends and Policy Options, No. 5. World Bank, Washington.

Hodel, M. (2008, Springer). The scramble for energy: China's oil investment in Africa. Edited by C. Pacheco. *The Journal of International Policy Solution*, Vol. 9.

Jiang, K. W. (2005). Globalization strategies of Chinese companies: A study of China's largest telecommunications equipment companies.

Kaplinsky, R., & Morris, M. (2009). Chinese FDI in sub Saharan Africa: Engaging with large dragons. *European Journal of Development Research, 24*(1). https://doi.org/10.1057/ejdr.2009.24

Kroeber, A. (2005). China's century is still a long march away. *Financial Times*, 22.

MOFCOM. (2018). *Statistical Bulletin of Chinese Outward Foreign Direct Investment*. Available from (mofcom.gov.cn) http://hzs.mofcom.gov.cn/article/date/201512/20151201223578.shtml

MOFCOM. (2019). *2019 Statistical Bulletin of Chinese Outward Foreign Direct Investment*. Available on www.fdi.gov.cn

Morck, R., Yeung, B., & Zhao, M. (2008). Perspectives on China's outward foreign direct investment. *Journal of International Business Studies, 39*, 337–350.

latecomer status and weak institutions into 'new' ownership advantages (Luo & Tung, 2007; Mathews, 2002, 2006a). Meantime, there is a predominant belief that the extant theories can generally explain Chinese OFDI by expanding the scope of the theories (Dunning, 2001; Rugman, 2010; Ramamurti & Singh, 2009) and rethinking the concepts with specific modifications (Child & Rodrigues, 2005; Buckley et al., 2007; Ramamurti, 2009), i.e. EMNEs are more likely to develop their internationalisation process with unorthodox approach due to their ability of learning-by-doing and trial-and-error rather than traditional expanding competitiveness (Ramamurti, 2012; Williamson et al., 2013). The researchers also notice that government involvement and political factors arise as significant participants in Chinese OFDI. Thanks to their home countries support, they tend to take more risks than those counterparts from developed countries (Guillén & Garcia-Canal, 2012; Mathews, 2006b). The interests of government in OFDI motivation as well as the relationships with Chinese firms, include the approaches of incentives toward different host countries, financial assistance, and political guarantees against investment risks and bilateral cooperation to secure investment opportunities in host countries (Deng, 2007; Morck et al., 2008; Luo et al., 2010).

A large number of recent contributions analyse the Chinese internationalisation process from a general demonstration of its tendency and distribution at the infant stage through to adoption of differentiated theoretical perspectives, such as OLI framework and FDI motivation, resource-based view, and institutional-based view (Hong & Sun, 2006; Buckley et al., 2007; Cross et al., 2007; Kolstad & Wiig, 2012; Deng, 2009) on Chinese MNEs at firm-level (Wang & Boateng, 2007; Rui & Yip, 2008; Deng, 2007), home-country level (Morck et al., 2008; Tolentino, 2008; Luo et al., 2010) and host-country level (Cross et al., 2007; Kolstad & Wiig, 2012; Cheung & Qian, 2009).

Another wave of discussion from both policy research and international business view (Alden & Davies, 2006; Broadman, 2007; Gill et al., 2007; Cheung & Qian, 2009; Kaplinsky et al., 2006; Kaplinsky et al., 2009) gains significance in the context of Chinese OFDI in Africa deriving from South-South FDI—the increasing phenomenon where FDI from developing country goes to other developing countries (Aykut &

Ratha, 2004; Gelb, 2005; WIR, 2006). The activities are often criticised as 'state investment' for resources and high political level motivations for development (Alden & Davies, 2006; Foster et al., 2008). Also, the scholars point out that the motives of Chinese investment in Africa increasingly diversifies (Wang, 2007; Brautigam, 2010, 2011) and become more market-oriented (Alden & Davies, 2006).

This chapter is structured into three parts (Fig. 3.1). The first section reviews the broad mainstream theories. The next section gives theoretical explanations provided for Chinese outward investment and Chinese MNEs. The third section deals with issue studies of China and Africa. In particular, the chapter focuses on discussion related to foreign direct investment in infrastructure sector and the development process. Reviewing the existing studies in two sections gives a literature background for developing the arguments of Chinese MNEs and their concrete investment in Africa.

3.2 Mainstream Theories

3.2.1 The Eclectic Paradigm

Underlying the studies by Hymer (1960), Vernon (1966) and Dunning (1977), MNE activity is considered as a procedure of competence accumulation at the firm-level in home country, and its exploitation and augmentation internationally.

Dunning (1977, 1988a, b, 1998) integrates early multinational corporate capital ideas on control and firms' advantages of being foreign (Hymer, 1960; Dunning & Lundan, 2009; Pitelis, 2002), transaction cost of external market from internalisation theory by Buckley and Casson (1976), Rugman (1981) and other theories, so as to outline a comprehensive view on cross border activities based on three interacted advantages:

Ownership (O) advantages are the first step of a process of exploiting competitiveness internationally. Dunning (1977) states that firms create their competitive advantages beyond those of their rivals in home

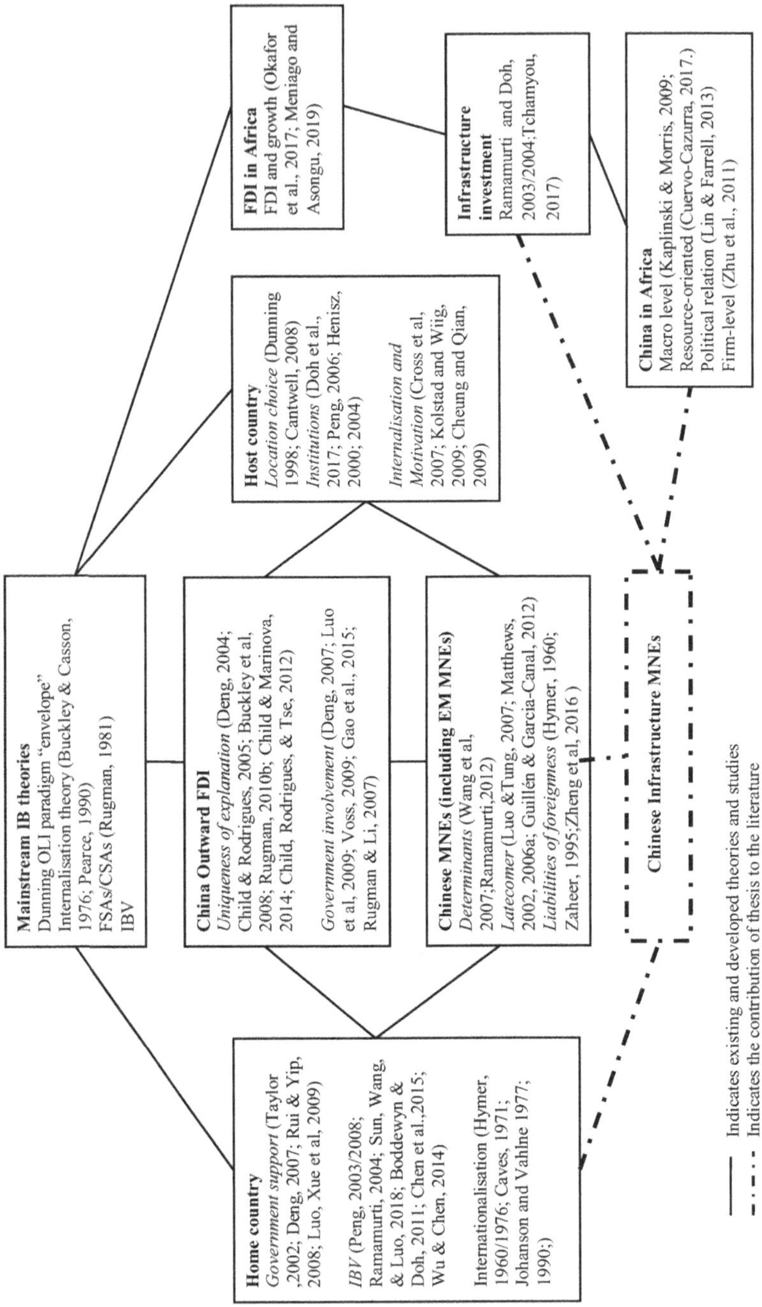

Figure 3.1 Literature structure

countries by building up their oligopolistic market power (Hymer, 1960; Knickerbocker, 1973; Graham, 1978), so that they have the competence to be a foreign firm and survive in other countries where they locate. These advantages generally take forms of the unique possession of assets and those which result from the abilities of cross-border value-added activities. In detail, the O advantages of MNEs depend not only on internally generated attributes, such as advanced technology, big market share in home country, highly-qualified managerial skills, innovation competence, brand name and coordinated networks (Pearce, 1997; Dunning, 1980, 2001), but also on the competence to sustain and exploit such existing advantages (Dunning, 2000; Rugman & Verbeke, 1998). Dunning (2003) concludes O advantages as the competitiveness that arises either from the firm's privileged ownership of, capacity to generate or ability to coordinate assets; i.e. firm- specific advantages (FSAs) that are also widely used in the FSA-CSA framework by Rugman (1981, 2007). In Chap. 5 this thesis generates a variation on this in discerning particular types of FSA that underpin the ability of Chinese IMNEs to expand internationally.

A *location (L) advantage* reflects the consideration of relocation into a host country depending on the characteristics of its inputs, in terms of natural resource endowment, production factors, institutions, and of market and other attractive elements for investment. The motivations of MNEs in choosing locations for their overseas operations are responding to particular macro-level unique advantages in host markets. In general, MNEs originating in home countries with O advantages invest in the host countries where the same industries have potential comparative advantages (Pearce, 1997) that they and can profitable exploit (Eden & Dai, 2010). In other words, the distribution of these resources is assumed be uneven, and hence 'depending on the different distribution, will confer a location advantage on the countries possessing them over those who do not' (Dunning, 1993). Besides political stability, many variables including market structure and government policies influence potential L advantages that firms face. Dunning (1980) also recognised that firms' O advantages were initially resulting from home country locational advantages, i.e. home-country CSAs. Location advantages, as such, relates to 'the endowment specific to the country they operate and to the country of origin' (Dunning, 1980). For a firm to gain benefit from making investments overseas, it must overcome the local advantages of existing firms in the host country. These ideas are complementary to those of Caves (1971) and Hymer (1976), who believed that foreign firms can gain oligopolistic advantages in less advanced, under-developed, countries, but often in a manner with negative welfare implications, if they are able to overcome their liability of foreignness. The framework in Chap. 5 evaluates these ideas to place strong emphasis on how home-country Chinese CSA condition the ability of Chinese IMNEs to access and operationalise particular CSA of African host countries.

Internalisation (I) advantages show that the MNEs will be more beneficial and effective as firms by using their specific advantages themselves instead of exploiting them through arm's length transactions. This advantage derives from internalisation theory, that a firm will consider explicitly the relative costs of servicing foreign markets by exporting to foreign markets with the FSAs embodied in final products, or engaging in FDI, or internalising a foreign producer. Imperfections are caused by issues such as asset specificity and information asymmetry that encourage foreign forms to overcome the foreign disadvantages and internalise foreign assets through application of their ownership advantages (Buckley & Casson, 1976). Hennart (1982) wrote this into a description of how communications and search costs occur in vertical and horizontal integration across national boundaries. Vertical integration occurs in industries such as oil industry and minerals. Horizontal integration is sometimes the case for mergers and acquisitions between firms. Buckley and Casson (1976) argue that the incentives of creating an internal market derive from the imperfections of markets for intermediate products. The internalisation of markets then allows interdependent activities of a single firm across national boundaries. This explains the question of why MNEs engage in geographically dispersed investments to add value to O advantages rather than through involvement with outside parties. MNE's control their operations and survive overseas in the long term. Based on arguments of Williamson (1975, 1981), transaction costs resulting from the uncertainty and inefficiency problems in external markets relate to firm investment in internalising specific assets. For firms running operations and competing in a foreign market that is highly imperfective, their

O advantages become intermediate goods which suffer risks from market failure, buyer and seller uncertainty and asymmetric information of technology (Dunning, 2000). Transferring such intermediate goods in an external market is costly with regard to the procedure of negotiation and bargaining on details so as to obtain the legal basis for an agreement. Therefore, MNEs gain benefits by internalising their OA and integrating all production parts into a firm. Internalisation reflects the organisational efficiency of hierarchies and the ability of adapting market power to exploit their new OA under their operation (Dunning, 1993).

3.2.2 Strategic Motivations

In an important perception Dunning (1993) suggested that a firm's international behaviour represents a 'gap-filling' approach that is exploring the developmental potentials of host countries (Pearce, 2001). Dunning (1993) then embodies his O-L-I framework into an extensively used typology of motivations for foreign direct investment in a strategic management perspective. Together with the 'international capital movement' (e.g. MacDougall, 1960) and Hymer's 'possession of advantages' insights, this approach indicates the motivations reflected in firms' global strategies (Pearce, 2006a, b). *O* advantage explains *'why'* motivation; *L* advantages determines *'what'* motivates by evaluating levels and types of inputs of host country; and *I* advantage identify 'how' to invest. Four main motives for MNEs' cross-border development are catalogued (Dunning & Lundan, 2009)

- Market-seeking (MS): MNEs' strategic activities designed to penetrate a particular/set of foreign markets on demand-orientation.

The traditional view of MS (Dunning, 1993, 2000; Pearce, 2001) reflects the response to trade constraints. It also allows MNEs to respond to particular tastes and distinctive needs of local markets. The frequently mentioned variables influencing MS investment in most studies, are size and growth of host markets, opportunities for expansion, cost of cross-border transaction, requirement of product adaption and customisation, as identified in Dunning's survey (1977).

- Efficiency-seeking (ES): MNEs pursue a more efficient specialisation of labour and assets. Firms seek to make the positive use of *L* advantages to maximise the economies of scale in their production.

By taking advantage of cost-effective factors in production, MNEs build up international supply networks in an highly cost-competitive manner. ES secures efficiency by MNE's ability to achieve economies of scale through competitive access to host country inputs (Dunning, 1993; Pearce, 2006a, b; Pearce & Papanastassiou, 2009).

- Resource seeking: MNEs aim at gaining access to unique resources of the location (e.g. notably natural resources) by looking at the supply side of investment.

Dunning (1993) identified resource-based investment as relevant to raw materials. This process can then be strongly related to the presence of particular industries. This facet of host-country OA or CSA become a major theme of the analysis of China's Africa strategy control to the analysis here.

- Strategic asset seeking (knowledge seeking): The strategies are designed to develop and protect the existing *O* advantages.

MNEs pursue new capacities in technologies and creative expertise that are available from particular host countries, but are not available at home, in order to extend the overall competence of the group (Menea & Pearce, 2004). Different from other motivations, firms respond to growing international technological and market heterogeneity by processes of learning (Pearce & Papanastassiou, 2009) and building the new ownership advantages that may support its long-term expansion.

Market-seeking and Resource-seeking investments are deemed as the static and initial motivations of internationalisation, whereas the Efficiency-seeking and Knowledge-seeking are more sequential and dynamic processes than the former two kinds (Dunning, 2000; Eden & Dai, 2010).

3.2.3 FSA-CSA Framework for MNEs

Rugman (1981) outlined an alternative approach to the firm and home-country factors for analysis of MNE activities. This framework is built on internalisation theory to construct a later matrix with firm-specific advantages (FSAs) and home-country specific advantages (CSAs). Conventional MNEs will be characterised by accumulation of FSAs in the home country with a duplication of home country production and managerial approaches in host countries (Rugman, 2010). To incorporate the framework into Dunning's OLI paradigm, it indicates O advantage and I advantage are combined in FSAs. In contrast on country level explanations, the traditional FSA/CSA matrix focused on home-country CSAs and FSAs whereas OLI indicates the factor-determinants of opportunities in host countries, i.e. host-country CSA. By drawing the second matrix for host-country L variables, host-country government behaviour, labour force, natural resources and market size are also precisely considered as a CSA axis of Rugman's FSA/ CSA (Rugman, 2010). This combination of impacts of the FSAs and CSAs, can range from low to high, and explains what most influentially drives MNEs activities.

Rugman (1981) emphasises that each MNE possesses a distinctive set of FSAs, which ensures its competitive advantage relative to other firms. The MNE transfers, deploys and exploits these FSAs through establishing foreign subsidiaries that make use of them abroad. These FSAs become strong when the MNEs are equipped with special knowhow or technological/managerial capability that is unavailable to others for a certain time.

MNEs expand internationally in response to imperfections in the goods and factor markets (Rugman, 1981). The CSAs of an origin nation provide a basic platform of comparative advantage accumulated by FSAs, internal to the MNE, and creating competitive advantage. Host CSAs affect the processes of transferring knowhow, deploying, recombining with other resources, and profitably exploiting FSAs across borders, which are always internalised to some extent (Rugman et al., 2011).

Both home and host country CSAs are important in terms of how the FSAs are managed. The factors recombination patterns provides useful analysis of which CSAs in the home and host countries can be leveraged by the firm, as well as the geographical dispersion of MNE internalising its network (Rugman et al., 2011). These insights then provide a platform for the application of home-country CSA to Chinese IMNEs (Chap. 5) where aspects of the institutional context like on a key relevance.

3.2.4 The Institutional Perspectives: Home- and Host- Country

Institutions of economies potentially influence internationalisation behaviour of companies on the macro-level due to the creating of market imperfection such as government intervention and market uncertainty. In terms of Institution-based view, political and societal aspects are often highlighted in IB studies for emerging market as the background condition, to capture the complex changing of relationships between organisations and environments (Peng et al., 2008). Business performance, decision-making, and strategic emerge choices as the outcome of such a dynamic interaction between institutions and organisations (Peng, 2003, 2006).

Institutions, as traditionally mentioned as part of the host-country location advantages, provides 'the rules of the game' on most aspects of an economy through formal or informal relationships between society and organisations and thereby influence 'how the game is played' (North, 1990). Institutions play an important role in supporting an effective market, in avoiding unnecessary risk and cost (Peng, 2006) and have attracted attention as explanations of multinationals' global strategies (Peng, 2003, 2006). Efficient markets, in recent years, not only depend on market size and natural assets of host country, but also quality of the institutions that can provide the formal and informal rules of the game allowing lower transaction costs and uncertainty (North, 1990). Buckley et al. (2011) indicate that host-country institutions can support its location advantage for attracting FDI. Host countries institutions can also lead to strategic problems for MNEs (Henisz & Swaminathan, 2008). Transparent and accountable institutions help the MNEs against those political and commercial risks of emerging markets (Buckley et al., 2011). As the economic and political pressures for globalisation expand the number of economies and the share of each economy, open to international competition and private participation, in these circumstances a firm expects the government to maintain an active role in the operation of these markets, even if its ownership stake is now partially or even fully liquidated (Henisz, 2003).

Location decision is influenced by changes in government policy and/or political institutions, resulting in the risk premium incorporated in any investment project (Busse & Hefeker, 2007). Many empirical studies indicate that political systems of a host country can pose uncertainty in terms of the institutional structure (Acemoglu & Johnson, 2005). Busse and Hefeker (2007) deem that the components of political risks are also linked to the quality of political institutions, i.e. the quality of the bureaucracy is closely associated with the institutional strength of a particular country, and a well-functioning legal system and the effectiveness of control of corruption are important effects of high-quality institutions.

The characteristics of MNEs correlate with the ability of such companies to manage 'institutional idiosyncrasies' (Henisz, 2003) that make a challenge for facilitating the application of firm-specific advantages through the interaction with diverse locations (Rugman & Verbeke, 2002; Bevan et al., 2004). For infrastructure industry such as ICT provision, government involvement in operation of the industry coexists with an opening to private ownership, so that multinational firms' resulting ability to manage institutional idiosyncrasies may be both a source of competitive advantages and a driver of internationalisation (Henisz, 2003). This relates to the concept of relational FSA (FSA-R) developed in Chap. 5.

3.2.5 Location Choice

Macroeconomic volatility has negative effects on decisions of multinationals (Aizenman, 2003). The dimensions of MNE investment aims and motivations suggest different objectives that are likely to be pursued for operationalising different location factors (Dunning 1993, 2000; Dunning & Lundan, 2008; Dimitropoulou et al., 2009). The motivations of MNEs in choosing different locations are responding to unique macro-level location advantages in each foreign market and their global interest, which also differs from one industry to another (Dunning, 1977). Dunning (1977) identifies the market structure at the country level and government policies as being potential location advantages. The concept of location advantage captures the abilities to shape the incentives to potential foreign direct investments (Dunning, 1998) reflecting foreign countries having host country-specific advantages (CSAs) (Rugman, 1981, 2007) in terms of natural resources, factors of production, demand conditions, etc. Location advantages also include elements of the broad institutional environment in which the firm operates, and that influence how the place to produce varies with the type of FDI and level of development of both home and host countries (Dunning, 1993). The distribution of these resources and foreign location capabilities is assumed to be uneven, hence, 'depending on the different distribution, will confer a location advantage on the countries possessing them over those who do not' (Dunning, 1993). A key theme here will be how Chinese IMNEs in Africa reflect the dynamics of LAs in both home and host economies as they undergo the charges implied in development.

FDI theory states that the location decisions of MNEs are determined by the relative location advantages of particular countries for certain activities. Market size is often regarded as a major location advantage that enables firms to benefit from advantages of large size and gain the benefits of scale advantages (Dunning, 1993). While market size is likely to have significant effect on the location choices of large firms, producing and selling products that enable standardisation and quantity production, it may have limited or no explanatory power for the location choices for specialised firms, whose core competitive advantage lies in a highly specialised technology (Nachum & Wymbs, 2002).

3.2.6 Political Economy and MNEs

MNEs are a distinctive feature of international political economy in recent decades. The MNE as the prime agent of FDI in the globalisation process, along with contracting and other new forms of internationalisation, is serving both domestic and international business activity, particularly through economy-wide effects that go beyond the individual enterprises' behaviour (Sally, 2013). Roughly speaking, MNEs can emerge as key economic links between state and state since they engage in FDI, which is popular with host governments seeking jobs, technology and the resources for development (Balaam & Veseth, 2008). Caves (1982, 1996) concentrates on efficiency and interaction of MNEs' activities and government regulation in an host country. The MNE is a centralised, hierarchical organisation to control international production by use of home-based FSAs. Based on distinctive interests of home and host governments, Caves (1982) suggests that taxation, competition policy and bargaining over the natural resources and technology protection issues can create conflicts between MNEs and governments. Later studies by Kobrin (1984, 1987), Henisz (1998), Ramamurti (2001), Eden et al. (2004), Buckley et al. (2007) recognise that political risk may a conflict issue for interaction between MNEs and governments. Firm-driven national responsiveness enables a firm to enjoy national treatment by government. The MNE strategic approach to government policy in terms of desired outcomes is driven by the MNE's resource base. The strategic perspective on government policy reflects either exogenous or endogenous effects on MNEs' decisions. MNE will attempt to build government policy in its favour though integrating FSAs with government when policy is taken endogenous; while MNEs will work under rules if it is exogenous (Rugman, 2010).

For both positive and negative effects of MNE on development, many studies point out that options and methods of host countries on bargaining with MNEs will vary under different circumstances. The outcomes of bilateral negotiation depend on the levels of knowledge and bargaining experience (Casson & Pearce, 1987). Indeed, the MNE will attempt to know much more about the host government plan for that economy than the government can find out about the activities of the whole MNE network and its future plans (Casson & Pearce, 1987). Business can internalise government decision-makers and leverage its bargaining power and support nation's competitiveness in long term (Boddewyn & Brewer, 1994).

Government is the vital external important player in international business: it is controller, regulator and adjudicator of business sectors

(Luo et al., 2010). The national governments understand the value of access to the MNEs' FSAs, known as 'acclaiming FDI as good news' (Dunning, 1994). Host governments should regulate MNEs through policy and changing the political environment parameters that MNEs are facing in the host markets. The relationship between bilateral governments is a factor which affects the investments of MNEs (Cohn, 2005). Thereby, political issues play a role in FDI, and MNEs seek to be involved in the economic decision making of government, especially in developing countries. In reality, the entry-level bargaining on home-host/ multilateral level is minimal as few governments now restrict inward FDI. MNE and host government engage in bargaining position when host government can prevail at the expense of MNE goals (Eden et al., 2004; Ramamurti, 2001). Therefore, MNEs must design an appropriate strategy to obtain benefit of policy or national treatment when interacting with home and host government (Rugman, 2010).

3.2.7 Liability of Foreignness

A key insight of MNEs activities is that they have to face a substantial liability of foreignness (LOF) so that they need to bear additional costs. The liability of foreignness represents the impact of various forms of weaknesses where MNEs have natural competitive disadvantages of being foreign in the host market relative to local companies (Hymer, 1976; Kindleberger, 1969). The importance of the choices firms can make to deal with these additional costs will vary by industry, firm, host country, and home country, deriving from distance for coordination, unfamiliarity with local market, environmental uncertainty, understanding of host country political-economic characteristics and cost from home country (Dunning & Rugman, 1985; Zaheer, 1995). Hymer's insight was his recognition that a MNE's possession of FSAs is required to offset the liability of foreignness when operating abroad (Hymer, 1960; Zaheer, 1995). In work on LOF and firm performance, some researchers have focused on firm strategies to reduce liability of foreignness. To overcome this liability, Buckley & Casson, 1976; Caves, 1996; Dunning, 1993) also emphasise that MNEs need to prepare their international activities with certain FSAs including endowment of resources and capabilities which are specified as strategic management (Bartlett & Ghoshal, 1991). Buckley (1983) noted that local knowledge should give domestic firms advantages, but only for first-time foreign investors, not to long established multinationals. Simple market-seeking subsidiaries suffer more liability of foreignness (Caves, 1982). Lacking of distinctive resources and specific advantages such as brands, technologies and management experience when they first enter foreign markets (Luo & Tung, 2007; Zheng et al., 2016), MNEs build up the subsidiaries for integrating with host CSAs. But vertical integration of efficiency- or resource- seeking MNEs use geographically dispersed subsidiaries to tap into a globally-integrated value-adding system in which it can exploit economies of global scale and scope (Zaheer, 1995). The MNEs that have differentiated roles and levels of integration in each subsidiary, may feel the liability of foreignness less (Ghoshal & Nohria, 1989).

3.3 Theoretical Perspectives on Rise of Chinese OFDI and MNEs

Many researchers acknowledge that EMNEs seem to have the potential for accelerated expansion into international markets as a result of several differentiating factors. To take into account emerging MNEs from developing countries, Caves (1996) recognised the third world multinationals by transaction-cost analysis. In Caves' opinion, most MNEs from developing countries concentrated in traditional manufacturing industries rather than those associated with advanced technology (Caves, 1996). The MNEs move abroad due to the domestic market conditions—running out of the growth sources and opportunities (Katz & Kosacoff, 1983 in Caves, 1996) and spreading of risks (Caves, 1996). Being the 'big tent' of international business theories, the OLI paradigm is widely adapted to analyse the issues of international activities of firms as well as the new features of recent internationalisation scenario of emerging MNEs (Dunning, 2006).

3.3.1 Competitive Advantages of Chinese MNEs

Mathews (2006a) focused on the strategies of a 'Latecomer Firm' and argued that such firms 'are able to exploit their late arrival to tap into advanced technologies, rather than having to replicate the entire previous technological trajectory.' MNEs from developing countries do not possess advanced domestic assets which can be strengthened abroad (Mathews, 2006a), but began their internationalisation already equipped with a global outlook (Mathews, 2006b). Matthews argues that latecomer firms (LCF) develop their competitive abilities by embedding themselves in the global supply chains of already operating firms in their sectors: as OEM or other subcontractors. They then leverage knowledge through these linkages as part of their own learning objectives. Though this LLL approach adds some useful ideas about practice and motivations of LCFs in some sectors, it cannot be seen as a fully-developed framework to show how LCFs can become MNEs. It leaves out some issues addressed by, for example, the OLI framework and understood in ways the FSA/CSA approach does address. Leverage is part of FSA how firm leverage in domestic market. Notably the ability of Mathews LCF to secure a beneficial 'linkage' position does not reflect possession of any FSA of theirs. It reflects their access to factors (CSA) of their developing home country that help them gain a position in another firms (established MNEs) global supply chain. This is likely to be low wage labour and other competitive inputs available to any firm- LLL does not explains which firms access these CSA to secure 'learning linkage'. The framework developed (see Chap. 5) in this thesis addresses these questions for emerging economy IMNE by showing how they are postured in Chinese development but firm-level attitude to do this.

Child and Rodrigues (2005) also believe that 'latecomer' explains how firms in this category develop their international competitive power. However, Child and Rodrigues gave greater attention on those latecomer firms which are initially disadvantaged and then acquire the necessary assets to offset these disadvantages through learning from foreign entities. In their research, Chinese firms internationalise by obtaining financial strength, in other words, support from governmental sponsorship to secure their advantage of redressing through purchasing and opportunities to learn (Child & Rodrigues, 2005).

Child and Rodrigues (2005) and Boisot (2004) argue that Chinese firms invest overseas to avoid and remedy competitive disadvantage in operating in their domestic market instead of by exploiting existing competitive advantages. Chinese firms expand globally in a way that is not driven by ownership advantage but by the expectation of securing sustainable global competitiveness (Deng, 2004). Wright et al. (2005) depict Chinese MNEs' strategies as exploiting competitive advantage in developing countries and exploring it in developed countries.

Buckley et al. (2007) talk about the financial structure of the Chinese economy and the idea that Chinese firms may have access to funds which are lower cost than in the world market. This is also an imperfection, which gives Chinese firms advantage in host markets through cheap access to investment capital.

Economic theory is that for a firm to gain benefit from making investments overseas in another country it must overcome local advantages of existing firms in that country that is the host countries (LOF). These ideas are from Caves (1971) and Hymer (1976) who state that home firms can gain oligopolistic advantage in less advanced countries. Regarding Chinese outward FDI, there are some other motivations based on China's own conditions, such as foreign exchange reserve, political support (Kolstad & Wiig, 2012; Luo et al., 2010; Voss et al., 2010).

Rugman and Li (2007) stated that Chinese enterprises creating their competitive advantages in the global economy are based on China's country-specific advantages in terms of low labor cost and resources. Consequently, successful Chinese firms are more likely to emerge from labor intensive industries where they can make use of their low-cost resource supply (Rugman & Li, 2007).

3.3.2 Motivations of Chinese MNEs

Dunning (1981, 1988a, 2001) put an emphasis on MNEs' expansion into developing countries, in search of natural resources. Market-seeking (MS) is the most common choice of strategy for developing countries'

MNEs in internationalisation process (Gao et al., 2015; Lattemann & Alon, 2015; Lin & Farrell, 2013; Rugman & Li, 2007; UNCTAD WIR, 2006; Dunning & Lundan, 2008), particularly Chinese MNEs towards large markets (Deng, 2004; Buckley et al., 2007). Cross et al. (2007) also found that Chinese FDI is positively related to host countries with small market size but abundant natural resources. With a similar stage of development, Chinese MNEs can exploit their ownership advantages of being low-cost foreignness (Cross et al., 2007). Chinese companies are first driven by home countries 'push' factors, MNEs do not simply compete in global market for maximising profit (Luo & Tung, 2007).

3.4 Debate on China in Africa

3.4.1 FDI and Infrastructure

Role of Infrastructure in Attracting FDI

Infrastructure is a key to integrating domestic economic development into the world economy (OECD, 2006). The provision of good infrastructure is an essential determinant of attracting FDI (Bellak et al., 2007; Asiedu, 2002, 2006) and consequently is necessary for foreign investors to operate successfully. In terms of arguments on infrastructure and FDI in Africa, an empirical study by Asiedu (2002) observed that the countries with enhanced infrastructure were rewarded with more FDI. Subsequent studies by him and his colleagues (Asiedu, 2006; Asiedu & Nandwa, 2007) confirmed the strongly positive link between infrastructure and FDI.

Although infrastructure consists of several elements, transportation construction is perhaps the most basic and necessary one for development and for attracting FDI. The obvious benefits of transport infrastructure are enhanced accessibility of certain sectors to the market and generally reduced transport cost. Khadaroo and Seetanah (2006) using both static and dynamic panel data approaches testing 33 SSA countries, concluded that 'transport infrastructure is observed to have been an ingredient in the attractiveness of the country as a FDI destination'.

With the rapid growth of information-based economy, ICT is believed to be the main new factor of FDI (Gholami et al., 2005). ICT becomes the core infrastructure in developing economy. It is not just a technological phenomenon in information industry, but a stimulating fundamental economic transformation. Its vital roles in advancing economic development and reducing poverty have been expanded (World Bank, 2011).[1] As a Report of the Regional Round Table on IT and Development claims 'the ever-developing ICT has fundamentally changed the nature of global relationships, competitive advantages and opportunities for economic and social development' (2000). ICT has strong spillover influence on long-run productive activities in other sectors. Individuals can unlock their potential human capital and creativity by easier accessing of global knowledge. Local companies, therefore, in developing countries are able to integrate into global production chains and markets. Governments could be more efficient and transparent by offering information and service to the public through internet. These are all contributing to long-term growth through efficiency and productivity. Gholami et al. (2005) also note that many studies have revealed that telecommunication infrastructure does not merely improve domestic economic development, but determines the ability to attract FDI to some degree and initially to increase competitiveness in the world market. As a key driver to a country's modernisation and growth, the improvement in ICT infrastructure has attracted substantial amounts of investment which generate significant revenues and employment in developing countries. Telecommunication based on information technology has improved the location advantage of a host country to attract FDI. ICT strengthens the ability of MNEs to coordinate their offshore activities because to the accessibility of both input and output markets.

[1] 2011 World Bank Strategy Sector Information & Communication Technologies Approach Paper.

Investing in Infrastructure

ODA has traditionally been considered as the major source of infrastructure financing (Estache, 2004). But its contribution to infrastructure investment started to decline in the 1990s since when the supply of infrastructure FDI has been impressively active (Ramamurti & Doh, 2004). Developing countries are discovered, in the rapidly globalising world economy, to attract commitments from private sources and MNEs. The quality of infrastructure becomes a major factor in MNEs' location choice (Dunning, 1998; Wheeler & Mody, 1992). Ramamurti and Doh (2004) point out that FDI infrastructure sectors in developing countries continue to be dependent on local government policies and actions in the operational stage. Special risks involved in infrastructure FDI combine the industry-specific and host-country-specific factors. Risks of infrastructure FDI in developing countries are higher because of the high political instability. TRIPS agreement had little impact on infrastructure service (Ramamurti & Doh, 2004). Infrastructure industries as a unique group differ from manufacturing because the individual firms are diverse but with common features. Investments in the industry are natural monopolies because of high-fixed cost and a single provider is traditionally most efficient. The investors also have no threat of import competition as infrastructure is a non-tradable service.

3.4.2 China and Africa

The scale of the rapidly and widely-growing involvement between China and Africa has generated debate, based upon extensive empirical and policy research, around two issues: motivations of this engagement, and its implications for sustainable development (Broadman, 2006; Chan, 2006; Goldstein et al., 2006; Tull, 2006; Wild & Mepham, 2006; Alden, 2007; He, 2007; Davies et al., 2008; Gu et al., 2008; ADB, 2008).

Kaplinsky et al. (2006) stated that Chinese multinationals' presence in SSA aims at raw materials rather than final markets or low-cost labour. At the same time, Alden and Davies (2006) considered that current Chinese multinationals are also seeking African markets and claimed that Chinese

MNEs can work for long-term objectives partly because the major Chinese MNEs are state-owned, so that they do not appear to pursue short-term profit maximising as Western firms, and partly owing to access to low-cost capital (Kaplinsky et al., 2006).

Corkin et al. (2008) also argue that the Chinese government and firms have a longer time-frame for strategic consideration in areas where they perceive medium- to long-term benefits. They note that determinant factors of Chinese interests of entering Africa are methods of operation, the capital and technology disposal and experiences in operating overseas. The success of Chinese firms which have entered Africa rely on the capability to leverage through loan agreements. Owing to the cooperation agreements between governments, as the loans and subsidies are taken to Africa, financial holding become another firms' ownership advantages which soften the MNEs' budget constraints (Gugler & Boie, 2008). The study also finds out the arising problem of lack of an institutional framework and government capacity to monitor and encourage FDI.

Most large scale investments are executed by Chinese SOEs as the statistics recorded. SOEs perform as 'contractors to Chinese-aid-funded projects in infrastructure and public building' (Kaplinsky et al., 2009) to obtain more chances of natural resource exploration.

Bibliography

Acemoglu, D., & Johnson, S. (2005). Unbinding institutions. *Journal of Political Economy, 113*(5), 949–995.

African Development Bank. (2008). *African Development Report 2007*. Abidjan, Côte d'Ivoire: African Development Bank.

Aizenman, J. (2003). Volatility, employment and the patterns of FDI in emerging markets. *Journal of Development Economics, 72*(2), 585–601.

Alden, C. (2007). Emerging countries as new ODA players in LDCs: The case of China and Africa. Paris, IDDRI, Idées pour le débat, 1, 2007.

Alden, C., & Davies, M. (2006, Summer/Autumn). A profile of the operations of Chinese Multinationals in Africa. *South African Journal of International Affairs, 13*(1). (original version: Chinese Multinational Corporations in Africa, Offshore Oil, Issue: 3–4, 1–11, Africa Institute of South Africa).

Asiedu, E. (2002). On the determinants of foreign direct investment to developing countries: Is Africa different? *World Development, 30*(1), 107–119.
Asiedu, E. (2006). Foreign direct Investment in Africa: The role of government policy, institutions and political instability. *The World Economy, 29*(1), 63–77.
Asiedu, E., & Nandwa, B. (2007). On the impact of foreign aid in education on growth: How relevant is the heterogeneity of aid flows and the heterogeneity of aid recipients? *Review of World Economics, 143*(4), 631–649.
Aykut, A. D., & Ratha, D. (2004). South-south FDI flows: How big are they? *Transnational Corporations, 13*(1), 149–176.
Balaam, D., & Veseth, M. (2008). *Introduction to international political economy* (4th ed.). Pearson Education.
Bartlett, C. A., & Ghoshal, S. (1991). Global strategic management: Impact on the new frontiers of strategy research. *Strategic Management Journal*, 5–16.
Bellak, C., Leibrecht, M., & Damijan, J. P. (2007). *Infrastructure endowment and corporate income taxes as determinants of Foreign Direct Investment in Central- and Eastern European Countries*. LICOS Discussion Paper, No. 193.
Bevan, A., Estrin, S., & Meyer, K. (2004). Foreign investment location and institutional development in transition economics. *International Business Review, 13*, 43–64.
Boddewyn, J., & Brewer, T. (1994). International business political behaviour: New theoretical directions. *Academy of Management Review, 19*(1), 119–143.
Boisot, M. (2004). Notes on the internationalization of Chinese firms. Unpublished paper, Open University of Catalonia, Barcelona, Spain.
Brautigam, D. (2010). *The Dragon's gift: The real story of China in Africa*. Oxford University Press.
Brautigam, D. (2011). *The dragon's gift: The real story of China in Africa*. OUP Oxford.
Broadman, H. G. (2006). *Africa's silk road: China and India's new economic frontier*. World Bank Publications.
Broadman, H. G. (2007). Chinese-African trade and investment: The vanguard of south-south commerce in the twenty-first century. In R. I. Rotberg (Ed.), *China into Africa—Trade, aid and influence*. Brookings Institution Press.
Buckley, J. P. (1983). New theories of international business: Some unresolved issues. In M. Casson (Ed.), *The growth of international business* (pp. 34–50). Allen & Unwin.
Buckley, J. P., & Casson, M. C. (1976). *The future of multinational enterprises*. Macmillan.

Buckley, J. P., Voss, H., Cross, A., & Clegg, L. J. (2011). The emergence of Chinese firms as multinationals: The influence of the home institutional environment. In R. Pearce (Ed.), *China and the multinationals: International business and the entry of China into the global economy*. Edward Elgar.

Buckley, P., Clegg, J., Cross, A., Liu, X., Voss, H., & Zheng, P. (2007). The determinants of Chinese outward foreign direct investment. *Journal of International Business Studies, 38*(4), 499–518.

Busse, M., & Hefeker, C. (2007). Political risk, institutions and foreign direct investment. *European Journal of Political Economy, 23*(2), 397–415.

Casson, M., & Pearce, R. (1987). Multinational enterprises in LDCs. In N. Gemmell (Ed.), *Surveys in development economics*. Blackwell.

Caves, R. (1971). The industrial economics of foreign investment. *Economica, 38*(149), 1–27.

Caves, R. E. (1982). *Multinational enterprises and economic analysis*. Cambridge University Press.

Caves, R. E. (1996). *Multinational enterprises and economic analysis* (2nd ed.). Cambridge University Press.

Chan, S. (2006). Scramble for China. Prospect 126, http://www.prospect-magazine.co.uk/article_details.php?id=7712

Cheung, Y.-W., & Qian, X. (2009). Empirics of China's outward direct investment. *Pacific Economic Review, 14*(3), 312–341.

Child, J., & Rodrigues, S. B. (2005). The internationalization of Chinese firms: A case for theoretical extension? *Management and Organization Review, 1*(3), 381–410.

Cohn, T. (2005). *Global political economy: Theory and practice* (3rd ed.). Pearson Education, Inc.

Corkin, L., Burke, C., & Davies, M. (2008). *China's role in the development of Africa's infrastructure*. SAIS Working papers in African Studies, 04–08.

Cross, A., Buckley, P., Clegg, J., Voss, H., Rhodes, M., Zheng, P., & Liu, X. (2007). An econometric investigation of Chinese outward direct investment. In J. H. Dunning & T. M. Lin (Eds.), *Multinational enterprises and emerging challenge of the 21st century* (pp. 55–86). Edward Elgar.

Davies, M., Edinger, H., Tay, N., & Naidu, S. (2008). *How China delivers development assistance to Africa*. Centre for Chinese Studies, University of Stellenbosch.

Deng, P. (2004, May–June). Outward investment by Chinese MNCs: Motivations and implications. *Business Horizons, 47*(3), 8–16.

Deng, P. (2007). Investing for strategic resources and its rationale: The case of outward FDI from Chinese companies. *Business Horizons, 50*, 71–81.

Deng, P. (2009). Why do Chinese firms tend to acquire strategic assets in international expansion? *Journal of World Business, 44*, 74–84.

Dimitropoulou, D., Pearce, R., & Papanastassiou, M. (2009). Strategic heterogeneity in MNEs and the integrating European economy. In M. Papanastassiou & R. Pearce (Eds.), *The strategic development of multinationals: Subsidiaries and innovation*. Palgrave Macmillan.

Dunning, J. H. (1977). Trade, location of economic activity and the MNE: A search for an eclectic approach. In B. Ohlin, P. Hesselborn, & P. M. Wijkman (Eds.), *The international allocation of economic activity*. Macmillan.

Dunning, J. H. (1980, Spring/Summer). Toward an eclectic theory of international production: Some empirical tests. Journal of International Business Studies, 11(1), 9–31.

Dunning, J. H. (1981). Explaining the international direct investment position of countries: Towards a dynamic or developmental approach. *Weltwirtschaftliches Archiv, 117*(1), 30–64.

Dunning, J. H. (1988a). The theory of international production. *The International Trade Journal, 3*, 21–66.

Dunning, J. H. (1988b). The eclectic paradigm of international production: A restatement and some possible extension. *Journal of International Business Studies, 19*(1), 1–31.

Dunning, J. H. (1993). Internationalizing Porter's diamond. *MIR: Management International Review*, 7–15.

Dunning, J. H. (1998). Location and the multinational enterprise: A neglected factor. *Journal of International Business Studies, 29*(1), 45–66.

Dunning, J. H. (2000). The eclectic paradigm as an envelope for economic and business theories of MNE activities. *International Business Review, 9*, 163–190.

Dunning, J. H. (2001). The eclectic (OLI) paradigm of international production: Past, present and future. *International Journal of the Economics of Business, 8*(2), 173–190.

Dunning, J. H. (2003). Some antecedents of internalization theory. *Journal of International Business Studies, 34*(2), 108–115.

Dunning, J. H. (2006a). Comment on dragon multinationals: New players in 21st century globalisation. *Asia Pacific Journal of Management, 25*(2), 139–141.

Dunning, J. H., & Lundan, S. (2009). *Multinational enterprises and the global economy* (2nd ed.). Edward Elgar.

Dunning, J. H., & Lundan, S. M. (2008). Institutions and the OLI paradigm of the multinational enterprise. *Asia Pacific Journal of Management, 25*, 573–593.

Dunning, J. H., & Rugman, A. M. (1985). The influence of Hymer's dissertation on the theory of foreign direct investment. *American Economic Review: Papers and Proceedings, 75*(2), 228–260.

Eden, L., & Dai, L. (2010). Rethinking the O in Dunning's OLI/eclectic paradigm. *Multinational Business Review, 18*(2), 13–34.

Eden, L., Lenway, S., & Schuler, D. A. (2004). *From the obsolescing bargain to the political bargaining model.* Bush School Working Paper 403.

Estache, A. (2004). *PPI partnerships vs. PPI divorces in LDCs.* World Bank and ECARES.

Foster, V., Butterfield, W., Chen, C., & Pushak, N. (2008). *Building bridges: China's growing role as infrastructure financier in Africa.* Public Private Infrastructure Advisory Facility, Trends and Policy Options, No. 5. World Bank, Washington.

Gao, L., Liu, X., & Lioliu, E. (2015). A double-edged sword: The impact of institutions and political relations on the international market expansion of Chinese state-owned enterprises. *Journal of Chinese Economic and Business Studies, 13*(2), 105–125.

Gelb, S. (2005). *South-South investment: The case of Africa.* Africa in the World Economy—The National, Regional and International Challenges Fondad. www.fondad.org

Gholami, R., Lee, S., & Heshmati, A. (2005). The Causal relationship between ICT and FDI. Research Paper No. 205/26. UNU-Wider, Helshinki.

Ghoshal, S., & Nohria, N. (1989). Internal differentiation within multinational corporations. *Strategic Management Journal, 10*(4), 323–337.

Gill, B., Huang, C., & Morrison, J. S. (2007). Assessing China's growing influence in Africa. *China Security, 3*(3), 3–21.

Goldstein, A., Pinaud, N., Reisen, H., & Chen, X. (2006). *The rise of China and India: What's in it for Africa?* OECD Development Centre.

Graham, E. M. (1978). Transatlantic investment by multinational firms: A rivalistic phenomenon? *Journal of Post Keynesian Economics, 1*(1), 82–99.

Gu, J., Humphrey, J., & Messner, D. (2008). Global governance and developing countries: The implications of the rise of China. *Journal of World Development, 36*(2), 274–292.

Gugler, P., & Boie, B. (2008). *The Chinese international investments: Corporate and government strategies. NCCR Trade regulation.* Working paper No. 2008/25.

Guillén, M., & Garcia-Canal, E. (2012). *Emerging markets rule: Growth strategies of the new global giants.* McGrawHill Education.

He, W. (2007). The balancing act of China's Africa policy. *China Security, 3*(3), 23–41.

Henisz, W. J. (1998). The institutional environment for international investment: Safeguarding against state sector opportunism and opportunistic use of the state. University of California.

Henisz, W. J. (2003). The power of the Buckley and Casson thesis: The ability to manage institutional idiosyncrasies. *Journal of International Business Studies, 34*, 173–184.

Henisz, W., & Swaminathan, A. (2008). Institutions and international business.

Hennart, J. F. (1982). *A theory of multinational enterprise*. University of Michigan Press.

Hong, E., & Sun, L. (2006). Dynamics of internationalization and outward investment: Chinese corporations' strategies. *The China Quarterly, 187*, 610–634.

Hymer, S. H. (1976 [1960]). The international operations of national firms, a study of direct foreign investment (Doctoral dissertation, Massachusetts Institute of Technology, only published in 1976).

Johanson, J., & Vahlne, J. E. (1977). The internationalization process of the firm: A model of knowledge development and increasing foreign market commitments. *Journal of International Business Studies, 29*(1), 45–66.

Kaplinsky, R., McCormick, D., & Morris, M. (2006). *The Impact of China in Sub-Saharan Africa*. IDS Working Paper 291.

Kaplinsky, R., McCormick, D., & Morris, M. (2009). *The Impact of China on Sub-Saharan Africa*. Working Paper 291, Institute of Development Studies, UK.

Khadaroo, J., & Seetanah, B. (2006). *Transport infrastructure and FDI: Lessons from Sub-Saharan African economies*.

Khanna, T., & Palepu, K. G. (2010). *Winning in emerging markets: A road map for strategy and execution*. Harvard Business Press.

Kindleberger, C. P. (1969). *American business abroad: six lectures on direct investment*. New Haven: Yale University Press.

Knickerbocker, F. T. (1973). Oligopolistic reaction and multinational enterprise. *The International Executive, 15*(2), 7–9.

Kobrin, S. J. (1984). Expropriation as an attempt to control foreign firms in LDCs: Trends from 1960 to 1979. *International Studies Quarterly, 28*(3), 329–348.

Kobrin, S. (1987). Testing the bargaining hypothesis in the manufacturing sector in developing countries. *International Organization, 41*, 609–638.

Kolstad, I., & Wiig, A. (2012). What determines Chinese outward FDI? *Journal of World Business, 47*(1), 26–34.

Lattemann, C., & Alon, I. (2015). The rise of Chinese multinationals: A strategic threat or an economic opportunity? *Georgetown Journal of International Affairs, 16*(1), 172–179.

Lin, X., & Farrell, C. (2013). The internationalization strategies of Chinese state and private sector enterprises in Africa. *Journal of African Business, 14*(2), 85–95.

Luo, Y., & Tung, R. L. (2007). International expansion of emerging market enterprises: A springboard perspective. *Journal of International Business Studies, 38*(4), 481–498.

Luo, Y., Xue, Q., & Han, B. (2010). How emerging market governments promote outward FDI: Experience from China. *Journal of World Business, 45*, 68–79.

MacDougall, G. D. A. (1960). The benefits and costs of private investment from abroad: A theoretical approach 1. *Bulletin of the Oxford University Institute of Economics & Statistics, 22*(3), 189–211.

Mathews, J. A. (2002). Competitive advantages of the latecomer firm: A resource-based account of industrial catch-up strategies. *Asia Pacific Journal of Management, 19*, 467–488.

Mathews, J. A. (2006a). Catch-up strategies and the latecomer effect in industrial development. *New Political Economy, 11*(3), 313–335.

Mathews, J. A. (2006b). Dragon multinationals: New player in 21st century globalisation. *Asia Pacific Journal of Management, 23*, 5–27.

Menea, J., & Pearce, R. (2004). *Multinationals and transition.* Palgrave Macmillan.

Meyer, K. E. (2018). Catch-up and leapfrogging: Emerging economy multinational enterprises on the global stage. *International Journal of the Economics of Business, 25*(1), 19–30.

Morck, R., Yeung, B., & Zhao, M. (2008). Perspectives on China's outward foreign direct investment. *Journal of International Business Studies, 39*, 337–350.

Nachum, L., & Wymbs, C. (2002). Firm-specific attributes and MNE location choices: Financial and professional service FDI to New York and London.

North, D. (1990). *Institutions, institutional change and economic performance.* Cambridge University Press.

OECD. (2006). Africa and China, Atlas on Regional Integration in West Africa economy series.

Pearce, R. (1997). Global interdependence, MNE strategy and technology. In *Global competition and technology* (pp. 3–12). Palgrave Macmillan, London.
Pearce, R. (2001). Multinationals and industrialisation: The bases of 'inward investment' policy. *International Journal of the Economics of Business, 8*(1), 51–73.
Pearce, R. (2006a). Globalisation and development: An international business strategy approach. *Transactional Corporations, 15*(1), 39–74.
Pearce, R. (2006b). Technology strategy in the competitive evolution of multinationals. *European International Business Academy conference.*
Pearce, R., & Papanastassiou, M. (2009). Creative transition and the role of MNE subsidiaries in host-country industrialisation. In M. Papanastassiou & R. Pearce (Eds.), *The strategic development of multinationals: Subsidiaries and innovation.* Palgrave Macmillan.
Peng, M. W. (2003). Institutional transitions and strategic choice. *The Academy of Management Review, 28*(2), 275–296.
Peng, M. W. (2006). *Global strategy.* Thomason South-Western.
Peng, M. W., Wang, D. Y., & Jiang, Y. (2008). An institution-based view of international business strategy: A focus on emerging economies. *Journal of International Business Studies, 39*, 920–936.
Pitelis, C. N. (2002). *Stephen Hymer, the multinational firm and 'multinational corporate capital.* University of Athens and Cambridge University.
Ramamurti, R. (2001). The obsolescing 'bargaining model'? MNC-host developing country relations revisited. *Journal of International Business Studies, 32*(1), 23–39.
Ramamurti, R. (2009). 13 What have we learned about emerging—market MNEs? *Emerging multinationals in emerging markets*, 399.
Ramamurti, R. (2012). Competing with emerging market multinationals. *Business Horizons, 55*(3), 241–249.
Ramamurti, R., & Doh, J. P. (2004). Rethinking foreign infrastructure investment in developing countries. *Journal of World Business., 39*(2004), 151–167.
Ramamurti, R., & Singh, J. V. (2009). *Emerging multinationals in emerging markets.* Cambridge University Press.
Rugman, A., & Li, J. (2007). Will China's multinationals succeed globally or regionally? *European Management Journal, 25*(5), 333–343.
Rugman, A. M. (1981). *Inside the multinationals: The economics of internal markets.* Columbia Press.
Rugman, A. M. (2007). Theoretical aspects of multinational enterprises from emerging economies, with particular reference to China.

Rugman, A. M. (2010). Reconciling internalization theory and the eclectic paradigm. *Multinational Business Review, 18*(2), 1–12.
Rugman, A. M., & Verbeke, A. (1998). Corporate strategies and environmental regulations: An organizing framework. *Strategic Management Journal, 19*(4), 363–375.
Rugman, A. M., & Verbeke, A. (2002). Edith Penrose's contribution to the resource-based view of strategic management. *Strategic Management Journal, 23*(8), 769–780.
Rugman, A. M., Verbeke, A., & Nguyen, Q. T. K. (2011). Fifty years of international business theory and beyond. *Management International Review, 51*, 755–786.
Rui, H., & Yip, G. S. (2008). Foreign acquisitions by Chinese firms: A strategic intent perspective. *Journal of world business, 43*(2), 213–226.
Sally, R. (2013). Multinational enterprises, political economy and institutional theory: Domestic embeddedness in the context of internationalisation. *Review of International Political Economy, 1*(1), 161–192.
Taylor, R. (2002). Globalization strategies of Chinese companies: Current developments and future prospects. *Asian Business& Management, 1*, 209–225.
Tolentino, P. E. (2008). Explaining the competitiveness of Multinational Companies from developing economies: A critical review of the academic literature. *International Journal of Technology and Globalisation, 4*(1), 23–38.
Tull, D. M. (2006). China's engagement in Africa: Scope, significance and consequences. *The Journal of Modern African Studies, 44*(3), 459–479.
Vernon, R. (1966). International investment and international trade in the product life cycle. *The Quarterly Journal of Economics, 80*(2), 190–207.
Voss, H., Buckley, P. J., & Cross, A. R. (2010). *The impact of home country institutional effects on the internationalization strategy of Chinese firms.* Multinational Business Review.
Wang, J.Y. (2007). *What drives China's growing role in Africa*? IMF Working paper 211.
Wang, Q., & Boateng, A. (2007). Cross-Border M&as by Chinese firms: An analysis of strategic motivation and performance. *International Management Review, 3*(4), 19–31.
Wheeler, D., & Mody, A. (1992). International investment location decision: The case of U.S. firms. *Journal of International Economics, 33*(1–2), 57–76.
Wild, L., & Mepham, D. (2006). The new Sinosphere: China in Africa. *The China Quarterly, 190*, 478–480.

Williamson, O. E. (1975). *Markets and hierarchies: Analysis and antitrust implications: A study of the economics of internal organizations*. Free Press.
Williamson, O. E. (1981). The economics of organization: The transaction cost approach. *The American Journal of Sociology, 87*, 548–577.
Williamson, P. J., Ramamurti, R., Fleury, A., & Fleury, M. T. L. (Eds.). (2013). *The competitive advantage of emerging market multinationals*. Cambridge University Press.
World Bank. (2011). *World Bank Strategy Sector Information & Communication Technologies Approach Paper*, available from https://www.unapcict.org/resources/ictd-infobank/2011-world-bank-strategy-sector-information-communication-technologies-approach-paper
World Investment Report. (2006). *FDI from developing and transition economies: Implications for development*. UNCTAD.
Wright, M., Filatotchev, I., Hoskisson, R., & Peng, M. W. (2005). Strategy research in emerging economies: Challenging the conventional wisdom. *Journal of Management Studies, 42*, 1–33.
Zaheer, S. (1995). Overcoming the liability of foreignness. *Academy of Management Journal, 38*(2), 341–363.
Zheng, N., Wei, Y., Zhang, Y., & Yang, J. (2016). In search of strategic assets through cross-border merger and acquisitions: Evidence from Chinese multinational enterprises in developed economies. *International Business Review, 25*(1), 177–186.
Zhu, Y., Lynch, R., & Jin, Z. (2011). Playing the game of catching-up: Global strategybuilding in a Chinese company. *Asia Pacific Business Review, 17*(4), 511–533.

4

Methodology and Data

4.1 Introduction

The research aims at exploring the specific phenomenon of China's economic involvement in Africa through both national-level and firm-level. The previous chapter introduced internationalisation of infrastructure investment in developing countries in the case of China's profile in Africa. As a nascent research field, the prior studies and statistics are limited. The nature of such exploration research can lead to differences in data collection procedures. For this study, it is foreseeable that non-response error would cause the problem of sample size if it completely relied on statistical data by a large spreading survey. Therefore, to give the broader view of the research context, multi-methods (Hurmerinta & Nummela, 2011) are adopted in course of the data collection. Primary sources of information include face-to-face interviews and multi-channel data digging. The secondary information comes from the background information related to China and Africa.

This chapter gives a detailed description of methodology and data collection strategies in two sections. Before this, there is explanation of the strategic approach on the mixed-method study. The first part is the modelling of the determinants and motivations of location decisions in two cases. It consists of model specification and the criteria for data selection. After econometrics discussion, the study focuses on the case studies by adopting interviews. It includes the design process of interview structure, characteristics of the sample, question layers and the summary of result.

Y. Tang, *The Operations of Chinese Infrastructure Multinationals in Africa*,
https://doi.org/10.1007/978-981-16-2562-6_4

4.2 Feasibility of Mixed-Method Strategy

Combining qualitative and quantitative research in one study is utilised as an alternative strategy for assessing the study more deeply where there is limited access to mass data and a large number of cases (Hurmerinta & Nummela, 2011). The considerable potential for mixing methods on data collecting and analysing has been acknowledged (Ghauri, 2004; Piekkari et al., 2009; Yin, 1994) and used in several IB studies (Fenwick et al., 2003; Clark & Pugh, 2001).[1] The strategies of combining multiple methods are diverse according to appropriate use of limited quantitative and qualitative data.

4.2.1 Mixed-Method Design for Telecommunication Cases

The case study of telecommunication MNEs aims at tapping 'an empirical inquiry that investigates a contemporary phenomenon' into 'its real-life context when the boundaries between phenomenon and context are not clearly evident' (Yin, 1994). After digging data from extensive online and official sources, the econometric study can be utilised for research objectives. However, the quantitative data are not fully stable as a standardised database. It may cause a few problems of interpretation. The study, therefore, designs interview questions of these firms to give better corroborated explanations of the test results. In such particular strategy of case design, the empirical analysis of the companies was applied with the interview cases context, and the cases then acted as a platform for better understanding, namely, 'aggregated strategy'[2] (Hurmerinta & Nummela, 2011). With this strategy, both the quantitative data and qualitative data were intertwined with each other. It can be applied to both single-case design and multiple cases. What matters is this integration of types of

[1] See the summary table of mixed methods case studies in Piekkari (2009) "Rethinking the case study in international business and management research."

[2] Another alternative strategy for mixed methods is 'Compartmentalised Strategy'. With this strategy, the studies are more likely reported as quantitative work, qualitative data formed supportive and illustrative examples but separate part.(see Hurmerinta & Nummela, 2011)

data and analysis to increase the weight put on conceptual development of the IMNEs in telecommunication perspective and interpretation of empirical findings.

Two phases of the research progress were built on: in a first stage of secondary data, I gathered quantitative data from country-related databases[3] including different possible explanatory data, which acted as a basis for the analysis and served as empirical-understanding; in the second stage, the two case companies (and also other construction firms, governmental department, research association[4]) were addressed by conducting semi-structured interviews. The interviews were firstly designed as the question sets and standardised questionnaire for supplementing the quantitative data. However, with the limitation of acceptance of interviewees, the interviews were restructured to provide more open questions in order to allow unexpected answers and perspectives to emerge. Because of the parallel data collection, the answers from open questions were blended for one perspective to incorporate quantitative results rather than fully used as descriptive examples.

Also the face-to-face interviews in practice in this study required a large amount travelling and time so that the interviews could only happen in selected countries in Africa instead of all objective countries. Two case companies were personally interviewed in both South Africa and Mozambique to obtain more in-depth information about the performance and strategies of individuals in two very different but usefully indicative host countries.

4.2.2 Single-Method Case Study Utilisation for Construction Sector

In construction sector, the study only uses interviews as the methodological approach for information. Doing primary data collection in interviews of Chinese SOEs context involves the practical challenges in gaining access and gathering data. The contextual sensitivity in asking

[3] See appendix in Chap. 6 on data sources.

[4] It will be explained in qualitative method in next section here

questions and interpreting findings impedes collecting quantitative data from large numbers of cases in similar types of firms. Chinese IMNEs occupy a large amount of construction projects in Africa, however, but provide limited published information. Case study method here is particularly well-suited to this research because it provides the chance to check the understanding of data and obtain the sufficient answers Ghauri (2004). Therefore, the study involves using deep contextualisation of case-study evidence to develop idiographic explanations. In this sector, comparative interviews based on different levels of ownership are considered. Buck (2011) notes that different 'polar' cases may offer contrasting patterns that may be useful for inductive propositions. This provides the opportunity for 'greater' depth, richness and case-oriented explanation in further analytical generalisation (Fletcher & Plakoyiannaki, 2011).

Single cases can be selected straightforwardly because their extremeness or uniqueness is useful for exploring the phenomenon (Buck, 2011; Yin, 2009). Extreme cases may comprise most features of the similar types of firms that are outstanding successes, though such cases lack of statistical representativeness to be exploited (Eisenhardt & Graebner, 2007). Although there are only one-firm responses to each kind of ownership level, the cases can inductively suggest important propositions. Small-N case studies still identify patterns of contrasts and similarities across cases. The findings of the cases will give insights on differences of performances among Chinese IMNEs under African conditions.

4.3 Quantitative Method

The quantitative data are collected for investigating the motivations and determinants of location choice in telecommunication sector. Looking into heterogeneity of responses on location choices between two similar firms, the study observes two groups of discrete outcomes that are time variant over African countries. Greene (2004)and Baltagi (2005) point out that the use of panel data allows controlling individual heterogeneity, to measure the effects that are not detectable in pure cross-section or time series data. It reduces measurement errors and biases and provides more accurate estimation for individual outcomes (Hsiao, 2003). Panel data model is a more robust way of modelling the effects on location decision. This is due to the availability of repeated observations on the same units allowing pooling individual time series of a number of countries and analysing them simultaneously (Verbeek, 2004).

The further model choosing as panel probit model since no sufficient statistic for v_i exists. This means that it cannot be estimated a fixed effects (FE) in probit model consistently for fixed T. In case of random effect (RE) model, the individual effects that are random and used for the key variable x_t do not vary over time. If there are various groups with dummy variable, RE estimator can control part of ε_i correlated with x_{it} (Wooldridge, 2010 [2002]). The error term in this model consists of two components: a time-invariant component v_i and a remainder component μ_{it} that is uncorrelated over time, written as $\varepsilon_{it} = v_i + \mu_{it}$. The regression will include the time-invariant individual effect v_i. Therefore, using RE, the model can efficiently be used for estimating effects of unobserved time constant elements, such as landlocked countries.[5] Verbeek (2004) states that RE approach allows making inference with regard to the population characteristics. Under the parametric estimation, the RE model concentrates on differences 'between' individuals, i.e. it is exploiting the between dimension of the data (differences between individuals).

4.3.1 Model Specification

The discrete outcome of y can be viewed as the observed counterpart of a latent random variable. In some micro-economic problems, the panel data may involve nonlinearities that requires discrete or limited dependent variables (Verbeek, 2004). When analysing binary response in context of panel data, through the information on intertemporal dynamics of individual entities allowing for a free correlation structure over time (Cappellari & Jenkins, 2003), unobserved effects probit model provides the possibility of a model of individual behaviour. The standard panel data model where the dependent variable is discrete is

[5] The variable will be explained in Chap. 6

$$y_{it}^{*} = \beta' x_{it} + \varepsilon_{it} \tag{4.1}$$

And

$$y_{it} = \begin{cases} 1 & \text{if } y_{it}^{*} \geq 0 \\ 0 & \text{otherwise} \end{cases} \tag{4.2}$$

Where $\beta'$is a vector of parameters to be estimated as partial effects of the elements of x_{it}, and ε_{it} as unobserved effects. The data on x_{it} are assumed to be strictly exogenous, which implies that $Cov[x_{it,}\varepsilon_{it}] = 0$ across all individuals i and all periods t (Greene, 2004). According to Wooldridge (2010 [2002]), the key assumptions for this model are:

Assumption 1: observed covariates are strictly exogenous conditional on the unobserved effect and x_{it} include enough lags of explanatory variables

$$\begin{aligned} D\left(y_{it}|,x_i|,\varepsilon_{it}\right) &\equiv D\left(y_{it}|,x_{i1}|,x_{i2}\ldots|,x_{iT}|,\varepsilon_{it}\right) \\ &= D\left(y_{it}|,x_{it}|,\varepsilon_{it}\right),\ t = 1,\ldots,T. \end{aligned} \tag{4.3}$$

Assumption 2: a response probability fully determines the conditional distribution $D(y_{it}|\, x_i, \varepsilon_{it})$

$$P\left(y_{it} = 1|x_{it},\varepsilon_{it}\right) = \Phi\left(x_{it}\beta + \varepsilon_{it}\right), \qquad t = 1,\ldots,T. \tag{4.4}$$

Assumption 3: responses are independent conditional on$(x_{it}, \varepsilon_{it})$, the y_{it} are serially uncorrelated, which involves T one-dimensional.

$$f\left(y_{i1},|,,,y_{i2}\ldots,|,,,y_{iT},|,,,x_{i1},|,,,x_{i2}\ldots,|,,,x_{iT},|,,,\beta\right) = \prod_{t} f\left(y_{it}|,x_{it}|,\beta\right) \tag{4.5}$$

Assumption 4: A strong assumption is that ε_{it} has a normal distribution and is uncorrelated with x_{it}. As $\varepsilon_{it} = v_i + \mu_{it}$ and μ_{it} is independent over time, v_i may not have normal distribution. Therefore, it assumes that the joint distribution of ε_{it} start from normal distribution

$$\varepsilon_i | x_i \sim \text{Normal}\left(0, \sigma_v^2\right), \tag{4.6}$$

4.3.2 Maximum Likelihood Estimator

Maximum likelihood estimation is a method to seek the value of the parameter vector that maximises the likelihood function that makes the observed data most likely. It often use logarithm to be equivalent to maximise the likelihood.

When ε_i are independent of x_{it} and is a random sample from a distribution G, indexed by a finite number of parameters ε, then the log likelihood function will be used as the estimator,

$$\log L = \sum_{i=1}^{N} \log \int \prod_{t=1}^{T} F\left(\beta' x_{it} + \varepsilon\right)^{y_{it}} \left[1 - F\left(\beta' x_{it} + \varepsilon\right)\right]^{1-y_{it}} dG\left(\{\varepsilon | \delta\}\right), \tag{4.7}$$

Maximising this with respect to unknown elements β and G, results in consistent estimators provided that the number of time periods T goes to infinity. For fixed T and N →∞, the estimators are inconsistent.

4.3.3 Criterion of Collection

The sample size is 40 countries out of 54 African countries with the criteria employed in the sample selection process.

Host country: selecting the major countries from each part of African continent the sample of 40 countries[6] based on the member countries that joined in the first FOCAC.

Time period: the years of records in different databases are various. Thus, the period was determined on maximum compiled from various secondary sources.

[6] Gambia, as the exception, is the one without diplomatic relation to China.

The companies: two case companies are used for comparison as their increasing involvement in local telecommunication sectors shows them as remarkable investors.

Time of first step into the country: this is the 'digging-data' part of the research. There are two approaches that I used for searching the time of first step into host countries. First, the companies' official websites provide the first entry and first time of investing in certain African countries in their publication. I took the recorded year as the time the company choose to invest in that country. The official publications do not give sufficient records. Therefore, I used a second way to supplement the rest of records from local and Chinese news website by typing into the country and year. The first entry year will be moved backwards when there is news reported on this firm's activities in the host countries until no reports appears.[7] Fortunately, sometimes, the news reports give the proper entry time of firms in certain host countries.

4.4 Qualitative Data

In IB studies, interview-based methods dominated in case study research to obtain deeper understanding (Piekkari et al., 2009). With a limited time to gather data, an interview is a quick way of providing qualitative perspectives. Sinkovics et al. (2008) in particular noted that text-based, in-depth interview is the most widely employed methodology for firm level international business research. The in-depth interview ensures the understanding of details of firm's decision-making (Ghauri & Holstius, 1996) and research phenomenon. Moreover, some issues of China's infrastructure investment in Africa are topics of interest researched without clear boundaries and an absence of sufficiently large numbers of sample units. The emergence of unexpected ideas from semi-structured interviews offer the explanation towards cross-boundaries propositions. Additionally, interviews with the companies and relevant organisations allow the participants to retain a greater degree of control over the

[7] I searched additional past three years if the reports stopped in the certain year to strengthen the validity of records. For example, if the last record of firm A was in 2005 and not any related reports in 2004, I continued to search in 2003, 2002, and 2001.

information which the researcher may obtain on other platforms. Thus, the findings will be more accurate to what the researcher looks for.

4.4.1 Sample Characterises

The population considered was Chinese MNEs in infrastructure investment in Africa during recent decades. First, several relevant press reports have listed a few of the companies and quantities of investment. This information, however, is not comprehensive and concentrated in particular information source. Most of them are mentioned generally in the infrastructure investment in Africa but never have clear and actual figures available in public. Second, regarding the feature of industry, most Chinese MNEs involved in African infrastructure are SOEs and usually are sensitive to questions. An ample response of survey data is not feasible in this case. Moreover, after cross checking on the official web sites and annual reports, the secondary information is too limited to get equivalent participation when the research is focusing on Africa. Therefore, to fully understand the detail of internationalisation processes and strategies of Chinese infrastructure MNEs, I narrow down the research objects into firms.

This part is based on field work in South Africa and Mozambique. The interview methodology used was qualitative and involved participant observation and intensive interviewing based upon semi-structured interview formats. The interviews were arranged via informal governmental, business and academic contacts acquired through face-to-face, in-depth interviews and conducted only by the author (English and Chinese in Africa).

In Africa, interviews were conducted in August–September 2012 in South Africa and Mozambique, involving a total number of 12 interviews with Chinese companies' participants and African government officials, research association (Table 4.1).[8]

[8] With the initial promise that any information given by participants will be treated in complete confidence and no participant will be named. The information of anonymity also requires non-records preference of the interviews.

Table 4.1 Summary of interviews

Date	Institution type	Duration	Format	Place	Topic
31-Aug-12	Private T1	1.5 hours	Face-to-face	Johannesburg	Telecommunication
10-Sep-12	Private T1	1 hour	Face-to-face	Maputo	Telecommunication
11-Sep-12	SOE T2	40 mins	Face-to-face	Johannesburg	Telecommunication
06-Sep-12	Private C	1 hour	Face-to-face	Maputo	Construction
06-Sep-12	SOE C1	1 hour	Face-to-face	Maputo	Construction
07-Sep-12	SOE C2	n.a.	Face-to-face	Maputo	Construction
31-Aug-12	Gov. 1	30 mins	Face-to-face	Pretoria	Host government
12-Sep-12	Gov. 2	30 mins	Face-to-face	Pretoria	Home government
13-Sep-12	Aca.1	40 mins	Face-to-face	Stellenbosch	Infrastructure investment
05-Sep-12	Aca. 2	50 mins	Face-to-face	Johannesburg	Infrastructure investment
28-Aug-12	Aca. 3	50 mins	Face-to-face	Johannesburg	Infrastructure
14-Sep-12	Gov.3	30 mins	Face-to-face	Johannesburg	Construction

4.4.2 Sample Selection

Host Country

I took two steps in course of selecting host countries. At the first stage of selection, looking for contact information without specific focus countries brings poor reception towards investigation requirements by Chinese firms. Multiple interviews around several countries are invalid for this case. As discussed above, it would be impossible to collect comprehensive data through the use of multiple cases in each type of firms in the China-Africa context. At the second stage, there are two ways to open the access to case companies. First, highlights the selection of information-rich cases for in-depth study, the purposeful sampling is appropriate rather than representative and random statistical sampling as in a quantitative study (Coyne, 1997; Hillebrand et al., 2001; Fletcher & Plakoyiannaki, 2011). South Africa and Mozambique, therefore, are chosen as the field work countries. The two countries are significantly different in economic development which brings extreme contrast to the sample. On the one hand, South Africa is one of the comparatively developed countries on the African continent. Here mature investment regulation and experience of attracting FDI may present a condition close to that of traditional investment. The regional HQs of the two telecommunication companies are in South Africa. Mozambique is one of the least developed countries in Africa with low level of infrastructure. The disadvantages of location incorporate the initial conceptualisation of infrastructure provision by Chinese MNEs. The findings from this country will be more evident for non-traditional MNEs' analysis. On the other hand, according to the local law and regulation, Chinese firms in South Africa provide more open information to the public. This means writing to prospective case companies or relevant institutions became possible. I contacted them with my research purpose and its impact to their Relations Department. Secondly, gaining access is through personal networks. Most Chinese firms in poorer African countries did not give any public contact information. They are only collected by government department. Obtaining internal information of register Chinese firms gives the access to some firms. Personal contacts helped me to interview Chinese companies in Mozambique.

Case Companies and Relevant Institutions

In the telecommunication sector, the interviews are used for integrating investigation on country choice through empirical results to understanding their internationalisation process. Additionally, the case companies are the major investors in telecommunications spread over Africa. Their performance can give a representative explanation of the phenomenon.

In the construction sector, the Chinese companies involved in construction projects in host countries are considered. After contacting with the companies from internal list, only three firms accepted to give interviews. And one interview was interrupted midway by one of those firms as they think the questions are sensitive to their confidential clause.

The relevant institutions are versatile from different perspectives. They are used for supplementing the investigation from home- and host- governmental levels, and local construction association and local consultancy research views. The selection of interviews for these participants is not strict in criterion but secures broadbased relevance to the issues of explored.

Numbers of Cases

Despite the 'more the better' view that can dominate case design, the limited number of cases design remained to constitute the optimum form for Chinese IMNEs. Based on real world discovery, one case is reasonable to generalise analytically towards theoretical propositions (Fletcher & Plakoyiannaki, 2011). According to the summary of merits of single case study,[9] my investigation's purposes on Chinese IMNEs suit single cases. It is valuable to make 1–2 comparative cases in each sector. Table 4.2 gives several features if the cases of two sectors for interviews in this study are rational to be selected as single case.

---

[9] Case study researchers Fletcher and Plakoyiannaki's work in 2011, they summarised the arguments of single case or multiple case selection by structuring a comparison table. The Table 4.2 used most features to measure if both sectors can apply to single cases investigation.

Table 4.2 Criterion of single case selection

Single case design	Telecommunication sector	Construction sector
Deep insights	Yes	Yes
Thick descriptions and better stories	Yes	Yes
Highly context specification	Yes	Yes
Within-case study	No	No
High level of flexibility	Yes	Yes
Inductive interpretation	Yes	Yes
Developing an understanding of empirical work	Yes	No
Conceptually-driven	Yes	Yes
Low resource intensive	Yes	Yes
Representing phenomenon	Yes	Yes

Taken together, the selection of the sample generates an inquiry that met the needs for this research well.

4.4.3 Structure of the Interviews

The study applies to semi-structured interviews with various categories of open questions designed towards the respondents. A semi-structured interview was chosen when questions were designed to obtain wide-range coverage for the purpose of the exploratory research. The major questions were developed in the form of general guiding statements which were then followed by a sequence of sub-questions for further probing according to the interviewees' answers. The choice of semi-structured in this study, rather than structured interview, was employed for two reasons. Firstly, it offers sufficient flexibility to approach different respondents differently while still cover the same areas from different perspectives. Secondly, it allows informants the freedom to express the interviewees' views in their own understanding of the topic which helps to develop relevant and meaningful conceptualising propositions. The yes/no questions' answers are required to give explanations. The interview questions consequently categorised into four groups with differences and similarities:

Question Structure of ICT Firms

1. Overview of Chinese telecommunication in Africa: this part gives general statement on my interview purpose that guides participants to address the following questions. The questions of this section provide general views of the interviewees on their investment.
   (a) Initial ideas of choosing location
   (b) The achievements and changes of telecommunication investment in Africa/South Africa/Mozambique over the decade years
   (c) Consideration of competition from home competitors and host countries
   (d) What are the advantages of Chinese telecommunication company?
   (e) What are the special/unique attributes your company provided in African infrastructure provision?

2. How to define your overseas activities: This part aims at investigating the general characteristics and performance of the investigated units.
   (a) Major works of your unit/company as a whole
   (b) Technology and innovation is always the core of your company, how do you adopt and adjust your technology to local customers?
   (c) Training centres and R&D centres (the purpose/location choice)
   (d) Advantages on bidding for programmes/projects
   (e) Approaches to get bid for projects: local governments/local co-operators/agreements on contracts provided by national government/provincial government.
   (f) Financing of the projects/contracts
   (g) Measurement of local market: market potentials/institutional factors/political relationship/etc.
   (h) Relationships with local government and Chinese government
   (i) Competition with local/international/home investors
   (j) Difficulties of investments in certain country

3. What is the operation trying to do for your group: this section asked questions on the role and localisation production of the investigated unit itself in the internationalisation process of the whole company
   (a) Any problems you ever met when you adapt the technology to specific projects
   (b) Solution of the technology problems: hierarchy/feedback
   (c) Adaption of the core technology to the locals needs
   (d) Managerial and technical staff transfer: within regions/ Africa/global
   (e) Communication and sharing technical information in-between other units. Frequency of it
   (f) Role of your unit in African Strategy /Global Strategy
   (g) Criteria of being regional headquarters
4. What is the operation trying to do for the local economy: this part asked the questions relating to the development issues of Chinese investment in Africa
   (a) Cooperation with local universities.
   (b) Work on the projects by yourself / with local operators? How many co-operators normally for one project?
   (c) Sub-contract from local partners
   (d) Partnerships in indefinite period for the support or ICT services to local consumers/enterprises(marketisation)
   (e) Maintaining of telecommunication infrastructure
   (f) The criteria of local recruitment
   (g) Evaluation of your contribution to infrastructure development of host country

Questions Structure of Construction Firms

1. General description of the investment in the country
   (a) Time of first projects in Africa.
   (b) Numbers of projects
   (c) Allocation of all units in Africa/regional headquarters
   (d) Major investments in Mozambique/Africa as a whole

2. Performance and major activities
    (a) Local government created projects/international institutions' projects/Chinese government ODA projects
    (b) Financing and leverage approach of projects
    (c) Roles of your companies, Chinese government and local governments in formulating, bidding and financing infrastructure projects
    (d) Bidding process for construction projects
    (e) To what extent Chinese government influences the choice of projects and areas
3. Competition and cooperation
    (a) Advantages of your company in bidding and operating on projects
    (b) Differences among Chinese construction MNEs/ MNEs from other countries/ local construction firms in Projects bidding
    (c) Main competitors in this country
    (d) Difficulties of investment in Mozambique /Africa as a whole (common/specific)
    (e) Institutional factors vs. market potentials
4. Contribution to the group
    (a) Sources of construction materials
    (b) Role of your unit in African strategy/global strategy
    (c) Investment in other areas to be localised
    (d) Communication with other units/headquarters
5. Development issues of China and local economy
    (a) Changes of infrastructure in Africa/Mozambique over years
    (b) Chinese MNEs' roles in development of infrastructure and China-Africa development, commercial impact or diplomatical impact
    (c) Prospects of Africa/Mozambique construction market
    (d) Criteria of local recruitment/level of labour force
    (e) Level of skills/technologies/managerial skills transfer. Approaches of technology/skills transfer

Questions Structure of Official/Governmental Institutions

I prepared two types of guiding questions for interviewing official institutions. Governmental or official institutions have stronger perspectives on their own sides. The guiding questions are set up on their direction of views. Furthermore, I also interviewed local commercial consultancy and academic organisations. The questions are mixed from both types and partially interview questions of companies.

Organisation Type A

1. Methods of bidding or cooperating with local telecommunication partners?
2. Relationship between Chinese construction firms and government? Directly contract?
3. Relationship between these two Chinese telecommunication firms and government? Indirect contract?
4. What is the difference of Chinese infrastructure provision from other international infrastructure provision?
5. Is ICT infrastructure provision marketised in this country? How do you think Chinese enterprise can fit into the development of ICT?
6. Improvement of local recruitment. Telecommunication firms? Construction firms?
7. What are the shortcomings of Chinese infrastructure provisions?
8. Angola mode. Does Chinese infrastructure investment also follow this mode, e.g. are resource potentials as basis of internationally-oriented development complementary with infrastructure provision in countries rich in resources?
9. The role of Chinese infrastructure companies in China-South Africa development?
10. What is the role of bilateral governments in formulating infrastructure projects? Difference in policy supports?

Organisation Type B

1. How did the Chinese IMNEs get to bid for participation in the ICT infrastructure creation projects?
2. How much is the company involved in formulating the details of the projects?
3. Did the Chinese investment in infrastructure seem to encourage or discourage local partners, i.e. technology spillover or crowding local enterprises?
4. Will the company be paid a fee for creation and initial operationalisation of the ICT programmes and then hand over to a local agency/firm? Or on the country?
5. To what extent are the ICT/construction companies seen as 'agents' of the Chinese government? Is it necessarily seen as a bad thing?
6. In what ways, did the Chinese government influence the selection of the Chinese IMNE? Financing the projects? Diplomatic pressure?
7. To what extent do specific competence/ capabilities of a Chinese IMNEs help gaining it a role in a project?
8. How much do Chinese ICT/construction MNEs involve themselves in infrastructure investment in your country? How much are they involved commercially in other investments?
9. What are the major parts of its rewards in commercial revenue/profit?

4.5 Concluding Remarks

To sum up, the mixed-method strategy allows gaining deeper understanding of the phenomenon under investigation and improving knowledge creation thanks to the integration of different types of data and joint interpretation of the findings (Hurmerinta & Nummela, 2011). To provide the theoretical contribution which may extend beyond the specific context in a nascent research field, this kind of methodological approach is particularly appropriate. However, in this study, the mixed-method strategy was not equally applied to both telecommunication and construction sectors. The emphases of qualitative data collection on the two sectors are versatile.

Bibliography

Baltagi, B. H. (2005). *Econometric analysis of panel data—Third edition.* John Wiley & Sons.

Buck, T. (2011). Case selection informed by theory. In R. Piekkari & C. Welch (Eds.), *Rethinking the case study in international business and management research* (pp. 192–209). Edward Elgar.

Cappellari, L., & Jenkins, S. P. (2003). Multivariate probity regression using simulated maximum likelihood. *The Stata Journal, 3*(3), 278–294.

Clark, T., & Pugh, D. S. (2001). Foreign country priorities in the internationalization process: A measure and an exploratory test on British firms. *International Business Review, 10*(3), 285–303.

Coyne, I. T. (1997). Sampling in qualitative research. Purposeful and theoretical sampling; Merging or clear boundaries? *Journal of Advanced Nursing, 26*, 623–630.

Eisenhardt, K. M., & Graebner, M. E. (2007). Theory building from cases: Opportunities and challenges. *Academy of Management Journal, 50*(1), 25–32.

Fenwick, M., Edwards, R., & Buckley, P. J. (2003). Is cultural similarity misleading? The experience of Australian manufacturers in Britain. *International Business Review, 12*(3), 297–309.

Fletcher, M., & Plakoyiannaki, E. (2011). Case selection in international business: Key issues and common misconceptions. In R. Marschan-Pierkkari & C. Welch (Eds.), *Rethinking the case study in international business and management research.* Edward Elgar.

Ghauri, P. (2004). Designing and conducting case studies in international business research. In R. Piekkari & C. Welch (Eds.), *Handbook of qualitative research methods for international business.* Edward Elgar.

Ghauri, P., & Holstius, K. (1996). The role of matching in the foreign market entry process in the Baltic States. *European Journal of Marketing, 30*, 75–88.

Greene, W. (2004). Convenient estimators for the panel Probit model: Further results. *Empirical Economics, 29*(1), 21–47.

Hillebrand, G. G., Miyamoto, K., Schnell, B., Ichihashi, M., Shinkura, R., & Akiba, S. (2001). Quantitative evaluation of skin condition in an epidemiological survey of females living in northern versus southern Japan. *Journal of Dermatological Science, 27*, 42–52.

Hsiao, C. (2003). *Analysis of panel data* (2nd ed.). Cambridge University Press.

Hurmerinta, L., & Nummela, N. (2011). Mixed-method case studies in international business research. In R. Piekkari & C. Welch (Eds.), *Rethinking the case study in international business and management research* (pp. 210–225). Edward Elgar.
Piekkari, R. (2009). International management. *The Handbook of Business Discourse*, 269–278.
Piekkari, R., Welch, C., & Paavilainen, E. (2009). The case study as disciplinary convention: Evidence from international business journals. *Organizational Research Methods, 12*, 567–589.
Sinkovics, R., Penz, E., & Ghauri, P. (2008). Enhancing the trustworthiness of qualitative research in international business. *Management International Review, 6*, 689–714.
Verbeek, M. (2004). *A Guide to Modern Econometrics* (2nd ed.). John Wiley & Son Ltd.
Wooldridge, J. M. (2010 [2002]). *Econometric analysis of cross section and panel data*. Cambridge, Mass: MIT Press.
Yin, R. K. (1994). *Case study research design and methods: Applied social research and methods series* (2nd Ed.), Thousand Oaks, CA: Sage Publications.
Yin, R. K. (2009). *Case study research: Design and methods* (4th Ed.), Thousand Oaks, CA: Sage Publications.

5

Conceptualising Infrastructure Multinationals' Provision: Case of Chinese IMNEs in Africa

5.1 Introduction

The booming of China's infrastructure investment has been continuously taking large account of China's involvement in Africa. The insight of Chinese MNEs extends to sectoral scope and arises as the context for bilateral developments in the form of provision and emergence of Chinese multinationals in infrastructure sectors. As noted Chap. 3 the established concern of IB theory is to understand and evaluate MNEs as firms. Currently, an extensive literature on emergence of Chinese MNEs begins to offer an explanation that the growth and opening of the economy provokes internationalisation of Chinese MNEs. In fact, it reflects specific needs of Chinese development as perceived through government policy. This exploratory chapter aims at drawing on these emerging contexts in terms of firms: the growing role of MNEs in the creation of infrastructure in developing countries and the emergence of MNEs from China, by elaborating on the positioning of Chinese IMNEs' operations in Africa. Thus, the analytical objectives are to explain how and why Chinese IMNEs, emerging as firms from the early stages of China's industrialisation and institutional reformulations, move to the current internationalisation of their operations. In the case of infrastructure, the rise of MNEs reflects the widespread privatisation of its creation and provision.

Y. Tang, *The Operations of Chinese Infrastructure Multinationals in Africa*,
https://doi.org/10.1007/978-981-16-2562-6_5

This is a leading impulsion within a wider nexus of needs, motivations and agents. The position of the sector is nevertheless still determined by government decisions in development programmes. The issues raised by participation of Chinese IMNEs in Africa therefore involve both the concerns of international business and the wider needs of economic development in Africa and of sustainability in China's own growth. These MNEs are projected into the interdependencies between the institutional bases for African and Chinese development.

The capacities of the Chinese IMNEs are seen to reflect their position in the achieved developments of the Chinese economy deriving from CSAs (e.g. access to capital and foreign exchange) and FSAs (e.g. technologies and skills) which are built up in participating in infrastructure creation in China's economic growth. The lack of necessary infrastructure and the capacities to finance and formulate it locally brings the major constraint on realising African development. Chinese IMNEs are well placed to overcome these constraints by implementing major infrastructure projects in Africa and this correlates simultaneously with China's growing need for resource access.

This chapter consist of four parts. Section 5.2 summarises the general features of companies involved in infrastructure provision. Section 5.3 discusses the IMNE's role in-between infrastructure and development. Section 5.4 conceptualises infrastructure MNE and the issues of international infrastructure provision within national development programmes. In the Sect. 5.5, it attempts to formulate a view of the IMNE in terms of its abilities in cases of Chinese IMNEs.

5.2 The General Features of Infrastructure Investment

Infrastructure is the core of development, so that increasing investment in this field is considered to be the priority for developing countries (WIR, 2008). UNCTAD (2008) provides a working definition of infrastructure as comprising 'the physical facilities, institutions and organisational structures, or the social and economic foundations, for the operation of a society'. The understanding of infrastructure in terms of its ownership and market orientation allows the formulation of private infrastructure enterprises and the international expansion of their operations as FDI and IMNEs.

First, infrastructure itself is not supposed to be value-added. It is not directly connected to commercial activities. They produce non-tradable services which are not tangible outputs. The competitions of infrastructure creation activities merely happen on the bargaining or bidding steps. Second, infrastructure sectors are 'natural monopolies' as they have increasing returns to scale with high fixed costs (Ramamurti & Doh, 2004). They are often involved in strong networks, which is an essential competitive advantage. Third, infrastructure sectors contain capital intensive activities and the infrastructure assets will last in to the long term, possess 'huge sunk costs' and are 'location-specific' (WIR, 2008). Fourth, many infrastructure investments relate to social and political issues. Their produced services are managed by governments as the public goods. Thus, firms in infrastructure industries in many countries are state-owned. Fifth, infrastructure industries do not make tradable products but mainly determine the economic competitiveness as a whole by their impact on other industries.

5.3 MNEs in Infrastructure and Development

In the processes of development infrastructure improvement is needed both to meet increased consumer demand for particular services and also to build endogenous capacities into the growth process itself. The infrastructure provision is inherently endogenous to achievement of economic growth. It will be most decisively crucial for countries which are at the initial level of development and targeting the initiation of an industrial sector or realising particular sources of potential comparative advantage (e.g. in resource-based sectors) (Tang & Pearce, 2011). The countries have to address the creation of new infrastructure capacity in sufficient scale and appropriate forms. The rise of IMNEs can be seen as the potential to help with both quantitative (financial) and qualitative (appropriate project formulation and implementation) concerns. Part of what these MNEs do is raise capital, so that they are also relevant to issues of funding of infrastructure. This is vital for countries at early stages of implementing development programmes which face an inevitable financing gap for infrastructure creation.

The creation or expansion of infrastructure supply capacity, especially in less developed countries at the early stages of an articulated development process, are likely to challenge the normal parameters of private enterprise decision making. Firstly, it is likely to supply direct services to consumers, thus comprising an important facet of what successful development is expected to provide to a population. The social benefits of such improvements to individual welfare, and their potential to provide positive feedbacks into the development process itself, suggests that the pricing of such infrastructure services might not be best left to the consumer market and private enterprise suppliers. Secondly, important elements of infrastructure expansion are intended to provide inputs and spillovers supportive of other value-adding parts of the economy. Thus infrastructure and its enhancement is an inherent part of the process of building for sustainable and self-reinforcing development. But this aspect of infrastructure performance is manifest in externalities that will be realised over long periods of time. How host government planners and potential private infrastructure providers predict and value these outcomes, and determine the firm's reward structures and conditions of operation, are again beyond the scope of normal investment decision processes.

China's ability and willingness to provide capital to its MNEs becomes at the centre of the participation in infrastructure provision in Africa. The role of Chinese IMNEs is considered as being major vehicles in operationalising precise synergies and interdependencies between the developmental needs and capacities of Africa and China. A central issue emerging in the sustainability of China's growth and international competitiveness is that the focus of this on the manufacturing sector has generated demand for many natural resources and primary product inputs that exceed the scope of domestic supply. This also generates a surplus of re-investable capital, alongside a build-up of foreign exchange reserves. Securing the growth already achieved has also led to familiarity with the need for infrastructure itself. It has therefore helped to generate an efficient construction sector that is familiar with a positioning in infrastructure creation. Another type of competitive and ambitious firms has emerged in China in other industries that can overlap with infrastructure provision and expand into manufacture, notably telecommunications.

Africa observes infrastructure limitations are a constraint on growth, along with the related infrastructure funding gap (Foster & Garmendia, 2010). The infrastructure limitations then become significantly relevant here; two constraints of development—the shortage of capital and the lack of domestic competence in infrastructure creation could be alleviated through access to Chinese capital and expertise. An infrastructure bottleneck constrains Africa's ability to build development and competitiveness around its extensive and varied resource-supply strengths. Alleviation of these bottlenecks can then provide a point of mutual benefits for Africa and China, with Chinese finance and expertise allowing Africa to realise its resource-supply potentials in ways that very precisely feed back into China's own developmental needs. These interdependencies play a role in both Chinese government policy towards Africa and its FDI there. The complementarities between the realisation of Africa's resource potentials and the creation of effective infrastructure there thus emerge as vital to the developmental progress of both Africa and China. The emergence and commitment to Africa of Chinese resource-seeking MNEs also becomes the major player in this network of interdependencies. Though these resource MNEs may be either state-owned or private there is no doubt that their commercial viability is positioned within and responsive to the twin needs of African and Chinese development. In many cases, the interdependence between Chinese IMNEs and resource MNEs may be strongly innate, or arms-length. An IMNEs' role in an infrastructure creation programme may help improve a host-location's capacity to support development of its resource potentials in which resource-seeking MNEs then find a viable position.

5.4 Conceptualising Infrastructure Multinationals

The increasing visibility of the internationalisation of infrastructure investment is attributed to two levels. Firstly, at the macro level, the reported flows of foreign direct investment (FDI) in infrastructure sectors dramatically increase. On one hand, it grows in the proportion of total FDI flows that the sector accounts for. On the other hand is the growing share of infrastructure creation which is provided by foreign enterprises in many countries. Secondly, at the level of specific high-profile cases of the companies, such as Chinese participation in infrastructure creation in Africa, resistance to privatisation of infrastructure supply is often articulated most strongly towards potential foreign ownership. Also notable trends within the wider phenomenon of infrastructure FDI have often attracted speculative contention. It is argued that in order to address the issues of *how* and *why* infrastructure FDI has emerged, and *what* its implications are in terms of achieving a sponsoring government's aims in the creation of infrastructure supply capacity, it is necessary to investigate the nature of the international firms that do it; i.e. infrastructure multinational enterprises (IMNEs). Such an investigation is facilitated by the adoption and, as necessary, adaptation of analytical frameworks that have already been operationalised effectively in the manufacturing and services sectors.

5.4.1 Central Activity of Infrastructure MNEs: Infrastructure Project

Infrastructure *project* (IP) is the centre of analysis. Infrastructure firm derives from privatisation of an existing source of infrastructure service supply and pursuit of the enhancement of provision in terms of quantity and/or quality. Whatever the arrangements to secure its implementation an IP will be legitimated through the authorisation of a host-country government or agency, for which it would be expected to target broadly defined developmental or welfare objectives (Tang & Pearce, 2011).

A significant benefit of a coherent commitment to infrastructure creation, and potentially of the participation of IMNEs in it, is likely to be an improved capacity to attract potential FDI into these wider sectors of the economy. Where infrastructure programmes are structured to support realisation of distinctive localised competitive resources (latent sources of comparative advantage) it may often be the case that the most complete fulfilment of these productive potentials may be through participation of established MNEs in the relevant sectors. Such MNEs are convinced that a country does represent a significant and viable new source of competitive activity (whether through market-seeking (MS) supply to the local economy or as efficiency-seeking (ES) production for international markets). Appropriate forms of supporting infrastructure need to be perceived as central to the host economy's projected development programmes (Tang & Pearce, 2011).

Confidence of the host countries may be considerably enhanced by the participation of IMNEs in the planning, building and initial operation of those facets of infrastructure on which other sectoral foreign investors expect to depend. An important element of this would be expected to derive from the view that where experienced international investors are prepared to commit significant resources to long-term infrastructure programmes, with major sunk-costs, it indicates a high level of trust in both the host government's acceptance of private business and its ability to generate sustained economic growth. Such an apparent endorsement by IMNEs should encourage the normally rather smaller and more flexible MNEs of other sectors to also commit to the economy's emerging competitive potentials. Similarly, the co-option of IMNEs by the sponsoring host government can again be seen, by other potential MNE investors, as indicative of the belief that such enterprises' participation will secure the most effective creation of the new infrastructure, in terms of its capacity to support the realisation of the wider-ranging developmental potentials.

Privatisation often raised capital for the government's other budgetary needs, it often also occurred at a point where more capital for expenditure on infrastructure expansion was perceived as a major developmental priority. The emergence of privatised infrastructure sectors in developing countries can be seen to derive from two possible sources. From the view of political-economy debate, the government supports passing into private ownership and control of previously state-owned infrastructure enterprises. Secondly, from funding perspective, the privately-funded and -organised expansions of infrastructure capacity are articulated to address specific aspects of government-perceived developmental targets through new projects. Additionally, of course, when infrastructure privatisation is carried out by IMNEs the capital committed will be imported and thus help alleviate balance of payments and foreign exchange constraints on development. For analytical purposes, in terms of deriving contexts amenable to particular contributions of IMNEs, both origins for privatised infrastructure operations can ultimately be seen as providing the basis of a discrete, development-oriented, infrastructure project. Though privatisation of existing state-owned infrastructure firms was often initially projected to reflect ideological motives or a short-term need for capital, a desire to expand and reposition supply of the relevant service was usually also present. Thus the capability of IMNEs to implement IPs depends on whether this constitutes significant regeneration and repositioning of antecedent State Owned Enterprises, or the creation of completely new enterprise and capacity.

An IP placed at the centre of the decision process of an IMNE immediately indicates a key difference with the decisions of MNEs in the manufacturing and service sectors. Thus in the latter sectors an MNE would normally formulate its own investment project, reflecting its perception of the potential for a country's location advantages (LAs) to support one of its range of strategic objectives (resource seeking; market seeking; efficiency seeking; knowledge seeking) and of the capacity of its existing sources of competitiveness (OAs) to access and operationalised these factors effectively. In the infrastructure sector, the broad parameters of an IP will normally be defined by a host-government ministry or agency, looking for a range of social and developmental objectives that are not inherently adaptable to the relatively short-term performance and profitability optimisation of private enterprise. There is a realistic acceptance by planners that *foreign* private, technologies, skills and practices will be needed to secure successful implementation of the IP. It is also likely to be accepted that the details of IPs will need to be bargained with putative IMNE participants, who will have access to these competences and the ability to package them effectively. The extent to which such a bargaining process is able to secure acceptable terms for the effective implementation of the IP in terms of its originally perceived aims, or whether some reformulation of these aims needs to be conceded to an IMNE, is an important facet of assessing the internationalisation of infrastructure creation.

Before substantive bargaining over the terms and detailed structure of an IP an IMNE is likely to assess it in terms of more conventional LAs. Thus the initial level, and the potential growth, of demand for the services of the IP would remain a plausible determinant of interest. Within this is the extent to which the benefits that an IP provides to the host economy can be marketised in a form that can be appropriated by the IMNE. On the supply side the ability of the host economy to provide adequate access to inputs that an IMNE will need to construct and operate the IP efficiently is also likely to be a significant decision determinant. Potentially relevant issue would be whether the IMNE would be permitted to utilise imported inputs in formulating the IP. This is most likely to affect evaluation of IMNEs on its scope for appropriating returns from the project, but can also influence its expectations for securing its most effective implementation in terms of both creation and operationalisation. A potentially significant factor in how an IMNE assesses a particular IP is the form in which it is intended to be structured contractually.

5.4.2 Participants of Infrastructure Investment

Foreign enterprise involvement with infrastructure generation is implemented through two tiers of IMNE, providing different types of input into IPs' formulation and operationalisation. Firstly, the IMNEs can be distinguished as 'sponsors' ($IMNE_{sp}$), who undertake the negotiations with host-country governments concerning the basic terms under which the IP will be created and then participate, to varying degrees, in formalising strategic details of its aims and structure. From this position at the core of an IP the $IMNE_{sp}$ will derive the responsibility for bringing together the resources and expertise needed to create and (at least initially) run it. Another categorised form towards a second tier role in the IP for subcontracted MNEs ($IMNE_{su}$), who will bring specialised capabilities to, in particular, the stages of building the physical supply capacity of the project.

An IP is often very wide-ranging and complex in its aims, technologies and processes, so that a consortium may need more than one $IMNE_{sp}$, as well as a varied multiplicity of $IMNE_{su}$. Different $IMNE_{sp}$ may bring different dimensions of existing political association (both in terms of home country and host country) and established connections with different subsets of $IMNE_{su}$. Sponsor IMNEs focus on bidding for the infrastructure projects at the stage (usually the early stage) with the host government. Here, the sponsors refer to the investors who are responsible to the whole IPs. The sponsor IMNEs can be the different bodies according to different purposes on an IP. The Chinese government plays a vital role in the bargaining process between IMNEsp and host government. The sponsorship of Chinese government ensures the financial support for the IPs and IMNEsp, the operational feasibility of investment and enhances the bargaining powers of Chinese firms in the process of infrastructure creation.

5.4.3 Realising the Infrastructure Creation in Host Countries

It is observed that the privatisation and internationalisation of infrastructure creation in poorer countries has been significantly driven by the need to access new sources of capital. This is achieved through foreign direct investment, rather than from *portfolio* sources. This suggests that the OAs of IMNEs are built around the need and ability to raise capital competitively. However, the ability of a *particular* $IMNE_{sp}$ to raise capital to support its participation in a *specific* IP will reflect distinct firm-level skills and capacities. Thus $IMNE_{sp}$ need to possess particular firm-specific and sector-specific competences that they can leverage to raise project-specific capital. This can involve the ability to clearly articulate and persuasively project in terms of the viable rewards (risk/return) of the IP to investors and its own distinctive firm-level capacity to secure them. While the organisational competences are likely to be needed to develop, operationalise and run the IP.

The type of OAs that are central to a successful $IMNE_{sp}$ would then focus on firstly, skill in bargaining with the host-country government or agency commissioning the IP; secondly ability to evaluate and access sources of more conventional types of OAs that are needed to build and operationalised an IP effectively. Alongside potential intra-group sources this places a high priority on locating appropriate $IMNE_{su}$ and building their inputs into a coherent realisation of the IP (see Fig. 5.1).

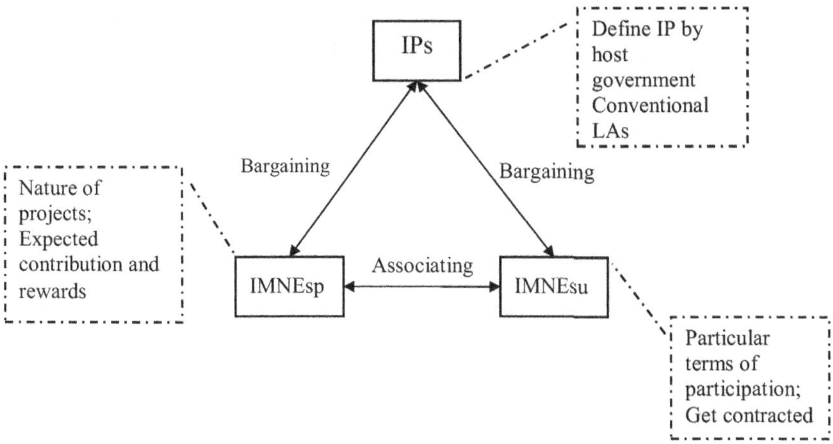

Fig. 5.1 How IMNEs work in host countries infrastructure creation

Here OAs directly related to operationalisation of an IP, including those that may be most effectively secured through $IMNE_{su}$ include technologies, effective familiar engineering and construction practices, and an ability to implement effective markets for infrastructure services where none had previously operated.

The defining attractiveness of an IP, taken over a long but often finite time period (e.g. in the case of build operate transfer (BOT[1] project) is its projected profitability to the potential IMNE (and its nexus of shareholders and stakeholders). A first, more direct, dimension of how an $IMNE_{sp}$ evaluates an IP will consider aspects of quite conventional LAs and reflect variants of familiar MNE strategic motivations, including (i) the likely demand for its services, reflecting a market-seeking (MS) motivation, (ii) the availability of the inputs (including the current state of infrastructure and restriction of using local inputs, materials, labours) that will allow the IP to be created and operated effectively, reflecting an efficiency-seeking (ES) concern.

However, the extent to which an $IMNE_{sp}$ can develop its commitment to, or evaluate its returns from, an IP in terms of unconstrained MS or ES

[1] BOT is same as other traditional MNEs. The operating process is the maintaining of infrastructure project.

calculations of normal LAs (i.e. as familiar from manufacturing or services sectors) may be compromised by the IP's context. Thus often an IP for which an $IMNE_{sp}$ may tender/bargain may be one component of its host-country's more widely defined development programme, with aspects of its perceived aims represented in externalities/synergies with other parts of the programme. Reflecting this, the social benefits to host-country development, as understood by government planners, may not be fully appropriable in the private rewards offered to IMNEs. The much discussed issue of prices/tariffs for infrastructure services is a prominent manifestation of this (which is likely to take an extra dimension of contention where the services derive from an IMNE).

A potentially important aspect of IMNE host-government tension may be the extent to which an IMNE is allowed to define the specific details of an IP, or to impose changes to the original dimensions of an IP as proposed by a host agency. This would, to some degree, allow an $IMNE_{sp}$ to define aspects of the LAs which its own operations would respond to and activate. In this, however, an $IMNE_{sp}$ may provide an ability to define the specifics of an IP to established levels of international capability in a way that might, indeed, elude local planners. This knowledge of received practice of $IMNE_{sp}$ (or indeed associated $IMNE_{su}$) may be a genuine benefit of their participation (a distinctive OA that adds value to the IP). But host governments may nevertheless have legitimate viable concerns that allowing too much IMNE influence at this stage of project articulation may permit opportunistic behaviour that can compromise the social-developmental contribution of the IP in terms of its wider contexts.

A second dimension of LAs that has a pervasive position in the early literature on IMNEs is the extent to which they will perceive a country's broader institutional environment as conducive to private and foreign participants as being able to securely realise the performance they expect and require from a specific IP. As expressed in a FIAS report (Sader, 2000) this 'requires detailed preparation by putting in place an effective institutional legal regulatory framework, supported by strong political commitment to sectoral reform and liberalisation'.

The context (defined around analysis of OAs and LAs) has seen an $IMNE_{sp}$ as operating, therefore, in a very complex and multipartied one. This suggests that an understanding of how such an IP is effectively developed by an $IMNE_{sp}$ would need to incorporate a multitude of contractual agreements and bargaining situations. This, in turn, indicates a vital role for transactions cost and internalisation analysis in fully understanding and evaluating IMNEs.

Two elements of this have already been indicated and may be drawn out here: firstly, the $IMNE_{sp}$ will bargain in depth with the host-country government or agency to define the nature of the project, and its expected contribution and rewards. Where this proves difficult (high transaction costs) it may lead to either the IMNE abandoning the project, or going ahead in a satisficing form that it sees as less than optimal; secondly, the terms of participation of $IMNE_{su}$ need to be bargained and contracted. Again trying to lower the transaction costs of this may compromise the achievement of an ideally configured IP.

In addition to the upfront MS and ES elements of developing its commitment to projects there is an, at least potentially, knowledge seeking (KS) component to IMNEs' (both sponsors and subcontractors) behaviour. Thus each new IP undertaken by an IMNE is likely to be an entry into a differentiated and complex situation, representing (i) distinctive opportunities and contexts, essentially articulated externally by the host government, (ii) different configuration of consortium partners ($IMNE_{su}$)—some familiar, some new.

So each new project represents a strong learning opportunity, so that there is an innate KS dimension within their expansion. This, in turn, suggests that more successful IMNEs will be augmenting their internal sources of competitiveness (OAs) most quickly. That raises issues of future global industry structure, with a potential for increased concentration and the emergence of clearly dominant players. Ultimately, the generation of the modes of analysis and articulation of issues suggested a key normative concern. This would be to discern the extent and ways in which the realisation of an IP's developmental potentials are enhanced, or compromised, by being executed by an IMNE.

5.5 The 'Traditional' and/or 'Enigmatic' Nature of Chinese IMNEs

The challenge in this section is to take an explanation of the issues on 'how' firms whose competitive origins had been very clearly contained within a specific economy then managed to expand successfully, beyond theorising on what have been acknowledged as traditional MNEs. The analytical framework indicates that Chinese and other developing economy MNEs will rarely be able to claim their position in a successful overseas operation purely on the basis of the superiority of a unique firm specific source of competitive advantage and need to co-opt external forms of home country support. The conventional types of competitive attributes that are unique to a particular firm will still be important for firm's capacities defined as asset firm specific advantages. The argument for the firm specific advantage (FSA-A) emphasised that these new MNEs have an effective operationalisation dependent on the ability to acquire supplementary advantages form home-country institutions. The ability draws benefit from external networks by building and maintaining relationships with the institutions and agencies. These can provide the resources and government-policy-based opportunities to achieve its internationalisation. Two special facets of Chinese and emerging market MNEs come from the characteristics of their developing country economies. The factors are important to the home-country's process of development which underwrites the ability of its firms to expand internationally and/or provide a reason for them to do so. AID programmes and diplomatic support that are directly integral to host-country development, such as infrastructure creation, are vital elements designated by government institutions (CSA-I). The argument will also suggest that the internationalisation of Chinese MNEs reflects an embedded positioning in the development of their home country. The success of many of these high growth economies has been associated with the introduction of market forces domestically and with an opening to international competition. This is likely to still operate within the continuation of carefully articulated development policies that seek to secure the upgrading and reinforcement of competitiveness. The process meets specific home

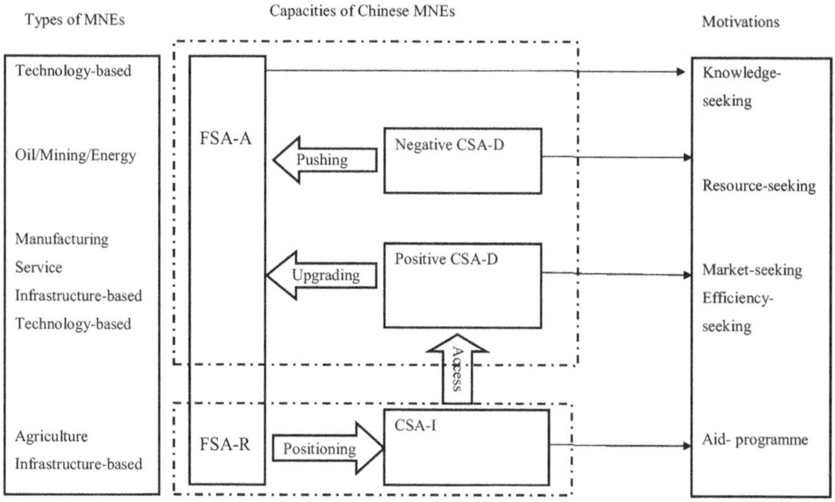

Fig. 5.2 The enigmatic natures of Chinese multinationals

country development needs if it's pushed by negative CSA-D (RS), or negotiates with a range of home-country institutions for supportive resources on its own purposes (MS/ES) (Fig. 5.2).

5.5.1 Asset Firm Specific Advantages

FSA-A are unique attributes of a firm that relate directly to its ability to perform particular value-adding activities in a competitive manner and which can be operationalised effectively when that firm wishes to expand internationally to benefit from a clearly perceived opportunity. In terms of the wider context of Dunning's eclectic framework we are here focusing on central intangible elements of asset-specific ownership advantages (OA_a) such as 'technology and information, managerial, marketing and entrepreneurial skills [and] organisational systems' (Dunning & Lundan, 2008). The positioning of these FSA-A in wider analysis of Chinese MNEs relates to two assertions. Firstly, that the presence of, at least emergent, elements of distinctive FSA-A will be essential to understanding these firms. Though it is a central theme of this framework that both the ability of Chinese firms to expand internationally and, probably, the definition of reasons for doing so, are dependent on the wider developmental context of their home economy, *which* firms access such external supportive resources and opportunities will still depend on the ability to convincingly assert relatively superior in-place capacities to fulfil expected roles. Secondly, that realistically at the current stage of China's industrialisation these extant FSA-A (even in the most plausibly competitive firms) are unlikely to be of a strength or originality to match those of other firms they will need to confront in international operations. Thus, internationalisation is mandated as a means of addressing needs of the Chinese economy through firms' overseas operations and the vulnerable FSA-As receive various supports to achieve this. Though not the central concern of our analysis here, one familiar manifestation of this scenario involves knowledge-seeking (or strategic asset seeking) FDI by Chinese firms very specifically to reinforce their FSA-A. This, of course, challenges central tenets of mainstream IB theorising and the practice again needs to be explained as a government supported part of a national learning process (or a pre-emptive internationalisation of aspects of China's national system of innovation). Here our analysis develops around the way Chinese IMNE are expected to operate in Africa as a component of a nexus of forces driven by resource-seeking objectives.

Another line of argument that was central to initial thinking on the international expansion of national firms that needs some degree of repositioning here is the idea of the 'liability of foreignness'. This suggested that a firm seeking to establish value-adding operations in a foreign economy would need notably strong and distinctive competitive advantages, in excess of those possessed by potentially rival local firms, since it would initially incur costs of adjusting to various aspects of the host-country environment that would not be affecting fully-acclimatised incumbents. These liabilities of foreignness can be found within a wide range of institutional arrangements, including the legal system, the tax system, other bureaucracies, the operation of the labour market, acceptable practices in marketing goods and services, the ability to understand and/or influence government policies and regulations, that the local firms are systematically embedded in but which may be significantly alien to new entrants attuned to different modes of practice. In our terms this assumes the competences applied by the new entrant are simply those directly related to the performance of its precise value-adding activities (i.e. FSA-A), with no expectation of a complementary firm-level expertise in building relationships that could be proactively applied to the need to overcome these particular institutional frictions. Traditional theorising on liability of foreignness thus made no allowance for the use of FSA-R to shorten the process of assimilation to an unfamiliar institutional context.

Indeed the implicit dominant focus on FSA-A in the context of FDI between mature industrial economies that provided the template for early theorising then seemed logical. At that time the expectation was that MNEs were emerging from a home-country environment that was institutionally neutral, in that it did not offer discretionary support and incentives to selected firms. With no systemic access to such supports potential MNEs, in this early scenario, had had no reason to generate distinctive relationship-building expertise; handling the external institutional context was a routine managerial practice. But here we argue that emerging Chinese MNEs have needed to make FSA-R competences central to their competitive development and strategic expansion; most notably overseas. These practices can then be potentially adapted to also build relationships in other developing countries in ways that can indeed facilitate adjustments to local institutional conditions, limiting the liability of foreignness and improving acceptance of their FSA-A.

Another adjustment to traditional perspectives on FSA-A is likely to come into play when placing the expansion of Chinese MNEs in the context of South-South FDI. Here it can be argued that the FSA-A of Chinese enterprises, in the process of being formulated within the large and fast-growing Chinese economy, will already considerably exceed the capacities of most possible local rivals. We should, therefore, define an alternative version of the firm-level advantage issue in terms of how Chinese MNEs can secure access to opportunities in other developing economies in competition with mature, fully competitively-evolved, rivals from developed industrialised economies. Within our framework we can suggest a number of possibilities. Firstly that, though Chinese MNEs' FSA-A may still fall short of 'state of the art', in the sense that they would not be capable of competing with the established MNEs in the more sophisticated developed markets that are those firms' natural terrain, they may be perceived as more appropriate to the needs of developing countries. This would simply reflect the fact that goods and services created to be competitive in the Chinese market (including a facility to produce them cheaply) through the relatively early stages of its development may transfer most effectively and logically to other emerging economies. For example, the abilities to create and secure the initial provision of infrastructure services that have recently been learnt at home by Chinese IMNEs may be more suitable to the similar early phases of building supportive foundations for sustainable growth and industrialisation in other low income economies.

Secondly, Chinese MNEs may be able to secure competitive entry into other developing economies due to their ability to augment their FSA-A due to preferred access to supportive external resources such as capital or foreign exchange (i.e. CSA-D). The very fact that many acts of FDI by Chinese MNEs are seen as integral to China's own developmental needs and policies provides them with considerably greater access to such preferential supports than available to possible developed country rivals, where a more neutral policy context prevails. Alongside this attributes central to the development potentials of many low-income economies (notably the presence of energy and raw material sources) may be more immediately influential on Chinese government policies and again condition support for Chinese MNEs' entries. Thirdly, the innately developmental context of many poorer economies may place a wider range of institutions at the forefront of determining the conditions under which MNEs may be allowed to enter. The ability to operate effectively within such an environment and build the sorts of institutional relationships that can facilitate the logical implementation of a new operation (i.e. FSA-R) may be stronger in Chinese MNEs than developed country ones. This point is elaborated in the next section.

5.5.2 Relationship Firm Specific Advantages

Relationship firm-specific advantages (FSA-R) are a firm's managerial abilities to establish, nurture and draw benefits from external relationships through which they seek to secure preferred access to initially generally available sources of support.[2] These are, in our terms, the CSA-D, which can then be accessed through the generation of relationships with the CSA-I which mediate access to these CSA-D. This includes the negative types of CSA-D where building relationships with institutions whose concern is to generate programmes to alleviate particular developmental bottlenecks may secure for a firm a beneficial position in such a programme. Firms that have emerged in a country such as China, during periods of not only high levels of economic growth (and, therefore, economic change) but also of formulation and reformulation of significant elements of the institutional environment (potential CSA-I) will have learnt to deal with volatility and endemic change. We also argue that this ability (central to FSA-R) to understand, tolerate and derive flexibility within such change through *time* can also become an attribute in adjusting to institutional and environmental differences across *space*. Thus firm-level skills engendered in continually adjusting to institutional change within China can also be applied to entry into rather different overseas situations. They may, in effect, possess ingrained capacities useful in dealing with the liability of foreignness that might not be available to MNEs that come from relatively stable and consistently formulated backgrounds.

These points emphasise that, though initial the use of FSA-R is to embed the MNE in *home*-country institutional networks, these types of competences are likely to become equally relevant in negotiating positions in institution-driven infrastructure creation projects in *host*-countries. But it then becomes an issue as to the degree to which FSA-R learnt in the specific context of home institutions can transfer to building similar relationships with other countries' agencies and policy makers. Indeed it will be the case that differences in the most amenable types of FSA-R for effective positioning in terms of home- and host-country institutions will be, in effect, a central factor in determining the extent and implications of cultural/institutional distance affecting potential

[2] Dunning (2002) defines firm-specific relational assets as 'the stock of a firm's willingness and capability to access, shape and engage in economically beneficial relationships; and to sustain and upgrade these relationships'. In his later work Dunning tended to subsume his insights on relationship building and relationship assets into the new concept of institutional ownership advantages—O_i (Dunning & Lundan, 2008; Lundan, 2010).

acts of FDI. This may favour Chinese IMNEs' ability, relative to those from more developed home countries, to secure and operationalise positions in African IPs.

We can distinguish two facets of FSA-R which, in different ways, relate to the ability of a firm to secure effective access to internationalising potentials that originate beyond its own immediate scope but within the development (CSA-D) and institutional structures (CSA-I) of its home country. Firstly, a direct institutional mechanism in the form of government participation in the ownership of the firm, which can then be leveraged within state bureaucratic and power structures to secure favoured access to resources and policies supportive of specific acts of internationalisation. Secondly, a specific ability possessed by the firm to discern and evaluate the presence of supportive potentials that are not 'automatically' available and build up the relationships necessary to secure preferred access to them. Though the ability to develop this more 'arm's length' access to resources and opportunities is likely to be more essential to private firms, or those with very limited government ownership, it is also plausible that its variance between SOEs may still affect their ability to secure such benefits. Thus, an IMNE could use its FSA-R to advocate its potential in Chinese efforts to secure access to African resources where infrastructure provision becomes an integral element in the Chinese programme.

In their analysis of the determinants of Chinese outward FDI Wang et al. (2012) suggest that firm-level resources (FSA-A) 'trigger foreign expansion only when firms are strongly supported by government' and then add the stipulation that an emerging economy MNE's 'ability to employ its resources and internationalise depends on its effectiveness in managing government ties'; effectively FSA-R.

Peng et al. (2005) define *institutional relatedness* 'as the degree of informal embeddedness or interconnectedness with dominant institutions [which] confers resources and increases the legitimacy of an organisation'. This associates institutional relatedness with 'a dense network of ties with dominant institutions'. It helps firms to access economies of scope that are based on three non-market forms of capital; i.e. social capital, political capital and reputational capital.

The crucial overarching institution conditioning the emergence of Chinese MNEs is the State: its agencies and those policies that help define more specific aspects of the institutional environment faced by firms. Many studies have now emphasised the ways in which Government policies in China (and other emerging economies) have generated a context supportive of the internationalisation of business (Luo et al., 2010; Peng et al., 2008; Buckley et al., 2008; Wang et al., 2012; Cui & Jiang, 2012).[3] FSA-R reflects the way in which institutions and/or relatedness factors influence the ability of a particular Chinese enterprise to leverage access to environmental factors supportive of, and maybe influencing the nature of, overseas expansion. The most direct of such mechanisms, as noted, would be through state ownership of aspirant MNEs (Wang et al., 2012; Cui & Jiang, 2012; Duanmu, 2012; Alon, 2010; Luo & Tung, 2007).

Two potentially influencing aspects of this have been addressed analytically. Firstly, the extent of state ownership or the degree to which the enterprise can be considered a SOE and to derive its strategic postures from this. Thus, generally speaking, it would be expected that the higher is state ownership the more likely it is the firm will be expected to position its internationalisation in tune with state-defined strategic needs but also have a facilitating route to access to resources needed to play the role (an aspect of FSA-R). Secondly, emphasis has been placed (Wang et al., 2012; Child & Rodrigues, 2005; Sun et al., 2010) on the level (state, province, city, county) at which the predominant governmental affiliation of the firm is operationalised. It is then governments at the state or province level that 'are more concerned with globalisation, openness and integration of the country into the World economy' and, in effect, address the prescriptions of the Go-Global policy (Wang et al., 2012). It then becomes an important issue, relevant to our concerns here, as to how the association of significant components of China's OFDI with *higher* levels of government is perceived internationally.

The question is of *how* emerging-economy firms with an ambition (or, at least, willingness) to internationalise can secure access to supportive resources (CSA-D) beyond their internalised capacities? One aspect of this

[3] For detailed explanations of China's policy of an outward FDI and internationalisation of Chinese enterprise see Luo et al. (2010, pp. 72–75), Buckley et al. (2007, 2008), Cross et al. (2007).

in transition economies such as China, is that different ownership structures (an institutional factor in itself) can define different modes of access to the institutions (CSA-I) that administer access to these resources. But within each of these routes a number of institutionally similar firms may be competing for resource access. Here it becomes the firm's particular skills in FSA-R, including the ability to advocate the distinctive attributes of its FSA-A, that is central in differentiating their status as potential international operators. These lines of argument can then also take on evolutionary and cumulative aspects. In the early stages of the generation of a competitive industrial sector, within the wider institutional reformulation of a transition economy such as China, a particular firm may be assisted in its initial derivation through favoured access to various forms of discrete benefits. However, as these processes settle down and mature the firms will need to take increasingly individualised responsibility for articulating their own positions in these networks; perhaps building on and deepening the linkages engendered during their formulation but also seeking new relationships and access to different types of support. This means the in-house generation of FSA-R to secure the logical evolution in their process of competitive development. This becomes more necessary when the firms move towards international expansion. At this stage FSA-R become a crucial component of a wider relationship-based capacity to inculcate a mutual comprehension between firms and institutions of the scope for and potentials of internationalisation, and to perceive and activate new beneficial exchanges between them at relatively low transaction costs.

As noted a firm's FSA-R will not only affect its ability to secure home-country support for its international aims but are also likely to be very influential in how it can negotiate its position in a specific foreign project. The relative influence of FSA-R and FSA-A in asserting an IMNE's role in a particular infrastructure project (IP) may be crucial in determining the ultimate effectiveness and value of that project. Ideally *if* the IP has been effectively designed, in terms of the developmental needs and potentials of the host-economy, then selection of an IMNE with the most appropriate FSA-A would optimise the performance and benefits from it. But this will be a bureaucratised selection procedure, a long way from market forces, so that the IMNE will need to project the potential of its FSA-A in complex and multifaceted negotiation and bargaining processes. This would draw the firm's FSA-R into this new context. Then it becomes important, in terms of the effectiveness of the execution of the IP, whether the FSA-R operate as a complement or a substitute for FSA-A. If the relationship is complementary then what high-quality FSA-R will do is to ensure that FSA-A which are actually the most appropriate to secure optimal achievement of the IP are the ones selected. But alternatively very effective and persuasive FSA-R could substitute for weak FSA-A, to ultimately detrimental effect, by causing an IMNE with seriously sub-optimal FSA-A to be chosen for the project. One aspect of this will be that part of the package that the FSA-R will project here are likely to be supplementary external supports (not innate to the FSA-A central to the IMNE's competence) that will have been acquired (through the *home* country exercise of FSA-R) domestically. If these are complementary with the FSA-A, and genuinely augment the effective execution of the project, then the package still succeeds. But, again, this wider package may be advocated (by the FSA-R) as beneficial to the host economy, but in ways that are not directly related to the precise securing of the developmental benefits of the *project* itself.

5.5.3 Developmental Country-specific Advantages

Developmental country-specific advantages (CSA-D) are forces endogenous to a country's growth processes that generate resources and/or motivations that can support the international expansion of its firms. These factors become manifest at the macro-level and externally to the growth of individual firms, even though their operations are likely to have contributed to them. This means that MNEs will need to develop the competences to access them through the relevant institutions.

CSA-D is predicated on two broad propositions that are likely to be prevalent in a high-growth emerging economy such as China. Firstly, that the growth process generates imbalances that have the potential to constrain its sustainability. Secondly, that logical means of alleviating these constraints may lie within the economy's international relationships and that this may provide specific roles for the international operations of domestic enterprises.

The most visible macro-level manifestations of China's success in the preliminary export-oriented stages of its industrialisation have been the emergence of very substantial capital and foreign-exchange surpluses. The fact that these are now routinely described as surpluses indicates that they can also be seen as imbalances in China's development; in the sense that no immediate purpose for their recommitment in that development process has presented itself. This, in turn, means such resources become available as a positive result of development that could be accessed to support acts of FDI (positive CSA-D). Put another way, where these resources are activated towards overseas operations by Chinese MNEs it means that their use in that external role is being revealed as more positive in China's development than any alternative domestic investment. Our thesis then suggests that reasons for this may lie in particular constraints (negative imbalances) in the progress of domestic industrialisation that can most effectively be alleviated through international commitments.

Any process of export-oriented industrialisation, such as China's, will be driven primarily by the exploitation of its most immediately abundant resource (e.g. low-wage labour). This means that relatively little attention will be paid to optimal use, at that stage, of other necessary inputs. As a result domestic access to resources, such as energy and raw materials, may become a constraint sooner than expected and before any similar constraints emerge in the availability of the primary resource. This is, therefore, an imbalance within the central processes of competitive industrialisation. Though this points to the logic that any process of development will need to be refocused and upgraded over time, in ways that alleviate the sources of bottlenecks through applications of new technologies, more immediate short-term solutions may be desirable; especially if the central input factors are still seen as likely to continue to support the current trajectory of growth for some time. The international accessing of a now domestically-scarce resource then emerges as a high-value activity, in terms of its ability to sustain the impetus of domestic growth that can still draw abundant local resources into productive utilisation. When this becomes enshrined in government policy, with business expansion encouraged as a means of securing it, we see the opportunities opened up as another source of CSA-D; although a negative one from the macro perspective of the firms' home economy.

From this we can now depict the emergence of resource-seeking FDI as a central factor in determining policy-driven aspects of the internationalisation of Chinese enterprise, with its IMNEs being drawn into particular contexts for this. In an extensive review of China's resource policy, Moyo (2012) firstly observes that in a global context of emerging potential resource shortages 'China seems to be the only country that is preparing for this eventuality in a sustainable and deliberately constructive way, by making friends across the globe and systematically and continually investing across the commodities complex'. This 'foray into international resource markets' is then seen as involving 'a comprehensive three-pronged approach: via financial transfers (be it aid or commercial loans), through trade, and by means of investment' (Moyo, 2012). Thus, within the institutional evolution of China's 'going global' strategy, the National Development and Reform Commission (NDRC) and Export-Import Bank (EIBC) issued a circular in October 2004 defining a selective policy to encourage FDI through offers of preferential credit and other incentives. Amongst the areas to be encouraged in this way 'resource exploration projects to mitigate the domestic shortage of natural resources' received emphasis (UNCTAD, 2006).

A comprehension of the potential for resource shortages to compromise China's strong growth, and thereby provide a motivation for resource-seeking FDI, was reflected in its inclusion in most pioneering statistical analysis of the determinants of Chinese OFDI. These studies sought to explain the geographical distribution of China's FDI in terms of particular, potentially attracting, characteristics of host countries. Though these studies are often ambiguous in their conclusions as to the overall relevance of resource-seeking as a driving force in the internationalisation of Chinese business we can interpret aspects of the *ways* they differ as indicative of this as a key motivation in defining the context of Chinese commitments to Africa.

In an influential early analysis Buckley et al. (2007) used a proxy of resource strength as 'the ratio of ore and metal exports to merchandise exports of host countries' interpreted as reinforcing 'the view that the securement of natural resources has become an imperative in more recent years, in line with Chinese domestic growth'. Using the same proxy Duanmu and Guney (2009) and Duanmu (2012) also tested resource-seeking as a determinant of Chinese MNE investments, finding it to be insignificant. One explanation suggested (Duanmu & Guney, 2009) may reflect 'sample composition, since resource-rich countries, such as African countries, have a very limited presence in the sample'. They also acknowledge (2009) that resource-seeking is an important industry-specific motivation for FDI 'but not so strongly as to affect aggregate FDI which contains a broad range of industries'.

Other studies then addressed sample composition directly as a potentially contextualising force affecting resource-seeking FDI. Here the Buckley et al. (2007) study found their resource variable to be weakly negatively signed, for their full period, for OECD countries but quite strongly positive (though short of significance) for non-OECD locations. Similarly Kolstad and Wiig (2012) found a natural resource variable to be a significant positive determinant of Chinese FDI into non-OECD countries but insignificant for OECD. In an interesting extension of their methodology Kolstad and Wiig then applied an interactive term combining their resource variable with one reflecting host-country institutional strength. This was insignificant for OECD countries but becomes significantly negative for non-OECD countries, contrasting with the significant positive result for the resource variable alone. Kolstad and Wiig (2012) then suggest that these results show that whilst resources attract Chinese FDI to non-OECD countries the interactive effect 'indicates that the degree of that attraction depends on institutions, and that the attraction of resources is greater the worse the institutional environment'. Therefore, what this framework can allow to suggest is that Chinese MNEs may have experience and expertise (FSA-R) in dealing with difficult or under-defined institutional situations that is not available to many potential rivals, so that where an institutionally uncertain or insecure country does possess significant resource exploitation opportunities it is the Chinese enterprises that are most prepared to venture into them.

Indeed, Chinese resource-seeking is an essentially institutional context, driven and supported by the wider situation of China's evolving development processes and needs. Amongst other things, integrating with further aspects of international dimensions are being drawn in to support home-country growth, e.g. aid programmes and infrastructure creation. A possible implication of this policy embeddedness of resource seeking is that firms involved in it would be SOEs rather than private. Thus some of the studies of the determinants of Chinese FDI distinguish between how different types of ownership affect firms' response to the various location characteristics, including resource-strength proxies. Having found a resource-strength proxy insignificant on its own Duanmu (2012) also included it in an interactive term with ownership structure and found this to also be insignificant, 'suggesting that SOEs do not respond more strongly to the natural resource endowments of the host country' (2012). Alon (2010), however, found natural resource strength to be a significant positive determinant of FDI by Chinese SOEs but not for private MNEs. Wang et al. (2012) produced results suggesting that state ownership played a more important role in determining resource-seeking Chinese FDI than it did for market-seeking. But they also found that level of government affiliation did not affect the commitment to resource seeking (though it did for market seeking).

The origins and magnitudes of the two positive CSA-Ds that are most important to the framework are familiar and will need little elaboration at this stage. Firstly, the exceptional savings rate that has persisted through China's period of high growth means that FDI can be considered as a logical option that is likely to support, rather than compromise, programmes of domestic capital formation. The parallel growth of foreign exchange reserves clearly points to this potential. The documents records China's foreign exchange reserves as having grown from \$166bln in 2000, to \$1,066bln in 2006 to stand at \$3,197bln in June 2011 (Nolan, 2012). However, Nolan also points out (2012) that the current size of these reserves still constrain investment options so that China 'cannot simply use its foreign exchange reserves to buy the World' (2012). But, they are large enough that when activated as a discretionary element in pursuit of clearly understood policy objectives they become a CSA-D that supports specified acts of FDI. Thus the key driver within this framework becomes institutions which are able to allocate these resources within increasingly internationalised components of China's development policies (CSA-I).

A more diffuse and generalised association between CSA-D and CSA-I is where the nature of China's growth and development inevitably requires increasingly active participation in the international economy. Beyond the resource-seeking this can also involve support for enhancement of the market for Chinese exports and ways of accessing new technologies to deepen the scope of future industrialisation. Within the panoply of agreements, treaties, diplomatic associations and other instruments that supports this will be many that either explicitly or implicitly operate as CSA-I, in that they help define a favourable context for FDI.

5.5.4 Institutional Country Specific Advantages

Building on the classic exposition of North (1996), Buckley et al. (2011) indicate that institutions 'coordinate aspects of the domestic economy, are potentially codified and contain an element of enforcement and sanction'. A distinctive aspect of the institutional context addressed by potential MNEs from economies such as China is then the way that relevant domestic markets work, in terms of any discriminatory preferences (or other imperfections) that can make certain factors (or influences) more readily available to firms wishing (or encouraged) to exploit them as a basis for particular overseas investment projects. Thus, institutional country specific advantages (CSA-I) can be defined as those components of a country's institutional environment that determine, or to some degree, impose motivation for, a MNE to address particular overseas projects and/or allow them to leverage discriminatory access to resources to facilitate such internationalisation. Firms aim to expand internationally will need to negotiate with CSA-I to secure the forms of support to complement their FSA-A. The ability of building into the nexus of institutions, separated from FSA-A, becomes a vital firm-level competence. This types of advantages may be likely available to firms which have affiliated with government or are government-owned, to some degree. The infrastructure firms may generate strong FSA-R, i.e. opportunistic, relationship building expertise, in developmental contexts where institutions themselves are not fully structured and their access to CSA-D is crucial. Chinese firms extend to the impulse towards their international expansion by integrating with their home country developmental advantages, with this being supported and motivated by government-controlled resources and policies, i.e. CSA-I.

5.6 The Hierarchical Structure of Strategies

The general pattern of Chinese MNEs investing in Africa is a dynamic process. Their structural embedding activities in certain countries secure a sustainable contribution to their investments and operate in terms of a hierarchical global strategy. Chinese MNEs enter into Africa, as do all other firms, derived from inherent competitive advantages including FSA and/or CSA. China's global strategy is undertaken in two approaches (Fig. 5.3). On the firm level, long-run activities derive from the strategic objectives: the company's sustained international competitiveness. Short- and medium- run aims are more directly commercial-oriented, MNEs inherently pursue profits constantly as a part of global strategy. The firms seek profit from local market (MS) by exploiting FSA-A and taking advantages of positive CSA-D. Under this process, firms' strategies reflect entrepreneurial activities. On the national level, global strategy is building up the competitiveness in the world market of which the two approaches are usually embarked on through different types of firms. By leveraging negative CSA-D, Chinese MNEs are responsible to home demand with diplomatic and developmental reasons (RS).

China's infrastructure MNEs located in Africa initially due to an original national strategy with relatively single motivation or sector, i.e.

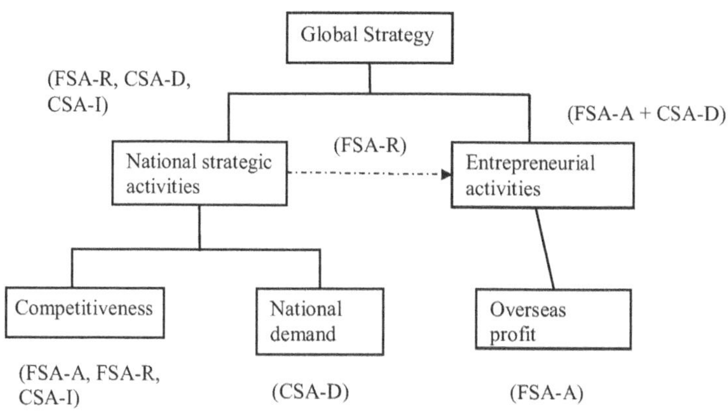

Fig. 5.3 The strategy hierarchy of Chinese MNEs

providing inputs into infrastructure projects' formulation and operation. New strategies towards the particular location then emerge that are attributable to the firms complete and integrated network under increasingly dynamic diversified motivations. The combinations of these strategies then create the new competitive advantages for long term investment. The generation of new ownership advantages appear from both CSA-D and FSA-A through FSA-R. The capability to build up internal coordination and control mechanisms relate to the production process which include the assessment of transactional advantages (Rugman & Verbeke, 2003). Chinese IMNEs' global strategy depends on how to link the exogenous (CSA-D) and endogenous (FSA-A) and effectively exploit the CSAs for further expansion. Support for activities of FDI and the internationalisation of key enterprises will be one strategy. FSA-R enables a firm to integrate the external supportive purpose with its firm-level strategy. The CSA-D, such as capital and foreign exchange, will be treated as 'policy resources' to operate in support of the reinforcing of national development programmes. Though traditional forms of resources seeking are likely to reflect the influence of potential primary resource shortages provoked by high growth, other components of strategic activities can be part of the global strategies.

For different purposes of localisation in African countries, the international expansion is divided into national strategic activities and entrepreneurial activities. It is indicated by Bartlett and Ghoshal (1986) that MNEs localise to seek a variety of ways in which their foreign affiliates can help to enhance their core strategy in host countries. National demand is a particular aim of Chinese IMNEs, which reflects the potential benefit of commitment to infrastructure creation. For example, infrastructure MNEs under the Angolan Mode indirectly strengthen the national security back home whilst ICT firms are more likely to contribute to the innovation system and firm-level competitiveness. Chinese infrastructure firms will have developed a degree of FSA-A for designing internationalisation strategies, and leverage it toward infrastructure creation in Africa. Though these FSA-A may not be fully formulated to world-level standards, their ability will be augmented by designated participation (CSA-I) in African projects and secured by access to capital and foreign exchange (CSA-D).

5.7 Concluding Remarks

Chinese MNEs may indeed possess very particular technologies and practices that are distinctively appropriate to initiation of infrastructure capacities in emergent economies. The roots of these firm-level competences will have been learnt within the needs and conditions of earlier phases of China's development. This may render them more appropriate and viable as a basis for infrastructure creation in Africa than would comparable attributes of infrastructure MNEs from more developed economies.

With the digging into the process of Chinese firms equipping for investment in Africa, there are four new attempts to explain the nature of Chinese MNEs, particular in IMNEs. FSA-A serves to differentiate between Chinese firms in ways that determine the abilities of internationalisation, i.e. it becomes champion of micro-level player in the macro-level progression of China's development. In selecting firms to pursue particular international objectives and receive supports in doing so (aspects of CSA-D) their in-place capacities to fulfil such objectives will need to be taken under consideration. But this is very much a bureaucratised selection process, outside of normal market domains. This means that the ability of firms to present their case, around the projected strength of their FSA-A, becomes a separate but complementary attribute. Thus relationship firm-specific advantages (FSA-R) aim to build positions within the CSA-I which mediate the processes through which particular acts of FDI are activated to play roles within China's development strategies.

Bibliography

Alon, T. M. (2010). Institutional analysis and the determinants of Chinese FDI. *The Multinational Business Review, 18*(3), 1–24.

Bartlett, C., & Ghoshal, S. (1986). Tap your subsidiaries for global reach. *Harvard Business Review, 64*, 87–94.

Buckley, J. P., Voss, H., Cross, A., & Clegg, L. J. (2011). The emergence of Chinese firms as multinationals: The influence of the home institutional

environment. In R. Pearce (Ed.), *China and the multinationals: International business and the entry of China into the global economy*. Edward Elgar.
Buckley, P., Clegg, J., Cross, A., Liu, X., Voss, H., & Zheng, P. (2007). The determinants of Chinese outward foreign direct investment. *Journal of International Business Studies, 38*(4), 499–518.
Buckley, P. J., Clegg, J. L., Cross, A. R., Voss, H., Rhodes, M., & Zheng, P. (2008). Explaining China's outward FDI: An institutional perspective. *The Rise of Transnational Corporations from Emerging Markets: Threat or Opportunity*, 107–157.
Child, J., & Rodrigues, S. B. (2005). The internationalization of Chinese firms: A case for theoretical extension? *Management and Organization Review, 1*(3), 381–410.
Cross, A., Buckley, P., Clegg, J., Voss, H., Rhodes, M., Zheng, P., & Liu, X. (2007). An econometric investigation of Chinese outward direct investment. In J. H. Dunning & T. M. Lin (Eds.), *Multinational enterprises and emerging challenge of the 21st century* (pp. 55–86). Edward Elgar.
Cui, L., & Jiang, F. (2012). State ownership effect on firms' FDI ownership decisions under institutional pressure: A study of Chinese outward-investing firms. *Journal of International Business Studies, 43*(3), 264–284.
Duanmu, J. (2012). Firm heterogeneity and location choice of Chinese multinational enterprises. *Journal of World Business, 47*, 64–72.
Duanmu, J., & Guney, Y. (2009). A panel data analysis of locational determinants of Chinese and Indian outward foreign direct investment. Journal of Asia Business Studies, 3(2), 1–15. ISSN 1558–7894.
Dunning, J. H. (2002). *Global capitalism, FDI and competitiveness* (Vol. 2). Edward Elgar Publishing.
Dunning, J. H., & Lundan, S. M. (2008). Institutions and the OLI paradigm of the multinational enterprise. *Asia Pacific Journal of Management, 25*, 573–593.
Foster, V., & Briceno-Garmendia, C. (2010). *Africa's infrastructure—A time for transformation*. The International Bank for Reconstruction and Development, The World Bank.
Kolstad, I., & Wiig, A. (2012). What determines Chinese outward FDI? *Journal of World Business, 47*(1), 26–34.
Lundan, S. M. (2010). *What are ownership advantages?* Multinational Business Review.
Luo, Y., & Tung, R. L. (2007). International expansion of emerging market enterprises: A springboard perspective. *Journal of International Business Studies, 38*(4), 481–498.

Luo, Y., Xue, Q., & Han, B. (2010). How emerging market governments promote outward FDI: Experience from China. *Journal of World Business, 45*, 68–79.

Moyo, D. (2012). *Winner take all: China's race for resources and what it means for world*. Basic Books.

Nolan, P. (2012). Is China buying the world? *Challenge, 55*(2), 108–118.

North, D. C. (1996). Institutions, organizations and market competition. In *Keynote address to the sixth conference of the international Joseph Schumpeter society* (pp. 2–5). Stockholm.

Peng, M. W., Lee, S., & Wang, D. Y. L. (2005). What determines the scope of the firm over time? A focus on institutional relatedness. *Academy of Management Review, 30*(3), 622–633.

Peng, M. W., Wang, D. Y., & Jiang, Y. (2008). An institution-based view of international business strategy: A focus on emerging economies. *Journal of International Business Studies, 39*, 920–936.

Ramamurti, R., & Doh, J. P. (2004). Rethinking foreign infrastructure investment in developing countries. *Journal of World Business, 39*(2), 151–167.

Rugman, A. M., & Verbeke, A. (2003). Extending the theory of the multinational enterprise: Internalization and strategic management perspectives. *Journal of International Business Studies, 34*(2), 125–137.

Sader, F. (2000). *Attracting foreign direct investment into infrastructure: Why is it so difficult?* (Vol. 12). World Bank Publications.

Sun, P., Mellahi, K., & Thun, E. (2010). The dynamic value of MNE political embeddedness: The case of the Chinese automobile industry. *Journal of International Business Studies, 41*(7), 1161–1182.

Tang, Y., & Pearce, R. D. (2011). The political economy of infrastructure multinationals: The case of Chinese investment in Africa. In R. Pearce (Ed.), *China and the multinationals—International business and the entry of China into the global economy*. Edward Elgar.

UNCTAD. (2006). *World investment report: FDI from developing and transition economies: Implications for development*.

UNCTAD. (2008). World investment report 2008: Transnational corporations, and the infrastructure challenge.

Wang, C., Hong, J., Kafouros, M., & Wright, M. (2012). Exploring the role of government involvement in outward FDI from emerging economies. *Journal of International Business Studies, 43*, 655–676.

World Investment Report. (2008). *Transnational corporations and the infrastructure challenge*. UNCTAD.

6

The Determinants and Motivations of Chinese Telecommunication MNEs in Africa: Effects of Host Countries' Economic Environment on IMNEs' Location Choice

6.1 Introduction

The determinants of location choice of MNEs have a comprehensive position in Dunning's (1980) eclectic theory as the location advantage of a geographic unit. There are two streams of literature that define the location advantages of a given country and these are the OLI framework and institution-based views. OLI thinking of location advantages based on macroeconomic environments include market growth and size, natural resources and labour costs. Increasingly discussion of institution theory allows consideration for the way the market operates—known as 'rules of the game' (North, 1990). These two streams of literature have been discussing the conventional MNEs. MNEs in infrastructure sectors, which are generally observed to follow the government-driven strategy of development, particularly Chinese infrastructure firms in Africa, have different ways of explaining the location choice under these two theoretical approaches. China's infrastructure assistance is nothing new since the first offer in 1970s. Corkin et al. (2008) conclude that 'it is often the most resources rich states that are in dire need of infrastructure development and support', hence the apparent link between infrastructure assistance

Y. Tang, *The Operations of Chinese Infrastructure Multinationals in Africa*,
https://doi.org/10.1007/978-981-16-2562-6_6

and resources rich countries. Traditional thinking on China's infrastructure investment sees an important role in carrying out the programme of official development assistance and debt- creating finance. The general trend of Chinese infrastructure firms' aggressive expansion in African countries has been shown to be working under weak location condition, involved in building transportation, electrical, and telecommunications infrastructure. Under the encouragement of the 'going abroad' policy, Chinese infrastructure firms are highly motivated to conduct investments that benefit both economic and political objectives. Therefore, there are two strategic drivers of Chinese infrastructure firms in Africa. Pursuing country-level political objectives through official development assistance; seeking firm-level commercial competitiveness where infrastructure companies tend to seek African markets. Different types of infrastructure provision will change. Thus the need for information and communication technology (ICT) provision is likely to emerge more strongly once industrialisation processes become more complex and interdependent. Similarly, consumer demand for the services of ICT will become increasingly strong and sophisticated. The demand for this will emerge at a stage before the country's indigenous technological and enterprise capacities can provide for them adequately. Logically this can open up an important opportunity for international firms in the ICT sector to supply the equipment and build up the backbone of initial provision in such countries.

However, few studies have looked at mixed ownership structures in China and their motivations to invest in African countries. By mixed ownership structure, we refer to firms that have a combination of state ownership and private ownership. Ownership identity plays great significance for the oversight and incentives management and corporate goals (Milhaupt & Zheng, 2014). The privatisation process in China in the 1990s has created firms with both private equity ownership and residual government ownership. The incentives and motivations of these companies are less clear due to mixed ownership. To fill in the gap, this paper will examine antecedents for foreign market location choices and motivations of Chinese mixed owned enterprises and private firms in Africa in the sector of information and communication technology (ICT) infrastructure.

Infrastructure sectors are generally observed to follow the government-driven strategy of infrastructure investment. There are also significant discrepancies among industries within the infrastructure sector. Compared to other forms of infrastructure, the ICT sector in Africa has a strong market potential. The market need for ICT provision is likely to emerge strongly once industrialisation processes become more complex and interdependent. According to economic theory, the demand for building ICT infrastructure will emerge at a stage before the country's indigenous technological and enterprise capacities can provide for them adequately. Similarly, consumer demand for the services of ICT will become increasingly strong and sophisticated. Consequently, this can open up an important opportunity for international firms in the ICT sector to supply the equipment and build up the backbone of initial provision in such countries.

Nevertheless, the policy is not significantly explicit as to what extent the role of infrastructure investment in an individual country reflects political objectives. The degree of the influences of macroeconomic and institutional environment on Chinese IMNEs' location choice depends on the extent of the political objectives the company is pursuing. Overall analysis of Chinese MNEs' motivation is too inadequate to find out how infrastructure provision brings the ICT firms to the particular backbone opportunities that they are motivated to. The differentiation of how firms measure the market potentials also decides the location choice.

To start with, investment location choice is the primary decision-making choice of entry which profoundly affects overseas operations. Institutional environments are undoubtedly regarded as a crucial element of location advantage. Pressured by the host institutions and economic environments, ways of arranging the geographical distribution in the African continent ensures that the later performance of investments has become a key issue that Chinese infrastructure MNEs will have to face.

Practice shows that the main factors motivating FDI into Africa in recent decades appear to be the availability of natural resources in the host countries and investment in the oil industries such as those of Nigeria and Angola. Macroeconomic instability and uncertainty contribute to the weakness of locations. According to Wright et al. (2005), the role of institutions is to reduce the uncertainty and establish a stable structure. However, a few countries have been able to attract firms to set down subsidiaries, apparently by virtue of the quality of their domestic economic environment and institutions.

This Chapter combines two major drivers of IB theory: institution-based view and location choice of host country, and it also proposes to explain how the cross-country differences on macroeconomic and institutional environment affect strategic behaviour of Chinese IMNEs in Africa. Institutions are commonly used in the study of investment strategies, i.e. entry mode choice, because of the different institutions of host and home countries. Nevertheless, prior to deciding the entry strategies in African countries, Chinese firms have to consider where to invest at the first stage. Indeed, the political risk system (Henisz, 2000), which forms an essential part of institutional quality, 'has an equally if not more important influence on location choice', that is rarely addressed by Chinese firms in developing countries.

On the other hand, most literatures focusing on Chinese MNEs in Africa are only based on market-orientation and consider the influence of host countries inherent location advantage. Meanwhile, most ideas explain that Chinese MNEs, infrastructure firms in particular, are accompanying government guarantees. Towards firms themselves, the location choices are also motivated by specific market opportunities. Operating as traditional Multinationals, telecommunication firm are becoming well-organised MNEs in Africa with individual subsidiaries built on the use of group level OAs from parent firms in China. The motivations of Chinese telecommunication firms are significantly traceable in determining where and when to begin to open up.

Owing to the particularity of IMNEs in telecommunication sector, the Chapter is picking up two major Chinese players as cases. Those are equipment manufacturers Huawei Technologies and ZTE (Zhongxing Telecommunications Equipment Corporation). Of the 34 ICT projects in Sub-Saharan Africa that involved Chinese financing the WB-PPIAF database suggests (Foster et al., 2008) showed that 27 involve the participation of the two Chinese contractors: ZTE and/or Huawei. The purposes of this chapter are to examine institutions and host country environments in identifying the relative importance of these indicators for Chinese telecommunication firms' location choices over the years; and, in reality, what are the real factors driving the investments of Chinese telecommunication firms in Africa.

6.2 Study Propositions

6.2.1 New Varieties of State Ownership and Location Choices

The growth of Chinese telecommunications firms and their commitment in African ICT projects are sophisticated, owing to how the nature of their ownership advantages related to both business strategy and political economy.

Chinese telecommunication firms, among the most important Chinese investors, play two different roles in African markets since the companies are investing with mixed motivations. Telecommunications combine competitive and non-competitive segments (WIR, 2008). In terms of the two major Chinese telecommunication corporations in Africa, the two segments have driven their business behaviour commercially and non-commercially. For MNEs, it implies a need to evaluate certain location advantages with explicit reference to their own attributes, and make their location choices individually, rather than following the 'norm' in their industry. There is a strong idiosyncratic element in location choices, and location decisions must be undertaken based on a careful examination of the firm's specific attributes in relation to specific location advantages rather than viewing the latter on their own.

As can be seen on political prospect, governments' cooperation influences on telecommunication are not as vital and obvious as they are on construction sectors, where the bargaining between firms and governments are more influential. Telecommunication enterprise are encouraged towards foreignness (Hong & Sun, 2006) in Africa, at the beginning, as part of infrastructure contributors. As Chinese firms are financed in some infrastructure projects under the programming of the Export-Import Bank of China, this offered a potential participation in the future investments in telecommunication infrastructure.

The potential competition is also one of the determinants of the motivations of MNEs' investment in infrastructures. The rise of mobile telephone use increases the technologies and cost competitions of firms. On this prospect, multinationals are involved in market occupation—market-seeking. Offshore subsidiaries are founded for manufacturing locally over last decades.

The relations between Chinese government and firms are built on contracts (the landline and telecom system cases). With more than half state-ownership, Africa reasonably became the first overseas market of ZTE as a more likely infrastructure contractor for China's Official Development Assistance (ODA).

In terms of the two major Chinese telecommunication corporations in Africa, the two segments have driven their business behavior commercially and non-commercially. How much Chinese IMNEs investment derives from 'National' preference? How much are host countries' institutional and macro-economic environments determining Chinese IMNEs' embedding decision? What kinds of market potentials drive investment of the two companies? For MNEs, it implies a need to evaluate certain location advantages with explicit reference to their own attributes, and make their location choices individually, rather than following the 'norm' in their industry. There is a strong idiosyncratic element in location choices, and location decisions must be undertaken based on a careful examination of the firm's specific attributes in relation to specific location advantages rather than viewing the latter on their own.

Africa is a fast growing region for Huawei and ZTE two companies, where the business areas include solutions for operators, terminal, telecommunication equipment and global service. Huawei solutions are deployed by more than 60 operators in more than 20 African countries. In 2011, Huawei revenues reached US$ 3.42 billion from Africa, representing 13% of the company's total global annual sales revenues (Huawei.com). However, as with ZTE, Huawei had auxiliary access to finance for its overseas operations in the form of $600mln export sellers credit from the Ex-Im Bank (granted in 2004) and $10bln in credit financing from China Development Bank (also 2004).

The potential competition is also one of the determinants of the motivations of MNEs' investment in infrastructures. The rise of mobile telephone use increases the technologies and cost competitions of firms. On this prospect, multinationals are involved in market occupation—market-seeking. Offshore subsidiaries are founded for manufacturing locally over the last decade. Huawei technologies and ZTE have been investing through African markets. Owing to the African countries location situation, mobile phone usage is much more popular than landline usage. The mobile lines usage is up to 10 times of the landline usage (IT times weekly, 2007).

6.2.2 Propositions

The propositions[1] designated in Chap. 6[2] are empirically abstract and falsifiable statements of proven and disproven realities on Chinese MNEs in Africa projected within the international business theories. These propositions indicate themes that are likely to be illustrated or demonstrated by following a case-study framework but not proven in the way that would be possible with empirically tested data. Because of the data limitations (see Chap. 4), it is unable to ideally model with firm-level data and give strict results The econometric analysis in this chapter aims at giving more specific cases with quantitative findings to supplement the conceptual framework. In this chapter, the propositions are divided into two parts from two aspects: the determinants from push and pull factors of host and home countries; and motivations of firms towards the specific local industrial opportunities.

[1] Concluding from Bailey, Kenneth D. (1994), *Method of social research*—4th edition (internet access):

Proposition is created by a set of arguments developed through deduction based on findings. It is usually used in qualitative research from a subjective view;

Hypothesis is a testable statement that suggests possible relationships between variables measured that arise from critique of specific part of existing literature review. It is usually in quantitative research domain with an objective view.

[2] Proposition analysis applies to Chap. 7 owing to the same research purpose.

Propositions on Determinants of Location Choice

China's telecommunication companies' investment in Africa can be generally divided into stages. Initially, executing the infrastructure contracts is the earliest way to get access to the African market. Chinese telecommunication companies' African market strategies aim to get into the countries which are weak in telecommunication infrastructure. With their large number of investments and equipment donations, Huawei and ZTE obtained ample contracts in infrastructure. This is also a process of building reputation in commercial markets. Gaining experience and market in these countries through infrastructure contracts, Huawei and ZTE ensure their market share of telephone manufacturing in the future. The donation of equipment to a degree 'forces' the future use of their equipment since the customers become used to the facilities of the companies. In addition, locals may then decide to use matched products owing to the already fixed telecommunication facilities. Accordingly, the two main telecommunication investors are differently connected with government regulation. The relations between Chinese government and firms are built on contracts (the landline and telecom system cases). Huawei, established privately to compete and seek profit at home, enhanced competitive advantages through long-term domestic market competition. However, it to some extent operates to execute economic development support of Chinese government in Africa. IMNEs' home strategies decided the financing channel and ownership. ZTE, is another model of ownership, called the 'ZTE model' mixed with state-controlling, collective-controlling and private-ownership, as a stock company held by the state and executed by an authorised group. With more than half state-ownership, Africa reasonably became the first overseas market of ZTE as a more likely infrastructure contractor for China's ODA. Therefore, the location choice of Chinese telecommunication MNEs would be determined by the macroeconomic environment where the firm-specific objectives are stronger than political objectives.

At the broadest level this simply reflects the now established view, in analysis of International Business (IB), that a wide range of entry, ownership and operational modes are available to MNEs in their international expansion. The choice of mode for individual overseas operations is then contingent on industry, location and firm factors, i.e. the willingness of companies' decisions to enter the countries depends on factors of host countries' location. The projects themselves are set to be ultimately owned and controlled by African (often government) entities. Nevertheless, in terms of opening up the research agendas suggested in this chapter, we can still see these operations in Africa as an integral part of the international expansion of Chinese MNEs.

Proposition 1 *A company with dominant state-ownership is most likely to be encouraged to start operations in countries with weak market-oriented LAs. A private company, operating at a relative distance from home country government influence, must address more immediate sources of normal profitability; positive response to market oriented LAs.* Many African countries possess primary resources as a very plausible source of comparative advantage that can be leveraged to initiate and drive their development. These become an emphasis for Chinese national purpose of investment, while the exploitation of these resource potentials is often constrained by lack of the appropriate infrastructure (notably roads, railroads, ports, airports). There is an innate link between infrastructure creation and resource-based development. The ability of Chinese IMNEs to implement infrastructure projects, and link this with the alleviation of China's resource constraints, recognised in the 'Angola mode' of project financing, enables the natural resources to become an indirect attractiveness for investment related to infrastructure. Thus, relating primary-product access with the creation of infrastructure can then also provide spillover benefits into the wider economy. Moreover, the geographic condition has important effect on the economic condition of a country. The geographical situation is a key economic variable that impacts on economic performance of developing countries (UN-OHRLLS). Landlocked countries are generally among the poorest of the developing countries, with the weakest market capability, and poor infrastructure to attract FDI. Although this may increase the opportunities for infrastructure projects bidding, Chinese IMNEs continue taking account of the investment environment for dynamic development reasons. The above determinants are not directly related to the impact of firms' decision but provide latent considerations. Securing the general wave of foreign investment leads to a cascading effect of location decision in subsequent periods. Investors ponder to invest in countries that already received much FDI because the past FDI stocks reflect favourable local conditions that are perceived by existing investors but not yet known to them.

Proposition 2a *Possession of raw materials as a LA will need support of infrastructure development. But if the economy is poor attraction of ICT firms will need home-country support for participation. This is more likely if the ICT firm is government owned.* Proposition 2b *Landlocked countries have particular need for infrastructure creation, but are like to be poor. Where they can get home-country support, ICT companies may invest, but not where they depend on efficient market for their products.* Chinese relations with Africa in the form of infrastructure have a long history and have grown exponentially over the past decades. Dating back to 1970s, China's first engagement in African countries—Zambia and Tanzania, started diplomatic ties with strong political stance of 'One China'. With long-term expansion of Africa's developmental potential, in parallel with the deepening trade relationship supported by preferential policies of the Chinese government, foreign investment by Chinese companies in Africa has increased substantially and in depth of commitment. China's investments in Africa have grown significantly since 2000 when Forum of China-Africa Cooperation (FOCAC) was set up. By the end of 2010, Chinese companies have covered 50 African countries with 85% area of the continent. Meantime, Africa becomes the second major destination of Chinese multinationals.

Proposition 3a *Location choice of firms with state ownership is more likely to be impacted by bilateral governmental cooperation agreement of host country* Proposition 3b *The longer the country has historical diplomatic ties, the more likely Chinese firms would be to invest there.* China's current engagement in Africa, while more commercial in nature, has no less focus on infrastructure development including telecommunications which contribute heavily on Chinese outward investment in African countries.

Chinese ICT investment can be seen high amongst ranked investment in total statistics (MOFCOM, 2008). The popularities of engagement of Chinese OFDI reflect the familiarity on individual countries, supporting firms to measure the location advantages through such experience.

Proposition 4 *Chinese telecommunication firms are more like to invest in host countries where China has already experienced large amount of total outward FDI.* Political risk and institutional structure constrains the location advantage. Luo and Tung (2007) suggest that institutions drive Chinese firms to pursue country-level political objectives in strengthening diplomatic ties between home and host country. Within a cross-country study by Brunetti and Weder (1998), a negative link between institutional uncertainty and investment has been found in policy-related variables on FDI. According to their theoretical considerations, political instability and violence reduces investment.

Institutional environment is thus an important determinant of the geo-strategic motivation. Kolstad and Wiig (2009) show a noticeable relationship between natural resources and host countries institutional environment, so that poorer institutions of host countries attracted more Chinese companies in natural resource investment. To consider the background of an African country, institutional uncertainty is an inevitable factor which affects the decision of Chinese companies. A number of conflicts have affected mainly countries in the African continent related to ownership of natural resources, political and economic conflicts and extreme poverty. The political instability will directly affect the power of MNEs' assets in host countries. After all, the international expansions of the two telecommunication companies, following the 'going abroad' policy, have limited overseas experience compared to MNEs from developed economies. Infrastructure FDI are tangible, capital intensive assets and tied with host countries, i.e. have high location specificity are not relocated to another use and are deeply involved in governmental regulation and administration (Sawant, 2009). The finance for the projects is usually, in effect, government to government with rare and limited participation by the firms.

Proposition 5 *Chinese IMNE in general will have a strong tendency to invest in countries with higher ranked institutions. For these in ICT the SOEs may be relatively less concerned by risky institutions than private ones with more direct concern for profitability.* Propositions of Motivations *Market-Seeking Potential*

Host- and home- country factors affect location choice when a firm decides to resort to FDI in order to take advantage of foreign markets. These 'factors that drive FDI behaviour' (Blonigen, 2005) determine the generalised perception of which market to exploit. Dunning (1993) stated that the foreign firms are also motivated to host countries by taking advantage of availability and factor endowments in different countries. Thus, ultimately the driver of a particular firm is linked to the motives underpinning the decision so that the FDI is used to reach a particular aim.

The main issue underpinning MS strategy refers to the fact that a foreign market to be supplied is necessarily the market where the further production of the company takes place. Thus, the market of ICT can be either filling a gap of the host country which is negative driver, or more positively treats the market as a more strategic internationalisation opportunity. In the first case, the firm is more likely motivated by given infrastructure projects or government programmes while, in the second case, the firm is interested in the exploitation of the market of the country and the possibilities of building up the platform in the surrounding area to tap it into the firm's global strategy. In practice, Chinese telecommunication firms more motivated by considering the factors of forward link whether or not they influence the ability of localised production process.

Dunning (1993) terms as a residual motive, the investments where the purpose is mainly 'to support the activities of the rest of the enterprise of which they are part'. The cases of ICT infrastructure provision can be subsumed in into such support investment. The general trends of lacking infrastructure spur the investment in the sectors. Given their inner ancillary nature, the investments are highly complementary to more commercialised or outsourcing decisions. The motivation on infrastructure investments share the character of the main business they serve. The firms may gain access and primary information of the local market by involving in government projects of infrastructure, and meantime, building up the business relationship with local operators. Companies' decisions on affiliating in different locations may appear as 'opposite attract' (Kravis & Lipsey, 1982). MNEs choose host countries because the countries do not possess advantages in this industry. Relatively developed infrastructure MNEs may choose a country with low-level infrastructure. Filling the gap of infrastructure serves the first step of market-seeking strategy by increasing experiences of managing the relevant information and the network of clients in the market of destination (Franco et al., 2008).

Proposition 6a *The greater the infrastructure gap at a host country the more scope that exists for IMNEs to benefit from participation.* Proposition 6b *For ICT IMNEs the more positive the signs for a country's market growth the more likely they are to deepen their participation over time.* Efficiency-Seeking or Knowledge-Seeking

Most views of Chinese investment in Africa are concentrated in MS/RS and few see ES emerging from small private companies due to low labour cost. This is because Chinese domestic markets have sufficient supplies of low-cost migrant labour force (Deng, 2004; Buckley et al., 2007). To 'take advantage of the economies of scale and scope and of differences in consumer tastes and supply capabilities' (Dunning, 1993), learning experience and restructuring the existed technology are all important to knowledge-based companies. The two companies have well-developed products and the ability to diversify the products and services.

Motivations are considered to serve the primary objective of generating economic rents through the exploitation of some firm-specific assets. They are usually technological assets generated through R&D investments that the headquarters of the MNE transfers to the subsidiaries to contribute to its exploitation in a foreign market (Pearce, 1999; Cantwell, 1989).

KS was initially defined as the purpose of the investment being that of acquiring and implementing a new technological base rather than exploiting the existing assets. Firm invests abroad in order to obtain access to knowledge or competences that it does not possess. The OLI paradigm mainly describes this with various situations in which strategic considerations dominate. It is motivated by the trend of MNEs to establish internal and external networks for innovation (Zanfei, 2000). Thus, consideration of the market needs to support foreign production by adaptation of existing technologies/skills to host country markets and then, most of all, to tap into the capabilities available in host countries by locating subsidiaries close to the leading centres of research and innovation (Pearce, 1999; Niosi, 1999), thus benefiting from localised knowledge spillovers. To ensure the localised production of the service and product, a host-country high-educated labour force provides an access to better understanding of local needs which MNEs can internalise to their foreign affiliates.

Proposition 7 *The higher the level of human capital in a host country the more likely are ICT IMNEs to increase the level of their participation over time.*

6.3 Methods

6.3.1 Model Specification

The econometric methodology of Panel Probit Model described in Chap. 4, is applied in this chapter for two dimensions of purpose. Thus we are modelling the determinants of the location choices and motivation of firms. The purpose of using two separate datasets with the same independent variables is to qualitatively compare the results in order to find out the differences and similarities of motivations and determinants between the two companies under the same circumstances. Given 40 countries within 8-year period, each firm is tested by the time point where it chose to start investment in the country.[3] In the datasets, the only variable is the time when they decided to invest. Although country-level data applied to the datasets may not straightforwardly reflect firms' decision and motivation, these factors of countries would have more effect on firms'

[3] The criterion of selection on data has been explained in Chap. 4.

consideration of investment in infrastructure rather than in other industries because of strong connection to development of economy and degree of government involvement.

Effects of home-and host- country factors—locational determinants

$$Y_{it} = \beta_0 + \beta_1 MEE_{it} + \beta_2 INS_{it} + \beta_3 FDIE_{it} + \beta_4 NATT_{it} + \beta_5 DT_{it} + \mu_{it} \tag{6.1}$$

Where Y_{it}, a binary variable which = 1 if the company enter the country i at year t and = 0 otherwise. The panel data are balanced on year by dropping the observations with missing values.

The next set of regressions M9–12 utilises a similar mechanism for motivations of firms in particular market

$$Y_{it} = \beta_0 + \beta_1 MEE_{it} + \beta_2 NATT_{it} + \beta_3 FDIE_{it} + \beta_4 MS_{it} + \beta_5 ES_{it} + \mu_{it} \tag{6.2}$$

Where, MEE stands for the group variables of Macroeconomic Environment; INS stands for variables of institutional factors; FDIE stands for FDI experience; MKTATR has been changed to NATT which stands for variables in national attractiveness.

To avoid form multicollinearity, the institutions indicators are added one by one into the benchmark model by controlling economic environment and other influential variables.

6.3.2 Data

The dataset on the two companies' location choice is obtained from Data collections and consists of multiple sources. The information on firm-level choice and timing of entry are according to, firstly, the two firms' reports and documents on official websites, and secondly groups of reports of local newspapers. Macro-level information attributes to database from World Development Indicators by World Bank, UN Statistics, and China Ministry of Commerce. They are two separate panel probit datasets within same 8 year time period and crossing 40 countries but with different binary dependent variables in the two datasets. The dependent variables are from the investment decision of companies. The two companies may or may not decide to invest in the same country in the same year. Therefore, the dependent variable varies. Location decision is not continuous data; it is a binary response to the host- and home-country factors in the certain year. The decision only occurs once when the firm decides to locate in the country, i.e. either 0 before the firm invest or 1 once they entre (if the company disinvested or left, the decision would turn to 0). Therefore, the same project would not affect the data.

Variables

Dependent Variable

Two MNEs' first published record of starting business with the host country in the particular year are used as dependent variable (Y) to illustrate firms' decision on location choice in Africa (see Chap. 4). This is a binary discrete choice that 1 represents when the company choose the market in the given country and year; the antecedent years are coded 0. To define an entry in this context the company can set up a representative office to undertake the programmes and sell products independently. The dependant variable (Yit) is the time that the company choose to invest in the country. The two regressions are being run for different purposes. However, the time when firm decide to locate in the country is not changed. In the first group of regressions, it looks into the determinants of investment decision making, while in the second group, the model aims at finding out what motivated firm to invest. This is a more firm-level consideration. The second regression has taken away the variables on home country effect.

Independent Variables

Macro-economic Environment

The vector of MEE contains three market level variables: Real GDP (RGDP), GDP per capita (GDPPC) and GDP growth rate (GR). Market size of host countries, measures as Real GDP and GDP per capita are most frequently used in explaining investment (Kravis & Lipsey, 1982;

Cheung et al., 2012); Cheung et al. (2012) specified the measurement of GDP per capita from general market size for evaluating market opportunities; and GDP growth rate is the measurement for market potential which was also used in Cheung et al. (2012). GDP and GDP growth rate pick up different host country market characteristics of in different time. So there is a real potential that they could have separate effects. GDP growth rate can truly affect FDI independent of the other market characteristics. In general, GDP measures simple size of market; GDP per capita indicates the quality of market or indeed simply serves as a proxy for level of development. The growth of GDP can be seen as a measure of the potential of the market separate from size or level of development. Overwhelming empirical and theoretical studies confirm the importance of the link between macro-economic environment and FDI. The size of a particular market may indicate the attractiveness for investment when MNEs' aim at targeting local markets (horizontal internationalisation or market-seeking). The market potential, likewise, is the signal for future return to investment which is considered within location decisions.

FDI Experience for China

These two firms are comparatively new participants in China-Africa. The overall Chinese African experience provides certain guidance for the two firms considering the host country's environments. Annual data on China's outward FDI (COFDI) in the given countries from 2003 to 2010 indicate China's country-level evaluation of the host countries and degree of investment experience in such African countries.

National Attractiveness

The vector of national attractiveness consists of China's quest for African natural resources[4] (NTR), FDI inflows to GDP (FDIinGDP), total FDI stock (FDIS) and the geographic condition (Landlocked), (i.e. Dummy Variable Country is landlocked equal to 1). In the MME vector, we saw

[4] The variable chooses one of the major demanded natural resource, i.e. oil

FDI attractiveness as logically affected by market size, market opportunities and market potential. The more important FDI is as a proportion of GDP, the more the companies feel confident investing there. High percentage of FDI/GDP illustrates dependency of a country on FDI. This host country may have more attractive rules and regulations for investors. Huawei and ZTE would be stimulated by this to make their initial decision on the host country. But the dependent variables for Huawei and ZTE are the timing of investment. So it is not a part of cumulative stock investment. On the other hand, here the extent of market attractiveness is reflected in the existing trends or popularities of investment as well as the endowment of certain resources. China's 'going abroad' policy for African countries considerably reflects oil procurement rather than other natural resources variables. Top Oil-producer[5] is selected as the dummy variable of countries which are the major oil exporters to China. Share of FDI in GDP represents the dependency on foreign investment of an economy and the FDI stocks measure the total absorption and popularity of FDI in those given countries. Top oil producer reflects natural resources (NTR) variable. Oil is one of the major natural resources being exported from Africa to China. Certainly, natural resources is not only oil but also some other resources. However, there is not sufficient data to show all types of natural resources that China looks for in Africa. The importance of a country as an oil exporter to China will encourage FDI in that country. But the FDI may not be directly related to 'oil exploitation'. Thus the oil producer is not endogenous to wider Chinese FDI. Last, but not the least, landlocked countries are considered as a location where there is less openness because of inconvenienced infrastructure in communication and transport.

Diplomatic Ties

We measure diplomatic ties by the length of years of diplomatic association according to data from China's Ministry of Foreign Affairs website.[6]

---

[5] The records of China custom provide the major (top 20) countries export oil to China by amount annually. Those countries are not always constant.

[6] Diplomatic relations by 2010. http://www.fmprc.gov.cn/chn/pds/ziliao/2193/

Year Dummy

Year dummy is used to control for the year 2006 of China-Africa. In this year, a dramatic increase of cooperation and agreements between China and African governments shows a signal of policy-orientation. Firms may decide to locate in the countries resulting from the bunching of bilateral contract agreements.

Institutional Environment

The institutional environment can be defined by a political system through indicating the degree of political risk of the given countries (Peng & Khoury, 2009; Bulter & Joaquin, 1998). In this catalogue, to measure the quality of the institutional environment of African countries over the years, the source of political system data is rating provided by one of the major rating services—International Country Risk Guide,[7] which covers relatively comprehensive institution evaluation of six dimensions including 10 components:[8]

- Voice and Accountability (VA) contains two components:
  Military in politics measures the influence of the military regime of the country which leads to internal and external threat. It indicates the degree of effectiveness of the government function that affects the investment environment for foreign businesses. The greater degree of military involve in politics, the higher level of political risk and the poorer institution quality is. It means the government function is less effective. *Democratic accountability* is a measure of responsiveness of government to citizen. The less responsive it is, the more likely the government will fall.

[7] The Worldwide Governance Indicators, 2011 Updated, World Bank. www.govindicators.org. Higher values thus indicate better governance ratings. The indicators contain several groups of data sources which use different units and cover different sets of countries. Considering the components of the indicators, data from PRS group are chosen to measure institutional quality. Political Risk Services data—Commercial business information provider headquartered in Syracuse, United States. www.prsgroup.com

[8] In general terms if the points awarded are less than 0.5 of the total, that component can be considered as very high risk; between 0.5–0.6 indicates high risk, in the 60–70% range moderate risk, in the 70–80% range low risk and in the 80–100% range very low risk. However, this is only a general guideline as a better rating in other components can compensate for a poor risk rating in one component.

- Political Stability and Absence of Violence (PSAV) with four components:
  Government stability is an assessment both of the government's ability to carry out the declared policies and to stay in office. *Internal conflict* assesses political violence in the country and its actual/potential influence on governance. A low rating country would be embroiled in an on-going civil war or civil disorder. *External conflict* measures the risk to the current government from foreign action, such as cross-border conflict, which can adversely affect foreign business by the restrictions of operations by foreign investment sanctions, and distortions in the allocation of economic resources. *Ethnic tension* is 'an assessment of the degree of tension within a country attributable to racial, nationality, or language divisions'.[9]

- Government Effectiveness (GE)
  Bureaucratic quality is the institutional strength and quality of the bureaucracy, acting as a shock absorber that tends to minimise revisions of policy when governments change. The more effective, with a high-rate country, is the more strengthened bureaucracy so as to govern without drastic changes in policy or interruptions in government services.

- Regulatory Quality (RQ)
  Investment profile is an assessment of factors affecting the risks to investment that are not covered by other political, economic and financial risk components; including notably contract viability and payment delay.

- Rule of Law (ROL)
  Law and order assesses confidence in, and independence of, the legal system and popular observance of the law, including the quality of contract enforcement, property rights and the likelihood of violence and crime.

- Control of Corruption (CC)
  This is an assessment of corruption within the political system. The most common form of corruption met directly by business is financial

[9] Definition of methodology on indicators, ICRG

corruption, in the form of demands for special payments and bribes connected with import and export licenses, exchange controls, tax assessments, police protection, or loans. Such corruption can make it difficult to conduct business effectively, and in some cases may force the withdrawal or withholding of an investment.

Market of Telecommunication Sector

The idea of the ICT vector is built on market-seeking motivation (MS) for assessing the target business of African market. Telecommunication investment of these two firms focuses on providing telephone lines, mobile phone subscription and phone and internet networks. Kinoshita and Campos (2006) use the number of mainline telephones as an infrastructure proxy. The densities of population in African countries are different and may affect the usage and needs of ICT infrastructure. Thus, population density and telecommunication situation both affect the motivation. This vector is constructed by two statistics as follow:

Market of mobile usage = Mobile phone usage[10] × Population density
Market of telephone lines = Telephone lines × Population density

Knowledge Seeking/Efficiency Seeking

Quality of human capital is one of the major contributions for exploring new technology and managerial skill. The variables consist of the education rate in the particular year, total population and population growth rate. According to World Bank definition, Secondary education provides the gateway to the opportunities and benefits of economic and social development. It is recognised as a cornerstone of access to learning and developing advanced technology and for a country to increase its more sophisticated labour force. This variable may measure the potentials for localised production and adaption of existing technology. Labour forces

[10] Mobile usage is measured by number of subscriptions to a public mobile telephone service. source: World Bank data

in tertiary education provide a knowledge-based investment climate for advanced skill and technology supporting 'how-to' and 'know-how' as learning outcomes. Multinationals usually benefit from the dynamics of the knowledge economy. The capacity for host countries to adopt, disseminate, and maximise rapid technological advances is dependent on adequate population with tertiary education. Tertiary education determined the effective national innovation systems and the potential driver of knowledge-seeking (Table 6.1).

Table 6.1 Descriptions of descriptive statistics and expected effect

			Expected effect[a]	
Variables	Mean	Std. Dev.	Huawei	ZTE
GDP per capita	6.463094	1.158416	+	-
Real GDP	7.52973	4.733086	+	-
GDP growth rate	1.981437	1.253468	+	-
FDI inflows of GDP	1.702884	1.085981	+	-
FDI in stocks	7.836898	1.587183	+	-
Top oil producers	0.250784	0.434145	-	+/-
Landlocked	0.275	0.447214	+/-	+/-
Year Dummy_2006	0.5	0.500783	+/-	+
Diplomatic Ties	36.45395	10.47949	+/-	+
China OFDI in Africa	3.283742	2.195365	+	+
Institutions factors				
VA	-0.7781	0.460412	?	?
PSAV	-0.35739	0.169539	?	?
GE	-2.03113	2.737356	?	?
RQ	-0.69574	1.255787	?	?
RoL	-0.70623	0.370545	?	?
CC	-1.36569	1.37712	?	?
Telecom market				
(Telephone lines)	15.36675	2.383301	+	+
(Mobile subscribers)	17.91382	2.323031	+/-	+/-
Human capital				
Secondary	9.281948	1.187115	+/-	+/-
Tertiary education	7.249566	1.449767	+/-	+/-

[a]This is an anticipant result of each proposition from the generalised understanding. It can be partially, entirely or oppositely supported

Note: +, - and ? donate positive, negative and unpredicted influence on two firms' location decisions

6.4 Results

Tables 6.2a and 6.2b provide correlations of descriptive statistics. The correlations of benchmark models M1 and M2 are fairly low at acceptable level of 1%. Some of the components of institutions variables are closely correlated to others (e.g. control of corruption, rule of law) since they are measured from similar points of view. The influence of political stability and military in politics, for instance, which are correlated at 0.53, as can be seen in Table 6.2a. Similarly, rule of law is closely related to corruption, with correlation of 0.78, indicating that law and order systems have an effect on potential existence of inherent instability of public power for private gains. To avoid multicollinearity problems, models 3 to model 8 are estimated one by one. Among statistics of motivations contained in Table 6.2b some are again highly correlated to each other, for example, the double-counting problem of secondary and tertiary education. Therefore, in the following regressions, I combined the statistics into proper explanatory variables. Simultaneously, the variables are tested separately based on Model 1.

6.4.1 The Country-level Determinants of Firm's Decision

The compared results of Huawei and ZTE from Eq. (6.1) proceeded to a stepwise regression and are provided in M1–M8 on macroeconomic environment and institutions factors (Tables 6.3a and 6.3b). The influences on location choice of the firms individually are both affected by host countries LAs which are catalogued as pull factors and home-country (China) particular needs from host-countries, which are put into push factors. Model 1 includes control variables of host-country location characteristics. Home-country supportive factors are introduced in Model 2. To investigate effectively the influence of country-level determinants on both sides, M2 is considered as the baseline rather than M1.[11]

[11] M1 only include the host countries location advantages.

Table 6.2a The correlation matrix of host- and home- factors[a]

	1(H)	1(Z)	2	3	4	5	6	7	8	9	10	11	12	13	14	15	16	17
1. Subsidiary	1.000	1.000																
2. GDP per capita	0.448*	0.423*	1.000															
3. Real GDP	0.251*	-0.071	0.173*	1.000														
4. GDP growth rate	0.294*	0.006	0.092	0.346*	1.000													
5. FDI inflows of GDP	0.042	0.134	0.024	0.068	-0.035	1.000												
6. FDI stocks	0.005	-0.061	0.031	0.026	-0.197*	0.133	1.000											
7. Top oil producers	0.450*	0.4292*	0.414*	0.311*	0.145*	0.1485*	0.122	1.000										
8. Landlocked	-0.054	0.170*	0.164*	0.433*	0.121	0.076	0.028	0.347*	1.000									
9. CNFDI	-0.062	0.046	-0.067	-0.389*	-0.275*	-0.128	-0.011	-0.204*	-0.255*	1.000								
10. Political ties	0.092	0.2238*	0.233*	-0.003	-0.051	0.075	0.182*	0.121	0.064	-0.112	1.000							
11. Year_d (2006)	0.271*	0.284*	0.451*	0.107	0.017	-0.052	0.133	0.223*	0.016	0.000	0.188*	1.000						
12. VA	0.192*	0.067	0.017	0.154	0.476*	0.073	-0.200*	-0.019	-0.322*	0.060	-0.222*	-0.002	1.000					
13. PSAV	0.036	-0.064	-0.217*	0.485*	0.323*	0.038	0.061	-0.053	0.004	-0.330*	-0.136	-0.055	0.532*	1.000				
14. GE	0.334*	0.045	0.015	0.286*	0.511*	-0.010	-0.083	0.157	0.183*	0.043	-0.058	0.010	0.280*	0.258*	1.000			
15. RQ	-0.079	0.002	-0.087	0.160	0.010	0.3492*	0.119	0.082	0.098	-0.255*	0.076	-0.066	0.174*	0.214*	0.008	1.000		
16. RoL	0.183*	-0.018	-0.168*	0.354*	0.474*	0.148	0.016	0.084	-0.161	-0.148	-0.044	0.001	0.421*	0.528*	0.287*	0.087	1.000	
17. CC	-0.069	-0.004	-0.051	0.130	0.012	0.496*	0.193*	0.090	0.023	-0.305*	0.129	0.042	0.162*	0.199*	-0.038	0.781*	0.205*	1.000

[a]A combined correlation matrix consists of Huawei and ZTE. As the comparison models use same independent variables, the correlations between those independent variables do not change

* at significant level of 1%

Table 6.2b Correlation matrix of host country environment and firm motivation

	1(H)	1(Z)	2	3	4	5	6	7	8	18	19	20	21	22	23	24
1. Subsidiary	1.000	1.000														
2. GDP per capita	0.251*	-0.071	1.000													
3. Real GDP	0.294*	0.006	0.346*	1.000												
4. GDP growth rate	0.042	0.134	0.068	-0.035	1.000											
5. FDI inflows of GDP	0.005	-0.061	0.026	-0.197*	0.133	1.000										
6. FDI stocks	0.450*	0.429*	0.311*	0.145*	0.149*	0.122	1.000									
7. Top oil producers	-0.054	0.170*	0.433*	0.121	0.076	0.028	0.347*	1.000								
8. Landlocked	-0.062	0.046	-0.389*	-0.275*	-0.128	-0.011	-0.204*	-0.255*	1.000							
18. Population density	-0.051	0.072	-0.241*	0.055	0.135	-0.093	0.011	-0.286*	-0.107	1.000						
19. Total Population	0.285*	0.562*	-0.441*	-0.026	0.145*	-0.082	0.520*	-0.008	0.133	0.296*	1.000					
20. Population growth	-0.411*	-0.029	-0.490*	-0.314*	0.047	0.088	-0.402*	0.041	0.152*	-0.015	0.011	1.000				
21. Telephone lines	0.234*	0.270*	0.218*	0.238*	0.053	-0.026	0.545*	0.167*	-0.187*	0.132	0.401*	-0.322*	1.000			
22. No. of Mobile users	0.301*	0.360*	0.137	0.209*	0.076	-0.006	0.644*	0.181*	-0.190*	0.196*	0.523*	-0.247*	0.585*	1.000		
23. Sec_Education	0.319*	0.003	0.723*	0.220*	0.024	-0.052	0.421*	0.043	-0.248*	0.076	-0.177	-0.745*	0.555*	0.276*	1.000	
24. Ter_Education	0.286*	0.220*	0.729*	0.240*	0.067	-0.018	0.521*	0.303*	-0.370*	0.174	0.080	-0.609*	0.610*	0.521*	0.861*	1.000

* at significant level of 1%

Table 6.3a Panel probit regression (random effect) of institutions and host- and home- factors on Huawei location choice, 2003–2010

Variables	M1	M2	M3	M4	M5	M6	M7	M8
Host Country (Pull) factors								
GDP per capita	1.083***	2.477***	6.821***	4.729**	4.588*	4.336	5.022**	4.647
	[0.418]	[0.850]	[2.611]	[2.214]	[2.372]	[4.343]	[2.425]	[3.022]
Real GDP	0.300*	0.383**	0.359	0.367*	0.0726	0.358	0.383	0.366
	[0.154]	[0.194]	[0.268]	[0.214]	[0.197]	[0.342]	[0.249]	[0.242]
GDP growth rate	0.199	0.334	0.0503	0.275	0.0326	0.29	0.186	0.222
	[0.243]	[0.386]	[0.529]	[0.437]	[0.377]	[0.501]	[0.469]	[0.470]
FDI inflows of GDP	-0.00849	-0.332	0.0632	-0.209	-0.35	-0.304	-0.177	-0.196
	[0.299]	[0.470]	[0.937]	[0.742]	[0.747]	[0.768]	[0.812]	[0.743]
FDI stocks	3.118***	3.152***	5.636***	4.017***	3.608**	3.498	3.934***	3.680*
	[0.773]	[0.794]	[1.806]	[1.341]	[1.510]	[2.861]	[1.390]	[1.898]
Top oil producers	-6.052***	-10.52***	-12.47**	-9.987**	-11.83*	-8.242	-10.14*	-9.534
	[2.085]	[3.106]	[5.414]	[4.996]	[6.095]	[7.876]	[5.554]	[6.704]
Landlocked	0.781	0.813	3.089	3.19	-0.793	2.425	2.943	2.547
	[1.548]	[1.955]	[3.365]	[2.399]	[2.617]	[4.705]	[2.733]	[2.617]
Home Country (Push) factors								
CNFDI		0.868**	1.566**	1.107**	1.228**	1.025	1.171*	1.078
		[0.345]	[0.625]	[0.516]	[0.607]	[0.791]	[0.617]	[0.664]
Length of political ties (by2010)		0.0728	0.12	0.047	0.0161	0.0395	0.0466	0.0429
		[0.0891]	[0.125]	[0.0935]	[0.0835]	[0.143]	[0.106]	[0.0966]
Year_d (2006)		2.173*	3.444	2.62	3.356	2.746	3.014	2.682
		[1.187]	[2.153]	[1.997]	[2.310]	[2.587]	[2.325]	[2.324]
Institutions factors								
VA			6.237*					
			[3.349]					
PSAV				4.688				
				[5.375]				
GE					0.979*			
					[0.572]			
RQ						-2.088		
						[2.371]		
RoL							0.453	
							[2.162]	
CC								-0.167
								[0.546]
Constant	-28.99***	-41.75***	-84.60***	-60.89***	-51.64**	-57.64	-63.84**	-59.75*
	[6.696]	[10.13]	[27.05]	[22.72]	[24.05]	[53.20]	[26.26]	[32.72]
Observations	316	296	243	242	242	242	242	242

***$p < 0.01$, **$p < 0.05$, *$p < 0.1$

Table 6.3b Panel probit regression (random effect) of institutions and host- and home- factors on ZTE location choice, 2003–2010

Variables	M1	M2	M3	M4	M5	M6	M7	M8
Host Country (Pull) factors								
GDP per capita	0.204	-0.581	-0.309	-1.192	-0.997	-0.835	-0.945	-0.554
	[0.510]	[0.622]	[0.629]	[0.907]	[0.856]	[19.20]	[0.937]	[1.001]
Real GDP	0.0435	-0.106	-0.116	-0.193	-0.11	-0.0596	-0.182	-0.0683
	[0.132]	[0.274]	[0.199]	[0.237]	[0.219]	[1.089]	[0.271]	[0.211]
GDP growth rate	-0.0894	-0.122	0.167	0.21	0.244	0.239	0.239	0.235
	[0.142]	[0.264]	[0.382]	[0.444]	[0.446]	[2.202]	[0.406]	[0.406]
FDI inflows of GDP	-0.248	-0.237	-0.868*	-0.765	-0.808	-0.856	-0.841	-0.826
	[0.166]	[0.274]	[0.520]	[0.611]	[0.574]	[0.829]	[0.598]	[0.598]
FDI stocks	4.127***	1.831***	2.138***	2.581***	2.148***	2.146**	2.203***	2.108***
	[0.486]	[0.503]	[0.588]	[0.643]	[0.768]	[1.085]	[0.758]	[0.619]
Top oil producers	0.772	1.037	2.491	4.289*	1.978	3.107	3.483	3.252
	[2.027]	[2.307]	[2.000]	[2.427]	[2.370]	[7.271]	[3.719]	[2.772]
Landlocked	4.706**	2.751	3.866*	5.789**	4.754	4.549	4.030*	4.535
	[2.154]	[1.867]	[2.137]	[2.777]	[2.891]	[14.62]	[2.392]	[2.956]
Home Country (Push)factors								
CNFDI		1.033***	1.026***	1.284***	1.050***	1.045	1.065***	1.072**
		[0.338]	[0.317]	[0.397]	[0.329]	[5.084]	[0.400]	[0.538]
Length of political ties (by 2010)		0.202***	0.273***	0.340***	0.308***	0.29	0.300***	0.290***
		[0.0684]	[0.0841]	[0.0823]	[0.103]	[0.690]	[0.0817]	[0.0968]
Year_dummy (2006)		2.796**	3.765***	4.613***	3.333**	3.274	3.648**	3.443*
		[1.112]	[1.173]	[1.516]	[1.297]	[18.36]	[1.655]	[1.928]
Institutions Factors								
VA			-0.747					
			[1.984]					
PSAV				15.07**				
				[6.001]				
GE					0.203			
					[0.314]			
RQ						-0.0387		
						[0.894]		
RoL							3.33	
							[4.600]	
CC								-0.164
								[0.611]
Constant	-32.50***	-19.32***	-25.84***	-21.17**	-22.06**	-23.14	-20.22*	-24.55***
	[4.617]	[5.423]	[7.705]	[8.584]	[9.204]	[139.6]	[11.00]	[8.175]
Observations	302	290	237	236	236	236	236	236

***$p < 0.01$, **$p < 0.05$, *$p < 0.1$

The first comparison built on effects of conventional location advantages variables. The results reveal that GDP per capita and Real GDP of host countries have a positive coefficient on the location decision for Huawei, at statistically significant 5%, which suggest that Huawei is more likely to invest in large-scale markets with more opportunities. On the contrary, the results did not find any market size variables to be significantly associated with the location decision of ZTE. Thus, considering the ownerships of the two firms, the first entry decisions of Huawei in African markets were motivated by firm-specific objectives, (i.e. market-seeking for location advantage), but the boot is on the other foot, for ZTE where advanced markets are not the determinants for its geographic strategies in Africa. At the initial point of location choice ZTE is non-market oriented. The two firms have different target purposes on different markets at the first stage. However, to view the background of the companies, they are both ICT companies and producing the telecommunication and information related products. Thus, the forward commercial-driven investment would have fewer differences. It underpins the point that IMNEs, especially in ICT, are likely to move towards conventional (mainly MS) motives as they become embedded in a host-country's development. The Proposition 1 is supported, suggesting that ownership of firm determines the likelihood of initial motivation of investment.

Towards national attractiveness, ZTE and Huawei may be expected to have opposite consideration on choosing the location according to whether the host country is major oil producer for China (sources for import oil),[12] because the telecommunication investment may involve in the underlying bilateral benefits between two countries, i.e. Angola Mode. However, a very notable result of national attractiveness is the insignificant coefficient of top oil producers, indicating whether the countries are among the major oil exporters to China. This is statistically insignificant to the probability of investment decision of ZTE, whilst Huawei's entry decision has a strongly negative response to the abundance of oil in host countries (-6.052***). Natural resources are indirect factors to the firms only if the firm has strong ODA responsibility or is

[12] Some of the countries may be sufficient in oil and/or other mining resources but they are not counted in the model since they are not the major oil importing countries for China.

bidding for projects based on China's infrastructure loans. The telecommunication MNEs dealing with oil producer not expected to be systematically and directly related to allocating ICT FDI, but a politically influential characteristic of the host country. The fact that the country is an oil producer does not affect its direct commercial attraction to ICT firms. The influence could have come from oil's attraction to China and, therefore, to CSA-D and CSA-I support for ICT IMNE. This confirmed the hypothesis which suggested that State-owned ownership must drive a positive objective on oil production in Africa. Huawei as a private ICT company (less government affiliation) has barely responsibility for opportunities oil exploitation. Most top host oil producers for China have relatively high investment risk (e.g. frequencies of conflicts); it might cause the long-term instability on Huawei's commercial investment. Thus, Huawei is less likely to invest in the countries where it is not obligated and less interested in. Another pair of opposite results of the two firms: Huawei's decisions to locate in the countries were not influenced by the geographic conditions; ZTE started more likely (4.706**) in the landlocked countries, meaning ZTE provided infrastructure based on geographic strategy compared to Huawei. ZTE nominal private company but with government as large stakeholder so is considered as a State-control company or highly associated with government. China specific factors would have more influence on its decision. Meantime, by taking on the responsibility of ODA, ZTE invested initially in those landlocked countries which maybe least developed. However, ZTE is also a profit-driven company in the consumer market. FDI stocks as one sign of the attractiveness of host country would be considered. Total FDI stock (FDIS) of host countries generally indicates attractiveness for FDI worldwide, i.e. the opportunities to make impact of FDI. Both MNEs' decisions are highly significantly affected by this indicator interpreted as the general consideration of economic risk factors. Like traditional MNEs the location decision here are impressed by the previous performance of attracting FDI. The share of FDI inflows of GDP is not significantly relevant to the likelihood of both firms' investment. The level of government affiliation and ownership bring the difference in location choice. In other word, the investment replying on strong FSA-R are unlikely to be decided by market-related factors because their capabilities to easily access CSA-D and interpret into their investment decision. Whereas the company with less association with government/institutions may invest in a host country through their own FSA-A, thus more market-related variables matter Huawei. Proposition 2 is partially supported statistically.

Model 2 incorporates variables for home countries' indirect incentives on firms' investment. The larger the amount of China's total FDI in a given country and in a given year, the larger the possibility of both companies deciding to set up offshore representative office in this country and year. Internationalisation theory suggests a firm's international expansion pattern is a function of its past international experience and knowledge base (Johanson & Wiedersheim, 1975; Johanson & Vahlne, 1977, 1990). The driving force of this internationalisation process is 'experiential market knowledge' (Johanson & Vahlne, 1990).

Telecommunication investments contribute to the amount of China's total FDI experience in Africa, but the small coefficients (0.868** Huawei and 1.033***ZTE) show that the FDI experience merely brings a weakly positive trend of possibility of establishing subsidiaries. The Chinese telecommunication FDI is concentrated in a few firms more than investments in other manufacturing industries, i.e. less home country rivals. Their experiential market knowledge may not come from the investment from the same sector, i.e. the specific knowledge base, but a general perception. The experiences of investment are slightly positively related to their decision seen as if the host country is a popular and stable market for all types of Chinese FDI as a general investment location. This corroborates Proposition 4.

Year dummy of 2006 measures the relevance of companies' decision on policy-orientation. After year 2006 (China-Africa), the bilateral governmental cooperation suggests that many new governmental level contracts or government joint contracts were signed during the period. The results support Proposition 3a that bilateral cooperation has a positive effect on ZTE's location decision with coefficient 4.492 significant at 1%, whereas Huawei's decision has slightly responded to the policy-driven investment with coefficient of 2.173*. Year 2006 as the China-Africa summit has important influence on positive consideration of host country. An interesting result shows that a diplomatic tie has insignificant influence on location choice of both ZTE and Huawei. This can be interpreted that the telecommunication infrastructure assistance is an integral part of firm's investment in Africa rather than needing institutional foundations for their international expansion. China's early age infrastructure investment in Africa was based on such diplomatic ties; however, the new Chinese investors, acting as more conventional MNEs, get access to African market with less responsibility of official assistance. Proposition 3b cannot be accepted.

Model 3–Model 8 apply the specifications of institutional factors. All the conventional location advantages are controlled as baseline. Political risk indicators are tested within six specifications. It was expected that the location decisions of the two firms would be sensitive to different indicators of the six specifications resulting from the organisational structure of parent companies and the policy-function of being Chinese investors in African countries.

The results show that the two firms' first location choices have different statistical significance for these institutions' indicators. It can be argued that Chinese infrastructure multinationals will respond only partially to differences in political variables, due to the influence of another layer of political relationships between governments. However, it remains in partial support of Proposition 5, which suggests that Chinese IMNEs continue to consider quality of institutions of host countries, although some of the investments are responsive to governmental contracts. The different reaction of location decisions of institutions, once again are towards the ownerships of firms. Proposition 5 is a generalised idea that has to be analysed individually here.

Voice and accountability reflect the influence of effectiveness of government functioning on the investment environment. Strong V&A represents an open attitude by government generally that is then perceived by the MNEs as a positive aspect of the investing environment. It does not represent a direct element of how the conditions in the environment work for FDI attraction, but is a potential indirect factor as perceived by MNEs. Regarding wholly privatised enterprises, less uncertainty of government should relate to probability of making an investment in the host country. Moreover, Huawei is more likely to choose these low-risk countries of government effectiveness in order to reduce the cost of dealing with the frequent changes of local policies. 'The bureaucracy tends to be somewhat autonomous from political pressure and to have an established mechanism for recruitment and training' (Brink, 2004; ICRG, 2012). A change in government tends to be disturbing in terms of policy formulation and day-to-day administrative functions. The uncertainty of the changes increases transaction cost that is the most influential on MNEs decision making.

V&A and regulation quality have more effect on commercial aspects of host countries. These, therefore, are more important factors for Huawei. Huawei's private nature determines their long-term commercial plans with less consideration of government affiliation. High degree of conflicts attributed to racial nationality or language divisions negatively affected political stability and economic environment. The Chinese government has strong political ties with most African governments. The political stance on ethnic tension or any conflicts will affect the security of the firm that is responsive to the governmental projects. The more linked to government relationship the more likely the concern for better political stability. For ZTE, as a listed company with state shareholder, the investment may partly represent a political purpose. The political instability has stronger influence on investing in government-related projects, e.g. the investment project may be interrupted by changing government or ethnic conflict if the investment is signed by political opponent. Therefore, ZTE emerges as more likely to locate in countries with higher political stability because of its state ownership would have to measure the political instability of each country.

Corruption is a threat to foreign investment owing to distortion of economic and financial environment, eliminating efficiency of government and business by enabling people to assume positions of power through patronage rather than ability and then the potential existence of inherent instability in political processes. However, corruption is more likely to impact those MNEs with large financial commitment and seeking high profit. Corruption is considered to be some form of calculated malfunctioning within an institution-based decision process. This is executed by an individual (or coordinated group) for the purpose of personal gain. It will represent the implementation of a decision that differ from the one that would have resulted from an undistorted application of rules laid down by the institution to achieve objectives mandated by wider policy agendas. In IB terms this can occur both in the home country (in an approval and/or subsidising process), or in a host country (distortion of entry regulation and/or terms and conditions of establishment and operations). Clearly then FSA-R become firm-level attribute that are most likely to at least discern the presence of corrupt potentials in an institutional context that it is its precise task to understand and operate within.

Regarding to the economic background of African countries and industry features of these two firms, corruption is less relevant to their location choice.

6.4.2 The Firm Specific Motivations on Decision

Table 6.4a and 6.4b present the results for propositions on the motivation of the companies. These models look into specific variables related to the particular industry and aim to find out concrete motivations on locating in a certain country in a certain year. This model use the baseline with M1 as the consideration of specific factor related to the sector is little affected by home-country general factors. Notably, the determinants of location choice rely on the external factors derived from home- and host-country. It is more like a response towards general country-level factors in FDI (M1–8). Based on established IB theory that a MNE's investment decision can be determined by a range of strategic objective (MS/ES/KS) that allows different locations to attract different parts of MNEs' expansion. For a MNE itself, the consideration of some particular elements of host countries will be narrowed down to what is the firm-level purpose of expansion. On this dimension, MNEs' location decisions are more likely to be commercially motivated. Therefore, these are the two different models. The variables on market level are seen as MS factors in M9–M12.

M9 and M10 test the stimulative effect of the specific markets for telecommunication, regarding the current telecommunication situation of

Table 6.4a Motivation on Huawei location choice, 2003–2010

Variables	M1	M9	M10	M11	M12
Host Country					
GDP per capita	1.083***	1.110***	2.779***	9.305***	4.652***
	[0.418]	[0.424]	[0.740]	[2.587]	[1.414]
Real GDP	0.300*	0.282*	0.508*	0.491	0.656*
	[0.154]	[0.159]	[0.294]	[0.320]	[0.350]
GDP growth rate	0.199	0.226	0.324	-0.417	0.0305
	[0.243]	[0.251]	[0.502]	[0.711]	[0.745]
FDI inflows of GDP	-0.00849	0.0605	-0.2	-0.64	-0.694
	[0.299]	[0.326]	[0.683]	[0.956]	[0.884]
FDI stocks	3.118***	3.084***	3.401***	5.648***	7.955***
	[0.773]	[0.681]	[0.921]	[1.171]	[1.398]
Top oil producers	-6.052***	-5.644***	-9.269**	-20.01***	-19.07***
	[2.085]	[1.960]	[3.638]	[7.378]	[4.885]
Landlocked	0.781	1.218	3.425	3.399	-1.233
	[1.548]	[1.615]	[2.765]	[2.531]	[3.095]
Market Potential (MS)					
Telephone lines× population density		0.38			
		[0.324]			
Mobile usage× population density			2.404***		
			[0.612]		
Human capital potential (ES/KS)					
Secondary education × population growth				3.440***	
				[1.284]	
Tertiary education× population growth					0.856
					[1.090]
Constant	-28.99***	-34.73***	-82.59***	-123.4***	-86.35***
	[6.696]	[8.110]	[14.95]	[18.51]	[14.44]
Observations	316	316	311	203	169

***$p < 0.01$, **$p < 0.05$, *$p < 0.1$

host countries, on location decisions of ZTE and Huawei. Huawei and ZTE are motivated in differentiate submarket owing to their slight difference in business focus. M9 provides positive sign of the investing aim on telephone lines market. However, only ZTE shows the statistical significance of treating telephone lines market as part of the future market. In terms of Proposition 6a, it was naturally considered a negative

Table 6.4b Motivation on ZTE location choice, 2003–2010

Variables	M1	M9	M10	M11	M12
Host Country					
GDP per capita	0.204	-0.524	-0.487	4.110**	-2.05
	[0.510]	[0.584]	[0.609]	[1.647]	[1.934]
Real GDP	0.0435	-0.2	0.00138	0.0535	0.757***
	[0.132]	[0.189]	[0.189]	[0.471]	[0.235]
GDP growth rate	-0.0894	0.0636	-0.222	-0.889	0.0289
	[0.142]	[0.163]	[0.354]	[0.651]	[0.645]
FDI inflows of GDP	-0.248	-0.385*	-0.21	-0.109	-0.442
	[0.166]	[0.202]	[0.387]	[0.681]	[0.422]
FDI stocks	4.127***	3.847***	1.155*	1.202	2.139**
	[0.486]	[0.462]	[0.699]	[1.034]	[1.047]
Top oil producers	0.772	2.745	6.686***	2.131	3.228
	[2.027]	[3.119]	[2.205]	[3.692]	[5.021]
Landlocked	4.706**	5.270***	5.733***	5.483*	8.750***
	[2.154]	[1.671]	[1.851]	[2.914]	[3.187]
Market Potential (MS)					
Telephone lines× population density		1.604***			
		[0.363]			
Mobile usage× population density			3.008***		
			[0.435]		
Human capital potential (ES/KS)					
Secondary education × population growth				13.00***	
				[2.131]	
Tertiary education × population growth					9.634***
					[1.686]
Constant	-32.50***	-48.55***	-58.27***	-151.1***	-79.96***
	[4.617]	[5.561]	[7.356]	[20.95]	[11.42]
Observations	302	287	283	190	159

***$p < 0.01$, **$p < 0.05$, *$p < 0.1$

relationship between gap of local infrastructure provision and opportunities of investment in infrastructure. Taken together, M9 results of two firms reject the Proposition 6a that the companies are motivated to fill the gap of infrastructure.

M10 suggests the usages of mobile phone with intensive population have positive link with both Huawei and ZTE location decision, at

2.404*** and 3.008*** respectively. Mobile phone manufacturing is one of the major businesses of both companies. Large size of mobile phone market will bring more profit for both firms in selling mobile cellular. Like most Chinese MNEs, the two companies are motivated in investing in the market where they can exploit their FSA-As in the sectors for international production. The results of Huawei and ZTE give the empirical support of market seeking on Proposition 6b.

The Models 11 and 12 test the education level and population growth on influencing the probability of location decision. The study supposes the increasing number of population obtaining high education brings high probability of potential localised production and technologies improvement. In Model 11, with higher population of secondary education, there is a positive relationship between location decision and human capital for Huawei and ZTE. Secondary education enables the companies to recruit qualified people to adapt their existing technology in host countries for local production, and take advantage of cheap labour instead of bringing migrant labour (Cheng & Stough, 2007; Cheung & Qian, 2009). Another component of the proposition is the tertiary education indicating the local human capital potential in developing advanced technologies (United Nations). The variables of population in tertiary education present a strong potential of restructuring and advancing the firm's assets to meet the local needs (Dunning, 1993). With different results in Model 12, Huawei has no statistically significant motivation in knowledge seeking when it considers the first step of the market, while the result verifies ZTE's long-term objective on seeking local innovation and localised manufacturing (9.634***). Partially corroborated on Proposition 7, the higher education level with the rapid population growth rate provides human capital of host countries which improve the probability of embedding in the countries.

6.5 Concluding Remarks

Macroeconomic and institutional environments of African countries have different effects on both the telecommunication companies owing to the differences of ownership advantage and MNEs' motivations that were created in China. The two Chinese telecommunication companies are considered as the token of emerging Chinese large enterprises that possess both inherent features of being Chinese MNEs and globalised companies. Facing to African markets, we draw from traditional theory of location choice and institutional theory in building a discussion on how these MNEs react to host countries' economic and institutional environments, respectively. According to African macro-level data and World Bank Governance indicators and IPR Guide, our main propositions are supported. Although Huawei and ZTE are both driven by political and firm-level objectives in Africa, the influence of host countries environment on firms' decision of location choice still differs though the ownerships. Home government provides foundations for both Chinese firms' international expansion (Peng et al., 2008), particularly in gathering of commercial investment opportunities and political incentives.

Location advantage of a host country in this case can be considered as both economic and institutional environments, which it remains necessary to take into account for Chinese infrastructure MNEs. The empirical study argues that Chinese infrastructure investment is not only based on political ties and ODA between China and African governments, but on the firms themselves, where seeking new markets and internationalisation strategies also motivate Chinese telecommunication investment in Africa.

In showing that the location decision is influenced by particular markets of telecommunication sector, the evidence points to these telecommunication firms being similar in motivations to traditional MNEs. This implicates firms' location decisions in Africa as not primarily taking chances to fill in the gap of inadequate infrastructure. But, on the contrary, this infrastructure provision by Chinese telecommunication MNEs is the complementary investment for further expansion. Chinese telecommunication MNEs are not a unidimensional construct for one purpose. From the differences of results of two firms, they do not possess similar ability to respond to different levels of host countries factors These purposes of investment depend on particular projects associated with firm's own capabilities and ownership position.

Appendix

Summary of Variable Construct, Measure Purposes and Data Sources

Proposition	Construct	Measure purpose	Source
1	GDP per capita	Market size	World Bank
	Real GDP	Market size	World Bank
	GDP growth rate	Market potentials	World Bank
2	FDI inflows of GDP	Dependency on FDI	World Bank
	FDI in stocks	Popularity of FDI	UNCTAD Statistics
	Top oil producers	Resources endowments	Chinese custom authorities
	Landlocked	Openness	Map of African continent
3a	Year Dummy_2006	Cooperation summit	FOCAC
3b	Diplomatic Ties	Historical link by 2010	China Ministry of Foreign Affairs
4	China OFDI in Africa	FDI experience in Africa	China Ministry of Commerce
5	Institutions factors	Effect of institutions	ICRG & WGI (PRS)
6a	Telecom market (Telephone lines)	Motivation of investment (MS)	World Bank Data
6b	Telecom market (Mobile subscribers)	Motivation of investment(MS)	World Bank Data
7	Human capital (secondary/ tertiary education	Potential of ES/KS	World Bank Data

Comparison of Two Companies

	Huawei	ZTE
Ownership	Private (collective)	State-holding listed company
Overseas Revenue (2011)	138.4 billion RMB	46.76 billion RMB (overseas)
Main business	Carrier Network Business; Wireless Networks; Fixed Network; Global Service; Carrier Software & Core Network	Wireless, Access & Bearer, handset &telecommunication software, Terminals, Network services, and ICT solutions for enterprises and government agencies

Source: Huawei financial annual report 2011 (https://consumer.huawei.com/cn/press/news/2012/hw-263368/); ZTE annual report 2011 (https://www.zte.com.cn/mi_imgs/global/investor_relations/348956/P020120917397063693372.pdf, pp. 12).

Early Achievements of Market Activities in Africa

ZTE[a]	Huawei
• In November 1998, ZTE won a contract from Kenya Posts & Telecommunications Corp. (KPTC) to supply ZXMVC 3000 videoconferencing system that connects Kenya's four major post and telecom departments. • In April 2000, ZTE's switching system with the capacity of 1200 lines was put into commercial operation in Mali. • In April 2001, ZTE signed a supply contract with Zambia Telecommunication Co. to provide switch equipment and transmission equipment to construct the telecommunication network covering 16 cities in Zambia. • In 2003, ZTE won the contract in Algeria to construct the largest CDMA WLL network in Africa. • In 2003, ZTE's GSM equipment was put into commercial operation on large scale in Nigeria and Ethiopia. • In 2004, ZTE won the contract from Telecom Egypt to help the latter construct a large scale CDMA WLL network with the total capacity of 60000 subscriber lines. • By 2005, ZTE provided Africa Flagship 3G Network for Tunisia to support the World Summit on the Information Society (WSIS). marked ZTE´s first 3G network win outside of China[b]. • In 2005, ZTE was contracted with Angola for Africa´s first CDMA2000-based NGN[c] • In December 2005, ZTE provided high-speed broadband equipment including DSLAM terminals, Power Supply and DSL modems with InternetGhana[d] • In 2008, ZTE signed agreement with Libya partners to Build First WiMAX Commercial Network in Africa[e]	• In 1999, Huawei was established in Algeria, and became the biggest CDMA equipment supplier by 2005[f]. Huawei has accessed to over 80% of all the operators and private network markets in Algeria by 2009[g]. • In 1999 Huawei was established in Zimbabwe and its intelligent network, switch, optical access, and CDMA wireless access products are now being deployed on a large scale in the networks of two of Zimbabwe's state-owned operators in 2004[h]. • Huawei arrived to Nigeria in 1999, by 2004 was bringing revenues of USD $400 million[i]; as part of a $200 million partnership agreement with Nigeria's Ministry of Communication in 2005, Huawei deployed CDMA450 wireless technology across Nigeria.[j] • In 2001, Huawei's representative office was established in Zambia. Huawei's products and solutions, including that of GSM, CDMA, IN, and NGN have been widely deployed in the Zambian telecoms market. • In 2004, Huawei won a US$34 million bid from Kenya's biggest mobile operator SAFARICOM to reconstruct and update SAFARICOM's Intelligent Network[i] • By 2006, the sales revenue in SSA reached US$ 1 billion; Built the first 3G commercial base in Mauritius[k]; Build a GSM network in Ivory Coast[l] • In 2009, contracted with South Africa's Neotel to expand its CDMA network and provision of a fourth generation (4G) base[l]

[a]"ZTE aims to be African telecom market leader", 2004 No.9, released in 2004-06-24, https://www.zte.com.cn/global/about/magazine/zte-technologies/2004/9/en_283/161350.html
[b]"ZTE Provides African Flagship 3G Network for Tunisia", 2004 No.11, released in 2004-08-25, https://www.zte.com.cn/global/about/magazine/zte-technologies/2004/11/en_294/161374.html
[c]"ZTE Advances African Telecommunications With First CDMA2000-based Fixed Next Generation Network (NGN)", 2005 No.8, https://www.zte.com.cn/global/about/magazine/zte-technologies/2005/8/en_241/161523.html
[d]"ZTE Supplies African ISP", 2006 No.6, https://www.zte.com.cn/global/about/magazine/zte-technologies/2006/6/en_156/161604.html
[e]"ZTE Partners with LTT to Build First Ever WiMAX Commercial Network in Africa", 2008 No.2, https://www.zte.com.cn/global/about/magazine/zte-technologies/2008/2/en_8/161977.html
[f]Economic and Commercial Office of the People's Republic of China in in Algeria, 2005-05-15, http://dz.mofcom.gov.cn/article/jmxw/200505/20050500091263.shtml
[g]Institute of Developing Economies-Japan External Trade Organisation, "China in Africa: A STRATEGIC OVERVIEW", October 2009, pp. 60, https://www.ide.go.jp/library/English/Data/Africa_file/Manualreport/pdf/china_all.pdf
[h]See news in China telecommunication and information forum (CN), released in 2004-11-05, http://www.ctiforum.com/news/world/258119.html
[i]Space Watch Africa, "Africa: Huawei ramps up its telecoms market", February 20, 2017, http://spacewatchafrica.com/africa-huawei-ramps-up-its-telecoms-market/
[j]People's Daily, "ICT cooperation: China and Nigeria ", 2005-4-15
[k]See news "Huawei and ZTE 10 years exploration in Africa" (translate CN), Frist Financial Daily (DiYicaiJing Daily),2007-05-10(C06). http://www.yicai.com/
[l]REUTERS,"Factbox: Africa deals by China's biggest vendors in Africa", FEBRUARY 16, 2011, https://www.reuters.com/article/us-africa-china-telecoms-fb-idUKTRE71E4YM20110215
Source: www.zte.com.cn. The publication series of ZTE Technologies; www.huawei.com/Africa

Bibliography

Blonigen, B. A. (2005). A review of the empirical literature on FDI determinants. *Atlantic Economic Journal, 33*, 383–403.

Brink, C. H. (2004). *Measuring political risk: Risks to foreign investment*. Ashgate Publishing.

Brunetti, A., & Weder, B. (1998). Investment and institutional uncertainty: A comparative study of different uncertainty measures. *Weltwirtschaftliches Archiv, 134*(3), 513–533.

Buckley, P., Clegg, J., Cross, A., Liu, X., Voss, H., & Zheng, P. (2007). The determinants of Chinese outward foreign direct investment. *Journal of International Business Studies, 38*(4), 499–518.

Bulter, K. C., & Joaquin, D. C. (1998). A note on political risk and return on foreign direct investment. *Journal of International Business Studies, 29*(3), 599–607.

Cantwell, J. (1989). *Technological innovation and multinational corporations*. B. Blackwell.

Cheng, S., & Stough, R. R. (2007, April). The pattern and magnitude of China's outward FDI in Asia. *ICRIER Project on Intra-Asian FDI Flows in New Delhi*, 25–26.

Cheung, Y. W., & Qian, X. (2009). Empirics of China's outward direct investment. *Pacific Economic Review, 14*(3), 312–341.

Cheung, Y. W., De Haan, J., Qian, X., & Yu, S. (2012). China's outward direct investment in Africa. *Review of International Economics, 20*(2), 201–220.

Corkin, L., Burke, C., & Davies, M. (2008). *China's role in the development of Africa's infrastructure*. SAIS Working papers in African Studies, 04–08.

Deng, P. (2004, May–June). Outward investment by Chinese MNCs: Motivations and implications. *Business Horizons, 47*(3), 8–16.

Dunning, J. H. (1980, Spring/Summer). Toward an eclectic theory of international production: Some empirical tests. Journal of International Business Studies, 11(1), 9–31.

Dunning, J. H. (1993). Internationalizing Porter's diamond. *Management International Review*, 7–15.

Foster, V., Butterfield, W., Chen, C., & Pushak, N. (2008). *Building bridges: China's growing role as infrastructure financier in Africa*. Public Private Infrastructure Advisory Facility, Trends and Policy Options, No. 5. World Bank, Washington.

Franco, C., Rentocchini, F., & Vittucci Marzetti, G. (2008). *Why do firms invest abroad? An analysis of the motives underlying foreign direct investments*.

Henisz, W. J. (2000). The institutional environment for multinational investment. *Journal of Law, Economics and Organisation, 16*(2), 224–364.

Hong, E., & Sun, L. (2006). Dynamics of internationalization and outward investment: Chinese corporations' strategies. *The China Quarterly, 187*, 610–633.

ICRG. (2012). *International country risk guide methodology*. Accessed March 12, 2012, from https://www.prsgroup.com/wp-content/uploads/2012/11/icrgmethodology.pdf

Johanson, J., & Vahlne, J. E. (1977). The internationalization process of the firm: A model of knowledge development and increasing foreign market commitments. *Journal of International Business Studies, 29*(1), 45–66.

Johanson, J., & Vahlne, J. E. (1990). The mechanism of internationalization. *International Marketing Review, 7*(4), 11–24.

Johanson, J., & Wiedersheim-Paul, F. (1975). The internationalization of the firm—Four Swedish cases. *Journal of Management Studies, 12*(3), 305–322.

Kinoshita, Y., & Campos, N. F. (2006, February). *A re-examination of determinants of foreign direct investment in transition economies*. IMF.

Kolstad, I., & Wiig, A. (2009). Is transparency the key to reducing corruption in resource-rich countries? *World Development, 37*(3), 521–532.

Kravis, I. B., & Lipsey, R. E. (1982). The location of overseas production for exports by U.S. multinational firms. *Journal of International Economics, 12*, 201–223.

Luo, Y., & Tung, R. L. (2007). International expansion of emerging market enterprises: A springboard perspective. *Journal of International Business Studies, 38*(4), 481–498.

Milhaupt, C. J., & Zheng, W. (2014). Beyond ownership: State capitalism and the Chinese firm. *Georgetown Law Journal, 103*, p. 665.

MOFCOM. (2008). Statistical bulletin of China's outward foreign direct investment.

Niosi, J. (1999). *The internationalization of industrial R&D: From technology transfer to the learning organization*. Research Policy.

North, D. (1990). *Institutions, institutional change and economic performance*. Cambridge University Press.

Pearce, R. D. (1999). Decentralised R&D and strategic competitiveness: Globalised approaches to generation and use of technology in multinational enterprises (MNEs). *Research Policy, 28*(2–3), 157–178.

Peng, M., & Khoury, T. A. (2009). Unbundling the institution based view of international business strategy. In A. Rugman (Ed.), *The Oxford handbook of international business* (pp. 256–268, 2nd ed.). New York: Oxford University Press.

Peng, M. W., Wang, D. Y., & Jiang, Y. (2008). An institution-based view of international business strategy: A focus on emerging economies. *Journal of International Business Studies, 39*, 920–936.

Sawant, R. (2009). The economics of large-scale infrastructure FDI: The case of project finance. *Journal of International Business Studies, 41*, 1036–1055.

World Investment Report. (2008). *Transnational corporations and the infrastructure challenge*. UNCTAD.

Wright, M., Filatotchev, I., Hoskisson, R., & Peng, M. W. (2005). Strategy research in emerging economies: Challenging the conventional wisdom. *Journal of Management Studies, 42*, 1–33.

Zanfei, A. (2000). Transnational firms and the changing organisation of innovative activities. *Cambridge Journal of Economics, 24*(5), 515–542.

7

Internationalisation and Development: Case Analysis of Chinese IMNEs in Mozambique and South Africa

7.1 Introduction

Infrastructure MNEs, to some degree, are likely to challenge some established parameters of being multinationals. But under the previous explanation here, Chinese Infrastructure Multinationals can be explained in line with our understanding of the Eclectic Paradigm. Infrastructure investment is generally observed to follow the government-driven strategy of infrastructure for natural resources. China's infrastructure assistance is not a new story. It has been occurring since the first large construction investment project in railways which was completely based on government ODA. Corkin et al. (2008) conclude that 'it is often the most resources rich states that are in dire need of infrastructure development and support' demonstrating the apparent link between infrastructure assistance and resource rich countries. Indeed, 'the bilateral relationship between China and Africa has to be mutually beneficial' (Xi, 2013).[1] With such understanding, Chinese infrastructure MNEs' activities are inescapably determined by bilateral governmental relationships

[1] The statement of President Xi Jinping in his foreign debut tour after visiting three African countries: Tanzania, South Africa and the Republic of Congo.

Y. Tang, *The Operations of Chinese Infrastructure Multinationals in Africa*,
https://doi.org/10.1007/978-981-16-2562-6_7

and demands. As is generally known, lack of well-developed infrastructure is one of the disadvantages of developing countries. Because infrastructure is the core of development, increasing investment in this field is considered to be the priority for developing countries (WIR, 2008). The provision of good infrastructure decides the level of countries' competitiveness and attractiveness in obtaining inward FDI. Host governments in Africa are keen on the investment in infrastructure to reduce their lack of preparation for absorptive capability. However, from an infrastructure MNE's perspective, there will be risk in bargaining with host governments. With the previous experience of 1990's boom of infrastructure FDI from western countries, the theory of 'obsolescing bargain' by Vernon (1971) explains why MNEs attracted by host government incentives on infrastructure investment are nevertheless exposed to the risk when they engage in projects (Doh & Ramamurti, 2003). Home country (China) involvement refocuses the bargaining process and changes bargaining power of each party. How Chinese IMNEs deal with the particular projects reflects what kind of roles the governments play in such investments.

The emergence of Chinese IMNEs in Africa provides a clear profile of the strategic process of emerging IMNEs in expansion of infrastructure within developing countries. For one thing, those infrastructure firms that will become the MNEs were set up by government to support the domestic economic development and accumulated important ownership advantages within that period of operation (WIR, 2008). 'State investment' as it is often called in Chinese involvement in infrastructure investment in Africa, reflects the ownership structure influence from prior motivation. For another thing, to get access to the international markets, the leading enterprises that are equipped for competing overseas have parlayed CSAs into the FSAs in domestic industries.

China's domestic economic growth also provokes firms to create more profits and finance themselves by engaging in market competition. In other words, marketisation enables more firms to turn into quasi-private enterprises in some sectors. Simultaneously, market-pull opportunities arising in African infrastructure sectors propel Chinese IMNEs toward market expansions. The involvements of Chinese firms in the generation of infrastructure capacity in Africa are generally divided into traditional infrastructure sectors (physical infrastructure) and telecommunications. The ability of Chinese IMNEs to establish international operations may derive institutionally from the wider competitiveness of their home economy. The investments in two major sectors are motivated by two different targets. Besides meeting country-level goals, the expansion of Chinese infrastructure firms is accompanied by further production and market participation in some particular countries. The changes of financing approaches have been diversified from merely being politically driven to being motivated commercially. Meanwhile, relationships between these MNEs, funding sourcing and governmental behaviours are drawing out important aspects of influences on African host countries.

The purpose of this chapter is to provide a comprehensive understanding of Chinese MNEs in infrastructure related investment by detailed explanation of each step of investment and how they work them together as mediator of two development processes. In this Chapter, the two sectors will be explained individually within an overall picture (Fig. 7.1) of the expanding processes of MNEs, based on different perspectives. The investigation focuses on interview findings from two countries we analyse: South Africa and Mozambique. Under six sets of propositions[2] in two sections: country-level views on home- and host-government's influence on general investment and the focusing firms; firm-level views with the comparison of telecommunication and construction firms in both countries and ownership structure.

7.2 Government Bargaining Process

It is not coincidental that the most extensive infrastructure investments are seen in the more resource-abundant African countries, such as Angola, Mozambique and Zambia. Indeed, many critics have commented on China's expanding attitude towards Africa, in the global race for energy security and raw materials, to secure China's burgeoning economy.

---

[2] Propositions 3a and 3b refer back to Chap. 5, i.e. the infrastructure MNE and infrastructure projects.

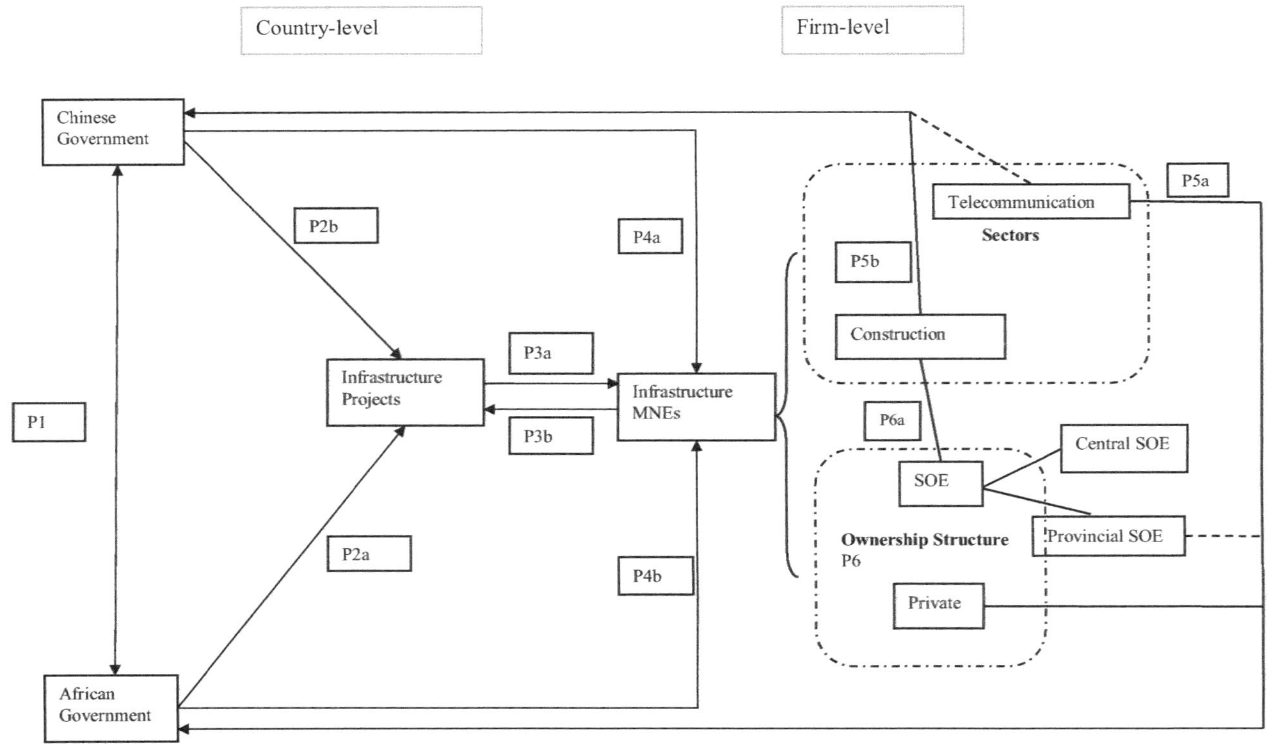

Fig. 7.1 The Structure of Chinese infrastructure Investments in Africa

Nevertheless, it is also worth noting that it is those most resource-rich countries that are in serious need of infrastructure development and support. Infrastructure projects undertaken by Chinese companies are often financed by loans from the Chinese government, on the condition that they are carried out by Chinese companies. This is in line with the access to substantial liquidity—driven by the Chinese government with the aim of promoting the internationalisation of Chinese companies in exchange for the exploitation opportunities of the natural resources; and the need of African governments to stimulate their economy. Under this bilateral development cooperation, the governments play a role in coordinating the investment and development assistance. This new diplomacy is based on MNE-government relationships concerning firm-level advantages, national-level competitiveness, political and social goals, provision of given and created factor endowments, market access in which the two actors have different objectives and interests with different bargaining resources (Grosse & Behrman, 1992; Stopford et al., 1991; Sally, 1994). More significantly, however, the investment entities—IMNEs are faced with bargaining with host governments that expose the risks of FDI incentives obsolescence. The obsolescing bargaining model (Vernon, 1971) suggests that the bargaining power shifts to host government over time as MNEs' assets are locked in by sunk capital in the sector-specific investment. In the infrastructure sector, the probability of such risks is expected to be more prone because of its capital intensity and immobility. The demands of the bilateral requirements get the home government into bargaining process to stabilise the investment policies.

Proposition 1 *Bilateral developmental demands determine the bargaining processes of infrastructure investment*

7.2.1 Bargaining Processes

When examining the bargaining process, it becomes inevitable that the relationship among the participants of infrastructure provision is of key importance. The traditional bargaining model which focuses on the step of bargaining between MNEs and host-country governments has been extended by Ramamurti (2001). He highlights two tiers of bargaining: that between home and host-country governments, as well as that between MNEs and host-country governments. Based on the experiences of developed-country MNEs and governments in terms of infrastructure investments, the model is observed that before the MNEs start to bargain with host countries for specific projects, home-country governments get involved in the bargaining as the first-tier to help the MNEs embed and increase the second-tier bargaining power in firm-level individual negotiation with host governments. The home country governments are activated in developing bilateral or multilateral investment agreements with host countries that remove entry barriers and set better macro environment for its home country MNEs. The Chinese IMNEs become the operators of home-host country government negotiation outcomes that alleviate the obsolescing risk in the tier-two MNE-host countries bargaining. The two-tier bargaining model emphasises the important role of the home-country government in MNEs' overseas investments that offers important insight into the growth of Chinese MNEs in infrastructure provision as the sector itself is part of development support. The first-tier bargaining is more in the line of a general negotiation on development cooperation. However, this experience may not comprehensively explain Chinese government's activities, which go beyond establishing investment agreements in African countries; they also include strategic considerations on the provision of low-interest loans to support infrastructure development in both the market and assistance perspectives. The ability of controlling 'resources' that the counterpart wants yields potential bargaining power (Eden et al., 2004). The infrastructure investment itself, therefore, is the bargaining chip of home countries. Thus, the desires of bilateral cooperation can be seen as a broadened role of home government, rather than the more narrow role set out in the original two-tier model.

7.2.2 Building Up the Relationship for Tier-one Bargaining

Tier-1 bargaining is determined by country-level and political variables (Ramamurti, 2001). The bilateral relationship is often built upon such things as the magnitude of bilateral trade between the countries;

interdependences of economies; official aid the host country is receiving; historical and diplomatic ties; further market opportunities. The bargaining process between two governments will impact on MNEs-host country bargaining (Ramamurti, 2001).

Home Governments Perspectives

The Chinese government has devoted considerable diplomatic attention to Africa since 2000 (Alden & Davies, 2006) with development assistance promised in various areas in order to develop bilaterally beneficial relationships with African countries and create a friendly environment for Chinese MNEs' investment in Africa (especially, bilateral investment agreement in 2006)[3] (Table 7.1). This is expected to increase investment opportunities and lowers political risks facing Chinese MNEs (Alden & Davies, 2006; Broadman, 2007; Kragelund, 2010). Home government mitigates uncertainty by tier-one bargaining. On the one hand, the beneficial agreements enhance bargaining power of Chinese MNEs in tier-two; on the other hand, it internalises the competitiveness of infrastructure programmes within domestic companies. This idea will pave the way for large-scale participation in infrastructure projects in Africa and boost China's domestic economy by absorbing overseas operation capacity in Chinese construction and related manufacturing sectors.

The early-age developmental donation and ODA projects provision strengthens the bargaining power of Chinese government in tier-one. Infrastructure investment, then, becomes a key component in bargaining power for the bilateral agreements between China and African countries. The exercise of home-country bargaining power depends on how the relationship with each African country is valued for the domestic economy in the bargaining process. Accordingly, the first type of countries, valued as accessibility for natural resources, are offered China's assistance packages linking infrastructure investment to long-term supply contracts with oil-rich countries, namely Angola, Sudan and, more recently,

[3] FOCAC has elaborated further on Sino–African co-operation theory and practice in each of the three of its summit meetings by adopting declarations and action plans.

Table 7.1 Events related to infrastructure in China-Africa Relationships

Date	Events and main actions
2000	The First Forum on China-Africa Cooperation (FOCAC)—Ministerial Conference Beijing, China; 80 ministers from China and 44 African countries
2003	The Second FOCAC—Ministerial Conference, Addis Ababa, Ethiopia. The first China-Africa Business Conference was held in parallel with the 2nd Ministerial Conference; over 500 Chinese and African entrepreneurs attended the conference; 21 cooperation agreements were signed with a total value of US$ 1 billion
2006	Beijing Summit and the Third FOCAC—Ministerial Conference, Beijing. 1. The Heads of State, government and delegation of China and 48 African countries attended the Summit of the Forum on China-Africa Cooperation. 2. The Chinese Government decided to support Chinese banks in setting up a China-Africa Development Fund (CADF) whose total amount will reach US$5 billion for encouragement and support to well-established and reputable Chinese companies in making investment in projects. Priority will be given to infrastructure, information technology, etc. in Africa which will contribute to local technological progress, employment opportunities and sustainable socio-economic development. 3. Telecommunication: strengthen cooperation in information infrastructure building 4. 14 agreements signed between 11 Chinese enterprises and African governments and firms, worth US$ 1.9 billion, cover operation in infrastructure facilities, communications, technology and equipment, energy and resources development, finance and insurance.
2009	The Fourth Ministerial Conference of the Forum on China-Africa Cooperation Sharm El Sheikh, Egypt 1. China increases the size of the China-Africa Development Fund to US$3 billion for supporting the expansion of investment from Chinese businesses to Africa. 2. In the next three years, the Chinese will provide US$10 billion of preferential loans which will be used mainly to support infrastructure and social development projects
2012	The Fifth Ministerial Conference of the Forum on China and Africa Cooperation, Beijing 1. Strengthen China's cooperation with the AU and sub-regional organisations in Africa: The Chinese government will continue to encourage Chinese enterprises and financial institutions to participate in transnational and trans-regional infrastructure construction in Africa and provide preferential loans to support infrastructure building in Africa 2. Step up training process for African personnel in the information field; support and encourage competitive Chinese information, communications companies to participate in the building of information infrastructure in Africa

Source: Forum of China and Africa Cooperation

Nigeria; and then involved with minerals producers like Gabon, Mauritania and South Africa at a later stage.[4] The second type of countries are those with weak systems of infrastructure. Chinese government evaluation on relationship in the bargaining process can be political (e.g. political/diplomatic support can be delivered in diplomatic relations, such as their support of Beijing's 'one China' policy) or economic (potential markets for IMNEs or other industries).

Chinese officials mention that China also invests substantially in countries that are not rich in natural resources. As a firm participant pointed out *'the biggest natural resource in Mozambique is coal mining which is occupied by Brazilian companies. This is not the key natural resources that China needs. The infrastructure provision between China and Mozambique is not built on natural resources exchange but market potentials'* (Private C). The allocation of investment arrangements by Chinese government reflects the bilateral development relevance in economic importance for China, either in terms of resource security of the booming economy or diplomatic influence.

Although the infrastructure sectors are still in state hands, the urgent demand for infrastructure in African countries causes the governments to marketise projects to private investment and find the most reliable and responsible providers. In the initial stage infrastructure provision involves the inter-government cooperation on infrastructure that helps the IMNEs to get trust of major customers that are local governments. '*The Chinese firm do not really have bargaining power problem with African countries…most SOEs have bargaining power that more likely depends on relationship with home country that is… simply local government give programme to China side and China give it to firms*' explained by Frontier Advisory[5](Aca.2). Most (60–80%) projects are farmed out to Chinese enterprises selected in China by ExIm Bank and the Ministry of Commerce for the beneficiary government (Alden & Alves, 2009). Also, in terms of tier-one process, the beneficial relationship on increasing bargaining power is non-distinguished between private firms and state-owned enterprises (SOEs) (Li et al., 2013)

[4] According to SAIIA (Alden and Alves, 2009), apart from the traditional interests of fuel resources, China has shown an increasing interest in the mining belt that stretches from south-east DRC and Zambia (copper and iron ore) to Mozambique and Tanzania; also Zimbabwe (platinum) and Angola (diamonds, copper and iron ore).

[5] Investment Advisory and Research Company, South Africa.

Host Governments' Perspectives

African governments hope to accomplish broader economic and political objectives though attraction of foreign infrastructure investment. It reflects rational economic attempts to secure the greatest benefits from China's side. The motivation of China's economy on sustainable supply of natural resources enables African countries to have power to negotiate for better and low-cost provision of infrastructure from China. Although the country-level discussion is all based on demand for resources, the differentiation of need for resources has an effect on the bargaining power and process of infrastructure investment. The more resources-endowed are countries for China's needs, the more emphasis on infrastructure investment and the more complicated the process. In the oil-endowed countries, bargaining relies on the direct bilateral relations of the governments and are building on Sino–African complementarities. This is a strictly business relationship: the trading of infrastructure for resources (Alden & Alves, 2009). The process includes the bilateral signature of an intergovernmental agreement that establishes the purpose, amount and interest rate of the loan, followed by a loan agreement with interest subsidised by the Chinese government. To enhance the bargaining power, the countries can sign the wider bilateral investment treaties to ensure the continuous provision of infrastructure donation and assistance. Simultaneously, BIT recipients' countries may secure the initial bargaining power in tier-2 MNEs-government negotiation.

The bargaining power will be weaker when the host country has few country-specific advantages that are desired by China. For those which are not considered as major resource suppliers to obtain more provision in infrastructure, the bilateral governmental involvement in tier-one process increase the bargaining power by offering in political support.

Multilateral Relationship

Because political instability is higher in some African countries, institutional control in the investment projects tend also to be weaker. The risk that a new government may renege on promises made to investors by earlier governments or add more conditions on existing investment is higher. Building up multilateral relationships with a third party—multilateral institutions, e.g. IMF and Work Bank, can secure the leverage and sustainability of terms on infrastructure projects. International financial institutions such as the World Bank are responding to the security for development projects in Africa by teaming up with the Export-Import Bank of China. Leverage of the international financial institutions requires the host- countries to guarantee the relevant FDI policies.

7.2.3 Tier-two Bargaining

The bargaining process is driven by micro variables that have direct effects on MNEs. As mentioned above, most of time, the infrastructure projects are negotiated and completed by signing intergovernmental agreements. Because the investment is building on assistance for development, any difficult renegotiations need Chinese government involvement. Chinese IMNEs fulfil the Chinese government's signed-up commitments to the host country government. However, there is the opportunity for host governments to renegotiate infrastructure contracts once MNEs have committed to an investment project and would face difficulties where MNEs have to redeploy fixed assets, i.e. the obsolescing situation. Non-tradability of infrastructure implies that the MNEs in infrastructure cannot use exporting as a bargaining chip with host governments through the life of those investments. Infrastructure MNEs therefore are more vulnerable to the obsolescing bargain risk than the average manufacturing investment (Ramamurti & Doh, 2004).

In the tier-two process, the infrastructure MNEs become the negotiating participant now competing by way of their advantages, such as the uniqueness of technology or the size and potentials of the host-country market for their particular product or services. At this stage, the sector differentiations of infrastructure become more important. Host country and MNEs may have similarity of goals, either complementary or overlapping, so that each party can achieve more through cooperation (Eden et al., 2004). In the case of Chinese IMNEs, the host governments are willing to create more infrastructure projects for improving their international competitiveness, while Chinese IMNEs then obtain more opportunities and markets in their African expansion. Thanks to the sharing of goals, Chinese IMNEs FSA-As are protected in the contracts with host countries. Therefore, the negotiation at tier-two between Chinese IMNEs and African countries can be more cooperative rather than conflictual over the traditional bargaining issues. Instead of being 'obsolescing' the ongoing tier-2 bargains may reflect potential shared diplomatic gains for both sides.

In terms of micro-level support for firms, ExIm Bank[6] and China Development Bank[7] have been the major financial institutions for Chinese MNEs' projects' loan and leverage. The Chinese government provides indirect or direct (depends on the ownership of the firms) subsidies on infrastructure investment in general. Marketisation of infrastructure investments differentiates Chinese infrastructure investors, with an increasing range of influences over the 'going abroad' policy that includes provincial and lower-level local governments that are actively promoting their companies' investments in Africa. The central government that promotes and pursues foreign economic policy has given them the capacity to secure dynamic bargaining power in obtaining projects from African countries. China's provincial-level divisions, in cases like the interviewed company, are increasingly significant economic actors on the global stage. Provincial firms are also among the top recipients of infrastructure contracts funded by Chinese commercial banks, which doubled their financial power placing them at the forefront of engagement with particular African countries. In the case of SOE, these as civil engineering projects investors also have an impact on the shape of China's resource policy as it is expanding the mining investment in some African countries. Additionally, the Chinese infrastructure firms mediate the bilateral development agreements on introducing corporate social responsibility (CSR) clauses into their work in Africa and are more accepting of host governments changing terms of each requirement within the programmes.

---

[6] A state-run financial institution founded in 1994, is directly under the State and has been the leading financial institution involved in providing concessional loans for projects in Africa.

[7] Authorised by the State and handle the $5 billion China–Africa Development Fund launched at the FOCAC meeting in November 2006.

7.3 Bilateral Governments' Roles in Infrastructure Investment

The intangible assets namely OAs suggested in the OLI framework, such as technologies and marketing resources, help MNEs to expand internationally and enables them to develop in certain locations by differentiating themselves from international rivals (Dunning & Lundan, 2008). Meanwhile, the institutional theory states that the institutional environments construct the processes of FDI. As such, beyond commercial and strategic optimisation, the determinants of investment are shaped by the broader political context surrounding the decision (Oliver, 1997; Peng et al., 2008). The governments play vital roles as political influencers. Both host and home governments are increasingly the guarantors of investment. In the case of China and African countries, the home government offered counter-guarantees to protect Chinese investors, particularly SOEs (Morck et al., 2008) in the whole process of biddings, purchasing and finance commitments and building up strong political relationships with African countries (see the explanation in 7.2), so as to reduce liability of foreignness and secure further investment opportunities, can be seen as the promoter in the participation in competing for projects. Dimaggio and Powell (1983) categorised this institutional pressure as *coercive isomorphism* where organisational decisions are guided by the orientation of the state, regulators, and political support of a given set of practices. The host governments are increasingly serving as sponsors for investment by undertaking a range of preferential policies or indirect incentives to investment opportunities, such as natural resources exploitation licenses, to encourage development of infrastructure industries. Infrastructure FDI in developing countries is doubly vulnerable, because, as discussed earlier, political and institutional conditions in developing countries are less stable and predictable than these in developed countries (Ramamurti & Doh, 2004).

7.3.1 Host Government

The external relationship that facilitates the acceptance of the companies within host countries may sustain the monopoly returns. Basic infrastructure is viewed as the effective catalyst to accelerate overall economic development, and is particularly urgent for African countries. Attracting private finance for public projects to alleviate the burden of limited financial resources, African governments increasingly open their infrastructure projects to private investors especially foreign firms.

Governments sponsor a project and are involved in it as lenders, insurers or underwriters of infrastructure project debt (Doh & Ramamurti, 2003). As a result of IMNEs involvement, host governments are less directly involved in the operation and management of infrastructure projects. Because of political sensitivities and capital markets constraints, African governments are not always able to provide infrastructure as sponsors to the market but apply for the assistance programmes from international agencies, such as World Bank, which open the bidding to IMNEs, '*the local government request ODA projects on governmental level or to international organisation*' (SOE C2); or it is put into the developmental agreements with particular home country. Mozambique, for instance, has prioritised the intensification of bilateral political relations with China[8] collaborating on infrastructure development by an 'infrastructure package' including roads, bridges, railways, airports and ports from Chinese partnerships. Particularly, Chinese state-owned investors will reach the countries and will be better located to import raw materials or components needed for production and to ship products out of Mozambique. On the other hand, host governments become consumers of the outputs of infrastructure investment (Doh & Ramamurti, 2003) by contracting the specific projects with the IMNEs after negotiating the long-term outcomes in the development agreement. Or they may be the initial customers for the output of the IMNEs but then distribute the outcomes and outputs of the infrastructure packages to the public. Governments may privatise the upstream businesses, but remain active in

[8] Mozambique is listed in the 77 countries that comprise the SINO as being the particular long term strategic importance.

direct service delivery, setting off a sensitive arrangement where governments feel political pressure to keep prices low (often below cost), while generators seek efficiency and economic return (Doh & Ramamurti, 2003). In the case of South Africa the government picks up first class construction firms for projects. Both foreign and local construction firms have to experience a long time to meet the standard of the assessment on taking projects. Large scale investment in infrastructure has been accomplished in South Africa because of a number of well-developed construction firms.[9] Compared to other African countries, South Africa has well-developed infrastructure services. The local construction firms also possess long-term development in African market and have to a certain degree become multinationals; special rules[10] that specify the percentage of foreign contributions in infrastructure investment include cost, ratio of local labour and foreign exchange; high technology standard. The host government then puts itself as the customer to find the proper contractor for business and opens tender and looks for pre-qualified companies.[11] Hence, host government being a customer in the infrastructure provision may stimulate the competition of investment projects but jeopardise the political advantages of Chinese construction firms.

There is not a clear line to distinguish the roles of host government in regulation and/or contracting of infrastructure provision. 'This tendency of governments to negotiate a contract—and then renege on the financial obligations associated with that agreement—is part of the broader evolution in governments' role as a regulator of the general terms of investment and the regulatory of the conditions under which markets may be opened to competition' (Doh & Ramamurti, 2003). Governments are the ultimate arbiters for regulating the conditions under which foreign investment takes place. This role can support or frustrate investment. Often, changes in regulatory policy in negotiating /contracting on specific

[9] Construction "Big Five" companies, accordingly, undertook most construction projects in SA.

[10] BBBEE ACT—Broad Based Black Economic Empowerment in terms of series requirements on broadening ownership and control; skills transfer and preferential procurement. Emphasis was also placed on 30% partnership of SA local ownerships with foreign firms in infrastructure projects.

[11] Pre-qualification. The companies in public construction field are ranked and assessed for qualification to bid for programme. The companies which do not have the qualification or certain ranks cannot join in bidding.

contracts with firms are driven by an interaction among political and economic factors. Often the challenges and complexity is associated with host governments' tendency to seek to stimulate the local economy by the request for the local firms' participation in both national and regional projects. For example, '*the construction projects biddings by MNEs may be accepted by joint venture*' said by a municipal official in South Africa (Gov.1).

Particularly, African governments are increasingly assuming broader roles as advertisers of new political and economic interests, not historically represented in bilateral development between home and host governments. Governments act as the conduit through which MNEs interact with different elements of civil society, and may also generate further outcomes of infrastructure industries. Such initiatives will have a growing influence of host government on development, especially those involved in the politically and socially sensitive infrastructure sectors.

Proposition 2a *The role of host country governments in attracting infrastructure investments derives from the ways they define overall developmental goals and how this determines the initial definition of appropriate infrastructure projects.*

7.3.2 Home Government

In the study, the home government can refer to different levels of authority—Chinese central government, provincial governments and other authorities. As the government ties are not equally beneficial to all Chinese firms, the bargaining power derives from the extent of involvement.

The variations in government involvement influence not only the objectives and the competences of MNEs to invest abroad but also the location choices and motivations (Wang et al., 2012). The purpose of Chinese government involvement in infrastructure provision in Africa has been most frequently imputed as developing economic and diplomatic ties with countries with natural resources (Alden & Davies, 2006; Broadman, 2007). However, the field work shows that the role played by Chinese government varies in terms of purposes towards different African countries. First, the Chinese government provides information assistance to firms which aim to bid for the projects. '*We are often informed of the local government invitation of public bidding from the Economic and Commercial Counsellor's office (department of Chinese Embassy)*' said by SOE C1; secondly, financial supports are commonly used approaches for helping Chinese investors to be more competitive in projects' bidding processes and/or indirectly exchanging the exploration opportunities for natural resources export; building up the strong relationships with African countries so as to secure the future investment opportunities and get Chinese firms trusted in host countries.

One of the most important sources that contribute to bargaining power of Chinese government is the use of a loan. First, Chinese government provides loans for infrastructure projects in the countries to guarantee resource-exploitation without political condition (e.g. interference in domestic affairs; the change of governance or political reforms). The bargaining power is more efficient with the countries where the Chinese government aims to access the oil/ mining / other resources. Second, the authorities (Ex-IM Bank, development Bank) provide assistance loans for poor infrastructure systems with conditions in order to get Chinese infrastructure involved. This Chinese government-funded projects (e.g. the improvement of Tanzania infrastructure) transferred its domestic experience and knowledge as FSA-As of Chinese firms in localising in the host country. The leading natural resources firms or infrastructure firms are central SOEs and often leaders in multiple purposes projects. Chinese government can easily organise consortia of the firms so as to deliver the broad array of local benefits and provide affordable manufacturing goods.

Proposition 2b *The purpose of infrastructure investment determines the role of infrastructure provision in the home government bargaining power*

7.4 Country Specific Advantages

7.4.1 Home country CSAs

The motivation of Chinese IMNEs and their overseas expansion is not simply a decision shaped by the firms' and their own inherent attributes and strategic objectives. In other words, the initial forces driving the expansion are the exogenous country-level factors. Chinese IMNEs are motivated to expand into Africa by the CSAs arising from the development of home country, i.e. CSA-D. Again, this derives from development and exploitation of Africa's natural resources, access to local markets, employment opportunities for Chinese labour and service contracts for Chinese companies on infrastructure projects funded by Chinese authorities.

Chinese government attaches a significant amount of funding to the firms taking part in designated infrastructure projects as these underpin future development and target beneficial returns. Many of these projects require large investment and have long pay-back terms that traditional donors are reluctant to provide or accept. These projects usually require the participation of Chinese firms, raising the opportunities and securing potential advantages for such firms to expand in the African continent. Home-country-specific advantages created over the economic growth process are defined as developmental CSAs (CSA-D). The more developed becomes the industrialisation of the home country, the greater its needs for resources to support the rapid growth. Negative CSA-D derive from the process of economic development, which causes a shortage of energy and resources. To sustain its long-term development, China's consumption of scarce resources needs to be sourced from overseas. Firms are expected to respond to government's development objectives by securing resource-seeking in order to address home needs of economic development.

Positive developmental CSAs are accumulated from the large amount of foreign exchange reserves and high level of domestic saving. The early age development boosting of Chinese trade surplus and 'open door' policy on attracting inward FDI over last two decades, generates a tremendous amount of foreign exchange reserves. Recent appreciation of the home country currency now encourages outward investment. These factors provide capital support to internationalisation of Chinese firms, since MNEs are strongly related to their internal capital market to finance FDI projects (Herzer, 2008; Baker et al., 2009), and enables sufficient financial support directly and indirectly to IMNEs. Chinese firms, including both IMNEs or more indirectly related to infrastructure industry, are motivated by the incentives and preferential treatment in undertaking infrastructure related projects in Africa. The strong Chinese firms have been experiencing rapid modernisation and home growth so as to be capable of internalising the positive developmental CSAs towards their international expansion. Chinese firms enjoy unique financial and political advantages in promoting Africa's growth through their own vast governmental financing with few or no strings attached. Firms bidding on large infrastructure projects are also successful, due to their abilities to leverage relatively 'cheap money' and preferential treatment of borrowing on international projects. The interventions of the state government in the banking system underpins the preferential policy for those firms which are eager to invest in designated infrastructure projects. The verification of enterprises and projects approval are needed, where large amounts of foreign exchange are involved. And those approval projects by government agencies can be leveraged with a low interest rate. Particularly, the CADF, which is under China Development Bank, provides a special approach for investing in Africa above the general banking system's promotion of FDI. Infrastructure related investment is one of the focus industries that encouraged by the fund The Fig. 7.2 draws the general processes of Chinese firms obtaining support from the banking system and the institutions for investing in Africa.

Importantly, as part of economic reform, the Chinese government has maintained political control on large-scale companies and formulated a series of policies on outward FDI worldwide (Table 7.2). They have created a supportive institutional environment that enables an allocation of reserves of foreign exchange to meet national needs. The ability to reward and discipline firms aiming to get the preferential access to the capital is described as home country institutional CSAs (CSA-Is). Infrastructure related investment is inevitably affiliated to government sectors, particularly China's long-term involvement in African infrastructure

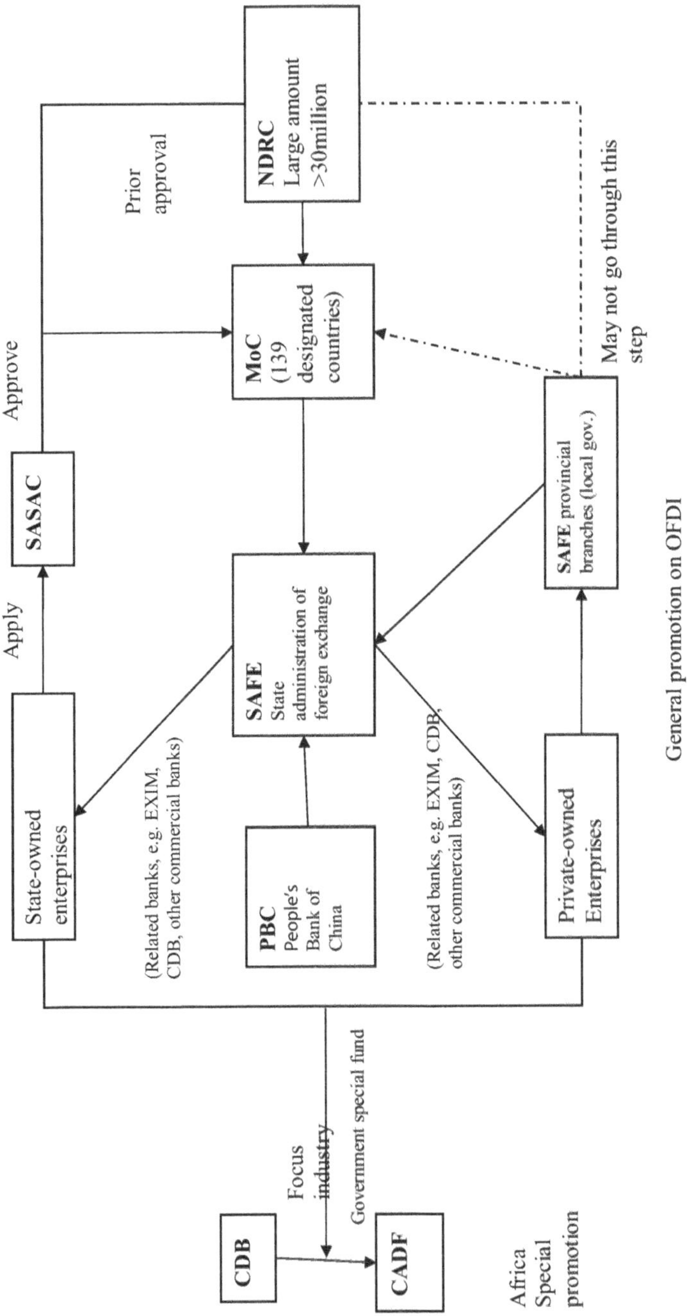

Fig. 7.2 China's banking system for investment encouragement in Africa

Table 7.2 Key institutions in China outward investment promotion system

Ministry of Commerce (MoC)
MoC authorise administrations on investment and guarantee and supervision system and leveraging system for approval of investment, including reasonable diversification of investments, safety, general investment environment in target country, political and economic relationship with China and international treaties.
The Export-Import Bank of China (EXIM Bank)
The China EXIM Bank is one of the policy banks established mechanisms to support investment with low interest credits reserved for exports, under the direct control of the State government. The bank officially implements government policies in industry, foreign trade, diplomacy and economy. It supports Chinese companies with a comparative advantage in order to engage with foreign partners in offshore construction contracts and overseas investment projects. Within the scope of the banks activities are international inter-bank loans, the bank engages in loaning to foreign governments and loans/mixed credits to foreign countries in general for securing the investment from China, to some degree. The bank's capital will be earmarked for key investment projects that are encouraged by the government.
China Development Bank (CDB)
China Development Bank provides medium- to long-term financing facilitates that assist China's cross-border investment and global business cooperation. Aligns with business focus with national economic strategy and allocates resources in China's economic and social development. CDB is committed to market-based practices.
The National Development and Reform Commission (NDRC)
NDRC was established it continued to take a central role in the economic development and central controlling and supervising outward investment. It outlines the criteria of examining and approving of investment and running enterprises abroad, along with MoC.
State Administration of Foreign Exchange (SAFE)
SAFE is an administrative agency undertake operations and management of foreign exchange reserves, gold reserves, and other foreign exchange assets of the state; managing state capital other international issues as assigned by the state government and the People's Bank of China.
The State-owned Asset Supervision and Administration Commission (SASAC)
The State Asset Supervision and Administration Commission (SASAC) was created in 2003 in order to control and supervise China's large SOEs. It safeguards the central government's right of ownership in non-financial enterprises. The SASAC's central task is to carry out the government role as investor and owner of state assets. The SASAC establishes procedures to approve of major enterprise operations and decisions. The most important sectors are petroleum and refining, metallurgy, electricity, military industry, telecommunication.

Note: Explanation of the functions of each institution are adapting and summarising from the official websites. Parts of them are adapting from the CASCC projects development. Government relates to firms' behaviour as outsiders through specific agent arrangements, such as the third-party held business-government committees and government agents in a common discourse (Child & Tsai, 2005). FOCAC is one of the government agents that provide relational frameworks that connect Chinese firms. The policies and information are particularly effective in conveying government expectations about corporate decisions and practices (Gould & Ruffin, 1993), which enable China to gain thrust with further implementation of its economic development.

The institutional CSAs also help Chinese firms to be more competent in tolerating risks because of their experience of insecure property rights protection, misty business-government relationship that gave more experience with chronically weak institutions in the process of China's development (Morck et al., 2008). These firms experience bribing and irregular leverage as part of their usual business operation, and as such they are aware of getting business done under corruption, to name but one. Ability to deal with institutional CSAs of home country enables the firms to deal with host-country institutions. Consequently, they are capable in dealing with burdensome regulations and opaque political constraints and reducing the cost and uncertainties.

Proposition 4a *The primary motivations in expanding Chinese infrastructure MNEs in African market are due to exogenous sources*[12] *of home country (1) developmental CSAs (2) institutional CSAs*

7.4.2 Host Country Specific Advantages

Dunning (2006) stated that the importance of the host-country environment, such as size and growth of domestic market, resource endowments and institutional environment, influence location specific decision of companies responding to different motivations. Accordingly, besides the

[12] The primary motivation in expanding Chinese infrastructure MNEs investment in Africa reflect home country factors exogenous to the firms; the factors related to Chinese development constraints (CSA-D) and the institutions that support FDI to alleviate the constrains.

endowment of resources, African countries with promising market size also influence China's global economic growth. Specifically to African countries, the conventional variables of the host-country advantages, to some degree, are not all theoretically applicable to Chinese IMNEs' in infrastructure.

The availability of natural resources stimulates the FDI from China as well as the non-resource exploration investment. The bad situations of macro-infrastructure of host countries attract large investment of Chinese firms in construction, and the telecommunication industry. Although weak institutions are considered as a limitation on access to capital and knowledge, some empirical studies have found the positive relations of Chinese firms in political risky countries (Buckley et al., 2007; Morck et al., 2008; Kolstad & Wiig, 2012). Here, the propositions address the host-country CSAs as the dynamics of CSAs. The IMNEs arrange the investment by considering the potential abilities of the countries, including potential sub-industries, and scope for further upgrading of industry. For example, the consumer markets of telecommunication in Africa can be based on the early age investment on telecommunication infrastructure investment.

Some of the African governments had little experience in long-term vision over possibility of foreign investment. These host governments do not have proper plans for using their rich resources for more sustainable investment in other fields. Weak infrastructure planning also places the host countries as those with 'bad' CSAs. Chinese infrastructure firms, however, can turn these host CSAs into good aspects following the early 1990 open door policy and associated domestic reforms. The Chinese Government has managed to maximise the benefits from the early FDI and from its moving up the ladder of the global industrial chain. Its experience could be inspiring for many African countries today. The similarity of institutions and government planning strategies enable Chinese firms which have experience to reduce the liabilities of foreignness. Chinese firms reduce the cost to deal with the distance of government regulations. They face lower liability of foreignness in weak institutions (He and lyles, 2008; Child & Rodrigues, 2005; Wang et al., 2012). Chinese firms are more experienced with such institutional features: bureaucratic, corruption, etc. in their home market and as a result are likely to be far more capable of dealing with burdensome regulations and surviving in another such environment (Perkins, 2005; Khanna & Palepu, 2010; Morck et al., 2008)

Since emerging market governments build ties with governments of other developing countries by providing aid and infrastructure, this ensures firms in which state-ownership is higher can take advantage of such government-government relationships and reduce uncertainty and contract failure (Duanmu, 2012)

Country Risk

The relationship defining the infrastructure investment is seen as the contract and how each party can use the information to improve their benefit (Estache, 2004). The infrastructure investment is strongly constrained by local institutions and economic environment. This involves the institutions arrangements that affect multinationals' performance in a host country. The common feature of weak institutions: the local law are not well developed, nor enforce the property rights; the governments are less accountable to their citizens; the regulatory agencies are not competent and are dependent on politics (North, 1990, 1996); the cross-country conflicts cause social instability, particularly in Africa continent. Chinese IMNEs experienced similar issues but have developed processes that can affect their reaction to the host country institutions.

Corruption

The familiarity of dealing with the institutions of a host country firstly requires understanding the requirements of the agents, i.e. their criterion of checking whether the prequalification of project bidders on contracts and enforcement of investment outcomes are consistent with contractual expectation. In African markets, the large programmes need multiple agents (various companies and regulators from different sectors) which bring more opportunities for getting multiplied corruptions. Chinese SOEs have experienced a long period time of dealing with the regulation system of monopolies in construction sectors under less transparent system. Secondly, natural monopolies in infrastructure sectors are strongly related to the degree of centralisation and financing of public services and the associated incentives for investment. African infrastructure sectors are seen with potentials by foreign investors because these increasingly needed projects tend to be bigger than in other sectors and services are granted with a monopoly delivery and control over the information by governments in most countries. The firms are able to attain massive benefits by contracting the projects. The process of infrastructure investment, especially in transport projects,[13] was illustrated to often allow the bidders to announce low cost to increase the chances of getting the projects and then to renegotiate. The Chinese SOEs are more able to lower their forecast expectation at the bidding process as the result of initial government supportive policy and funds, as well as the long period accumulation of group financial power. Thirdly, bribery is more likely to happen in the countries with greater concentration and constraints on utility capacity and state ownership. Inevitably speaking, most Chinese SOEs and large firms were born in similar circumstance at the early development stage as most African countries. Taking malign advantage of corrupt opportunities through FSA-R capabilities could, in theory either be perpetrated as tacitly understood firm level practice or independently by the FSR-R informed individuals (probably against the wider interests of their parent company and the institutional being subverted). These scenarios of corruption are seen as an illicit subset of FSA-R practices and the normal scope of FSA-R are viewed as potentially operationalising the firm/institution interface to the potential benefit of both. The firms benefit with dealing in competition with other bribe payers when they are profitable and expect greater returns from the project's investment. In contrast with other foreign investors from developed countries, corruption is not as strongly taken as the big obstacle of doing business in Africa by Chinese IMNEs. However, an exceptional case is the South Africa requirement of local participation in projects[14] for explaining in certain countries corruption may protect the short- and medium- term growth since they gratify the preferences of local infrastructure business (Rock & Bonnett, 2004).

[13] Flyvbjerg et al. (2002, 2003) undertook extensive review of transport projects to measure the abuse by monopoly.

[14] Explain in case of country comparison.

Democratic and Regulatory Environment

The logic of international production discussed above suggests the following implications that set the stage for our analysis of the effects of democratic institutions on FDI inflows. First, the MNE's ownership-specific and internalisation advantages often result from, and are further enhanced by, their oligopolistic or monopolistic market structures. Host government regulatory policies can limit the use of these advantages, particularly through the application of antitrust and other competition-oriented legislation. Second, endowed with the ownership-specific and internalisation advantages, the MNE is more competitive than local firms in the host country. The host government adopts industrial policy that either protects indigenous businesses from the MNE or favours the MNE. Third, expecting FDI to bring about managerial skills and production technology beneficial to economic growth, the host government may offer foreign investors financial and fiscal incentives. Such incentives not only affect the choice of FDI location, but also strengthen the competitiveness of foreign investors. Finally, the MNE must rely on the host government investment profiles for protection of its property rights in proprietary assets, without which its ownership-specific advantages would disappear.

The location-specific advantages existing in the host country facilitate the MNE's exploitation of its ownership specific and internalisation advantages. Regulatory risk continues to be high in infrastructure investments (Doh & Ramamurti, 2003). Lack of regulatory institutions are considered as weak LAs of a host country, where the conditions hinder the MNE from exploiting its ownership-specific and internalisation advantages. Firms that enjoy monopolistic or oligopolistic positions may lose competitiveness if the host countries exercise strong antitrust regulation. However, the feature of sole contractor for specific projects in infrastructure investment would not stand up for strong property right protection.

Democratic Requirement

Democratic institutions in host countries attenuate many MNEs' ability to exploit and enhance their monopolistic or oligopolistic positions. Firms invest abroad to take advantage of their ownership-specific and internalisation advantages, advantages that often result from oligopolistic or monopolistic market structures. Such Chinese IMNEs constitute large amounts of FDI that possess enormous market power. In the host countries, such MNEs seek to create and strengthen their oligopolistic or monopolistic positions that result in higher returns. The associated imperfect market structures, however, lead to less optimal allocation of resources in the host economy than would perfect competition. While MNEs consider the pursuit of monopolistic or oligopolistic positions a legitimate corporate strategy for greater returns, their desire to create, maintain and increase their monopoly or oligopoly positions can be perceived as dangerous and unwelcome by host countries.

Proposition 4b *Host countries CSAs impact on Chinese IMNEs location choice and strategies in African markets*

7.4.3 Countries Comparison—Political Implication

The African continent is now in a winning position of getting attention of international investors on winder access to funds for urgently needed investments in infrastructure and securing productive use of natural resources. As one of the remarkable donors, China's focus of investment shifts from traditional ODA managed by government institutions to commercial ties driven by both private companies and state-owned enterprises. The broad picture of African markets varies among countries in a detailed evaluation due to the resource components and degree of development. For China's long-term development, the countries can be distinguished as those rich in needed resources such as oil, copper ore etc. such as Angola, Congo, Zambia and Sudan. Then those countries with less relevant resources, i.e. abundant in resources that are less required by China, such as South Africa, Mozambique and Kenya and so on. For further internationalisation of domestic industries, the countries can be categorised by degree of development in certain industries. To deepen analysis of infrastructure sectors, the investigation has to look into two countries which have distinctive level of developments in infrastructure creations. The interviews are based on the official authorities on China's investment in infrastructure provision, including China's Counsellor of Economics and Business (Republic of South Africa), the Department of International Relations and Cooperation, investment advisory centre (based in South Africa).

Most Chinese SOEs investing in Africa operate under beneficial policy, derived from national loan and home authorities' underwriting. What concerns China's impact on companies' orientations of leveraging and localisation on infrastructure investment is whether the increasing FDI in infrastructure sectors of the countries are able to benefit the firms in a sustainable manner. The interviews in this part were taken under the consideration of the so-called 'Angola Mode'[15] but looking into the differentiations of investments derived from capacities of infrastructure creation market and further expansion opportunities.

South Africa

Chinese Investment in South Africa

The Republic of South Africa has been extensively involving itself in infrastructure investment with foreign firms.[16] With its high level of general marketisation and developed banking system, Chinese companies can enter more commercially and leverage their FSA-A to win infrastructure projects from an international market.

Differently from China's infrastructure involvement in other African countries, its construction companies seldom invest in South Africa; where large scale investment in infrastructure has been accomplished by a number of well-developed local construction firms.[17] Compared to other African countries, South Africa has mature infrastructure services. Its local construction firms also possess long-term developments into other African markets and have a certain degree of being multinationals.

[15] The barter mode between China and some certain African countries in bilateral development cooperation—infrastructure support for Resources.

[16] Such as the largest PPP—"Gautrain" project in 2000 established by provincial government.

[17] Big 5 companies, accordingly, undertook most construction projects in SA.

Thus South African firms and industry may see Chinese MNEs entering their market as competition. The regulations for investment in this sector sets special rules[18] which require the percentage of foreign contributions in infrastructure investment include cost, ratio of local labour and foreign exchange, as well as an high standard of technology application. The participation of Chinese competitors ensures that relevant development projects get implemented in the more effective way and sharpens the competition of SA companies in the sectors.

Traditional Chinese construction SOEs find it difficult to make full use of FSA-As due to the restriction of investment which constrains them in value chain operations within domestic markets. To be involved with local construction firms increases the cost of the whole process of investment, such as adapting the subsidiaries to meet the local requirements, joining in the companies' qualification assessment processes, etc. South African authorities have more experience in managing foreign infrastructure investment through a market regime.[19] Maketisation of infrastructure services in South Africa diversifies the selection in competition. Chinese companies hardly ever undertake projects without local cooperation.

South African construction department has comparatively comprehensive regulations in bidding and awarding projects in order to give infant industry protection to a local construction industry. '*Government picks up first class construction firms for projects. Both foreign and local construction firms have to experience a long time to meet the standard of the assessment on projects taking*', '*Most large scale projects are created by provincial and national government*', '*Private funding for public projects*' explained by Gov.3. Private-public partnership is more likely to be applied to South African construction projects. The government opens a tender and looks

[18] BBBEE ACT—Broad Based Black Economic Empowerment in terms of series requirements on broadening ownership and control; skills transfer and preferential procurement. Emphasis was also placed on 30% partnership of SA local ownerships with foreign firms in infrastructure projects.

[19] Business/projects information are normally reported by local government directly; The local government request ODA projects on governmental level or to international organisation.

for pre-qualified companies.[20] The bidding may be accepted by a joint venture. Subcontracting can frequently apply in large programmes and is encouraged by government, especially to local subcontractors. The main project contractor has to guarantee the quality by getting involved in managerial procedures of the whole project.

Under this situation, local firms normally have the priority on bidding for the programmes. According to DIRCO, Chinese SOEs in South Africa are normally provincially owned firms and seldom become localised as the local Act required. '*Once Chinese company started operations in Country B, they brought their labour from country A where they also had projects*', says Director (Gov.1), '*the labour movement within the company occurs in the continent*' The basic infrastructure-related company has no obvious technology transferring. Chinese control most ownership in the companies. The increasing cost of liability of foreignness weakens the advantages of Chinese construction SOEs.

However, South Africa retains high potentials for Chinese MNEs in infrastructure sectors. '*Few Chinese construction firms started enter South African market in last three years*' according the record from Academic participant (Aca.1). With a decade of internationalisation and domestic privatisation, some of those SOEs accumulate overseas experience and are more internationalised. The enhanced FSA-As and FSA-Rs enable them to meet different regulations of investment. '*Owing to constraints of funding, South Africa has lack of ability for maintaining existing infrastructure service*'. '*The Chinese infrastructure related company bring new areas*'; '*Long time working*', '*Low wage rate*', '*Vast markets for construction in roads/rails*' are generally mentioned[21] by both governmental participants (Gov.1; Gov.3) and academic participant (Aca.1).

Differently, the two telecommunication firms have been successfully bidding for South African telecommunication programmes. Highly internationalisation experiences, marketing research and long-term relationship with local operators satisfies the willingness of South African government in FDI.

[20] Pre-qualification. The companies in public construction field are ranked and assessed for qualification to bid for programme. The companies which do not have the qualification or certain ranks cannot join in bidding.

[21] These are the notes that are taken and repeated from different interviewees.

Mozambique

State-sponsored investments in the infrastructure sector are, as the previous chapter discussed, China's recent tendency to offer an 'infrastructure package' in order to win the attention of governments economically and diplomatically. One of the economic clusters that has been most affected by Chinese direct investment is the recent domination of Chinese multinationals in many construction sectors. Many of these projects are making use of preferential loans from China. Notably, a significant number of the infrastructure involvements in Mozambique are manifestly of a private nature, encompassing a wide range of business motivations across a wider range of sectors. Such private firms are, as compared with SOEs, motivated initially in manufacturing expansion because of limited competition from local firms in techniques and overall productivity, low-cost inputs and profitable outputs. These Chinese private firms were originally keen on manufacturing investment because of the competitive skills and manufacturing techniques, compared to the regional competitors, that drive profitability. But concerning the situation of Mozambique, the firms inevitably face high operational and transaction costs in every investment due to lack of existing infrastructure. Thanks to the lack of initial infrastructure, the whole series of self-sufficient investments of private firms can spread their outcomes to Mozambique infrastructure.

Despite of the significant participation of private Chinese firms involving in construction, the SOE investors are the major participants in Mozambique. Mozambique has prioritised the intensification of bilateral political relations with China[22] collaborating on infrastructure development of roads, bridges, railways, airports and ports where Chinese partnerships is the crucial contribution to reach the full potential of the nation. Mozambique is abundant in coal mines. Although China's tendency to source from Mozambique remains high due to rising levels of national demand, over past decades, China has not been a big participant in coal exploration.[23] Mozambique is on course for more projects in min-

[22] Mozambique is listed in the 77 countries that comprise the SINO as being the particular long term strategic importance.

[23] Mozambique Tate area that are abundant of coal mine are occupied by Brazilian Bale Group. Benga power by Australian company Riverside mining.

ing exploration that are expected to engage Chinese companies in the mission to overcome infrastructural challenges. Mozambique stands out in the strategic interest in natural resources.

As considering Mozambique, the degree of industrial development, the sea accessibility and competitive low wages may potentially attract Chinese firms' localisation. Simultaneously, multinationals must also be content with an investment environment which is high risk. The companies that are investing still remain 'local into arrangements with local government elites that inhibit profit-making' (Alden, 2005). The local economies do not offer the most inviting absorptive and institutional contexts. The potential returns through investing in Mozambique come with considerable risks, so Chinese investors in particular sectors are underwriting such risk by the large scale and early inter-governmental arrangements.

Concerning the employment of local labour, a great extent of local labour are employed in Chinese–sponsored investments. According to claims of three interviewees, the companies operating in Mozambique suggest a general tendency and business-sense of utilising cheaper labour for more efficient production.

7.5 IMNEs Firm-Level Performance in Africa

7.5.1 Sector Differences Drive Different Performances

Sectors Comparison—Chinese Infrastructure Investment in ICT and Physical Construction

Case 1—Two Giant ICT Multinationals

The ICT sectors have important common characteristics of an infrastructure industry but also key differences. Telecommunication is taken into account as a unique case within the whole infrastructure sector for three reasons (Ramamurti & Doh, 2004): the fierce competition and the possibility to be a natural monopoly owing to its high technology basis enabling more private and local rivals to work in any long-distance and value-added services to local services; for African countries themselves, telecommunications is not dominated by local SOEs or agencies as key buyers or suppliers, most governments issue the projects to the competitive markets; and telecommunication is important for development but less essential than other construction sectors for most African countries, which is then less sensitive to political purposes. Compared to other sectors in Africa, telecommunication takes up a shorter period and is less important in role of bilateral development ODA because the telecommunication markets have been dominated by western investors at the early stage. Much greater levels of private participation in infrastructure investment in African countries have been directed towards telecommunication because of the first and early experience of privatisation at home country

This case study looks into the ICT infrastructure investment in Africa as a whole. Two giant telecommunication providers—HUAWEI and ZTE-which have been noticeably successful expanding over recent decade in African market as well as global players, are both well-known telecommunication groups in their home market. Following Ericsson, they are the other two biggest suppliers for phone systems and network infrastructure in Africa. Huawei (2010) and ZTE (2009)[24] have also predominated through telecommunication equipment sales and contracts in US$ 3.5 billion and US$ 1 billion from Africa, respectively (eLearning Africa, 2011). This case provides a dynamic analysis of their motivation and strategic development, through investigating what creates the ownership advantages (OA) of the ICT infrastructure firms for being profitable investors in South Africa and the regions. Also, based on the interview questions, the cases represents their strategic performances and localisation process within the local economy.

Firm Specific Advantages

To analyse technology based multinationals in Africa, it is necessary to understand the evolution of China's innovation system that contributes to asset firm specific advantages (FSA-A). MNEs' international

[24] The data for ZTE in 2010 is not available.

capabilities are to access and utilise CSAs. China's national policy on innovation is aiming at pursuing long-term science and technology programmes. A series of encouraging High-Tech programmes, '863'/'873' programmes[25] for improving the innovative ability of R&D in high-tech and 'Torch' Programme[26] through project financing, to name but two, enhanced the overall competitive advantage of technology-based firms and therefore underpin their strategic formulation. Huawei and ZTE, as introduced above, were born at this stage.[27]

China's telecom market therefore has developed enormously over last two decades. A massive investment in telecom infrastructure derived from a policy task 'quickly building a modern infrastructure by leapfrogging over outmoded technologies with foreign technology, it also protecting and nurturing domestic manufactures'[28] The cases in this study are of the most representative national champions in this national innovation task. Both firms are competing in the domestic market but also have ambitious plans for globalisation.

Huawei and ZTE exploit late arrival on the market by tapping into technologies globally, rather than having to replicate the entire previous technological trajectory. This internationalising process, as 'catch-up strategies latecomers', is introduced by Mathews (2002, 2006).

Motivations

Facing very severe competition in domestic markets, the companies started to prioritise investing in Africa to keep their competitiveness, as the target countries were normally at the same level of development as

[25] The "863"Programme named as "National High Technology R&D Programme", which was launched in 1986, mainly focused on financial support of RMB 11 billion in areas of science and technology to narrow the gap between China and developed countries, including directly increasing funding provision for Chinese corporation for their R&D projects, academic research institutes. Followed by "873" Programme in 1987 was continuous implementation.

[26] "Torch" Programme was launched in 1988 to support high technology industry in creation or adaption of new products and services in the market quickly.

[27] Zhongxing Telecom (ZTE) and Huawei Technologies were both founded headquarter in Shenzhen, Guangdong Province, in 1985 and 1988, respectively.

[28] Ministry of information industry, source from *technology-based competition and Chinese multinationals* (Larçon & Barré, 2009).

China or lower, which is similar to western multinationals' expansion in Africa. Owing to the historically strong price advantage, which is normally cheaper by 20–30% than other rivals, the two firms rapidly occupied the African markets. *'Price is a more concern in small and least developed markets'* explained by (Private T1). Cheap price winning recognition in customer markets and for local industry is the first step conducted by both firms. The interviewee believes that *'there is a large market for Chinese telecommunication over a few years'* (Private T1).

Another influential element is the growth of the global market during the period: 'Push' effect of home country flags enterprises to go abroad, creates firms' willingness of internationalisation; with the economic growth in Africa, which need assistance of modern infrastructure, then providing such massive business opportunities.

Infrastructure Provision: Low Cost Technology to Fill in the Gap of Local Telecommunication

Provision of Low Cost Technology

'Our products have a significant advantage in pricing' (Private T1, Private T2), *'We sell our equipment and phones at low price to meet the needs of low income customer'* (Private T2), the infrastructure gradually become the small piece of the major business—*'it is a platform'* (Private T1). The two Chinese investors claimed that the main purpose of entry is commercially driven, starting at infrastructure investment and equipment donation to make infrastructure investment the platform for localisation. Small pieces of infrastructure create the recognition in African market and telecom industry by putting resources in at low cost. The previous discussion of location advantages LA, suggested MNEs in infrastructure investment may look for negative factors in host-country location advantages—the large gap of infrastructure—it is a strategy but not motivated by this.[29]

[29] See Model 9 and Model 10 in Chap. 6

Providing low-price services ensure the access to infrastructure projects (IPs).[30] Responding to the local laws and telecom construction qualification, Chinese infrastructure investment is based on their technology, then using the local materials and providing equipment and transferring technology along with the qualified local ICT construction firms and operators. BOT is the most popular method, setting up and commissioning the telecom switch. To win the participation in projects, low-price strategy attracts the qualified local operators.[31]

Infrastructure provision built up a reputation and pre-occupied the emerging market share. Huawei and ZTE both state that they have very long-term cooperation relationships with local operators and other subcontractors and the brands are already well-known in the telecommunication industry in Africa. Products and services in telecom industry require high-level compatibility and operational familiarity. So the early-age infrastructure contribution creates further market opportunities for equipment and services entering the consumption market and enables customers to be drawn into their product chain.

Source of Donation

In the telecommunication sector, '*donation is benefit as the voucher to the clients*' and also '*it is the part of CSR*' (Private T2). As the result of their financial background, Chinese companies provide loans and interest-free credit to enable their clients to buy their equipment.

[30] Huawei and its local partners ensured the telecommunication service for 0.4 billion subscribers and accomplished 32 3G network within 21 African countries. Because of lowering the cost by 40%, more than 0.25 billion population in rural area can access telecom service. For government projects, Huawei has built 20 national communication lines within African countries and 20 government e-government networks improving the ability of informatics and efficiency. ZTE's operation in Africa is comparatively smaller than Huawei.

[31] Participant mentioned the company usually give the equipment for free to the local operators.

Locally-Specific Production

A general pattern of Chinese MNEs investing in Africa is as a dynamic process and can be divided into stages. Initially, executing the infrastructure contracts is the valuable way to get initial access to an African market. Accordingly, the two main telecommunication investors are not strongly connected with government regulation. The companies set up whole-owned registered subsidiary and can then switch major business for further cooperation with local telecom operators, such as MTN, ETISALAT, VODACOM, ZAIN, France Telecom, etc. The major business of Huawei changes from infrastructure creation to customer supply market in telecommunication services. Chinese telecommunication companies operate dynamically differentiated networks to respond to strategic developments. An interviewee mentioned the second stage of telecommunication investment of the company has incredible changes:

> *Quality improvement…South African and the regional markets become mature under the impact of global economy…to compete with Ericsson, quality turns to be more important; Innovation within the group…the technology of Chinese firms at the early stage from copy culture through to the requirements of local partners which lead to copy and new invention…* (Private T1)

Regarding to the adaptation solution the initial product may be lagging for local needs and tastes. The products are made in China and adapted well there, but the applications of the core technology then need to be localised. *'The problems come from two sides: far lower level of compatible infrastructure, underdeveloped education; Local staff have to work in Chinese thoughts'* (Private T1). The technology adjustment happened in HQ once the requirements accounted for a major adjustment. If it is a smaller number of limited local adjustment issues, it may be solved locally. The subsidiary's new function is to redesign the product for local customers in an understanding version. In Huawei, the bottlenecks of technology are normally handed over to Huawei R&D in Europe/US. Before the bidding, local marketing research provides tailor-made product and services. The technical problems will be upgraded through the hierarchy.

In ZTE, at early stage of the market, cheap and single functional products (routers and mobile phones) quickly took the market share responding to the local consumption level. As the brand become known after a few years, the R&D team innovated higher-end products according to the known tastes and market demand (e.g. smart phones) with high price and quality level.

Leverage and Bidding

'Massive approaches of leveraging include World Bank loans for special programmes, other loans provided by Chinese commercial banks/policy banks/ other overseas banks. The parent company may provide financial support and loan from home country or international financial markets' (Private T1). Subsidiaries can also get loans from international financial markets/world bank/local banks based on their already contracted projects. Bidding for projects from local operators is the main channel. They also bid for the public projects which are launched through relevant industrial media as well as applying to agents of certain projects. They are more likely to be interested in long-term returns, so that the project's immediate returns are only required and designed to meet a modest quarterly target. Parts of the winning contract rely on overpromising to the partners or customers at extremely cheap price at the beginning for building up business relationship.

Role of Subsidiary: Structure of Company

Accordingly, both firms are still highly centralised because the initial role of most subsidiaries and their laboratories is the transfer of established technology into a new environment. The parent company dispersed subsidiaries depending on the factors that related to their market orientation and the availability of production processes (Manolopoulos et al., 2009). The role of the subsidiaries are motivated by demand-side factors, such as the importance of the markets, a responsiveness of local customers and market potentials, allocated within MNEs' overall operation and supported by basic technologies from the group's established knowledge capacity (Papanastassiou & Pearce, 1997). The major functions of subsidiaries are adapting the established technology and applying it to the local market.

The structural embedding activities in certain countries secure a sustainable contribution to their investments and operate in terms of a hierarchical global strategy. The diagram below is the comparison of two hierarchies between investigated companies (Fig. 7.3). Parent company is dominant in the group and created the product range. Innovation decentralisation is not yet coming into the story. Market-seeking is mainly applied to subsidiaries scope, which has a wide range of functions in host countries. The subunits do not possess basic creative flexibility but do have a certain degree of management autonomy. The marketing researches are only based on the area where they are located. Notably, below the parent HQ, regional HQ appears in-between parent and subsidiaries for relatively higher-level management functions.

The Huawei subsidiary in South Africa acts as a regional headquarters and contains Regional functions, Country-level functions, Customer functions. Formalised communication and sharing ideas in a focused Working Team deals with information access and relationships. It normally happens between regional executives and the director of engineering in annual meetings in the parent company. Informal daily technical communication is the same as most firms through telephone.

A similar structure of management hierarchy in ZTE is named '3-2-1 structure'. Subsidiaries/ representative offices/customers report the information to regional Headquarter through regional customer services; regional HQ hand in issues to parent HQ for major adjusting. Three regional customer service centres in African markets (Kenya, Algeria, and Ethiopia) provide customers with technical support and field troubleshooting services with quick responses, and are under control of The Global Customer Service Centre of the group.[32]

---

[32] It boasts nine product sub-centres, several advanced laboratories, one technical support team of engineers, perfect technical issue solution banks, an advanced laboratory environment, and quick and effective control and use of technical resources within the global range.

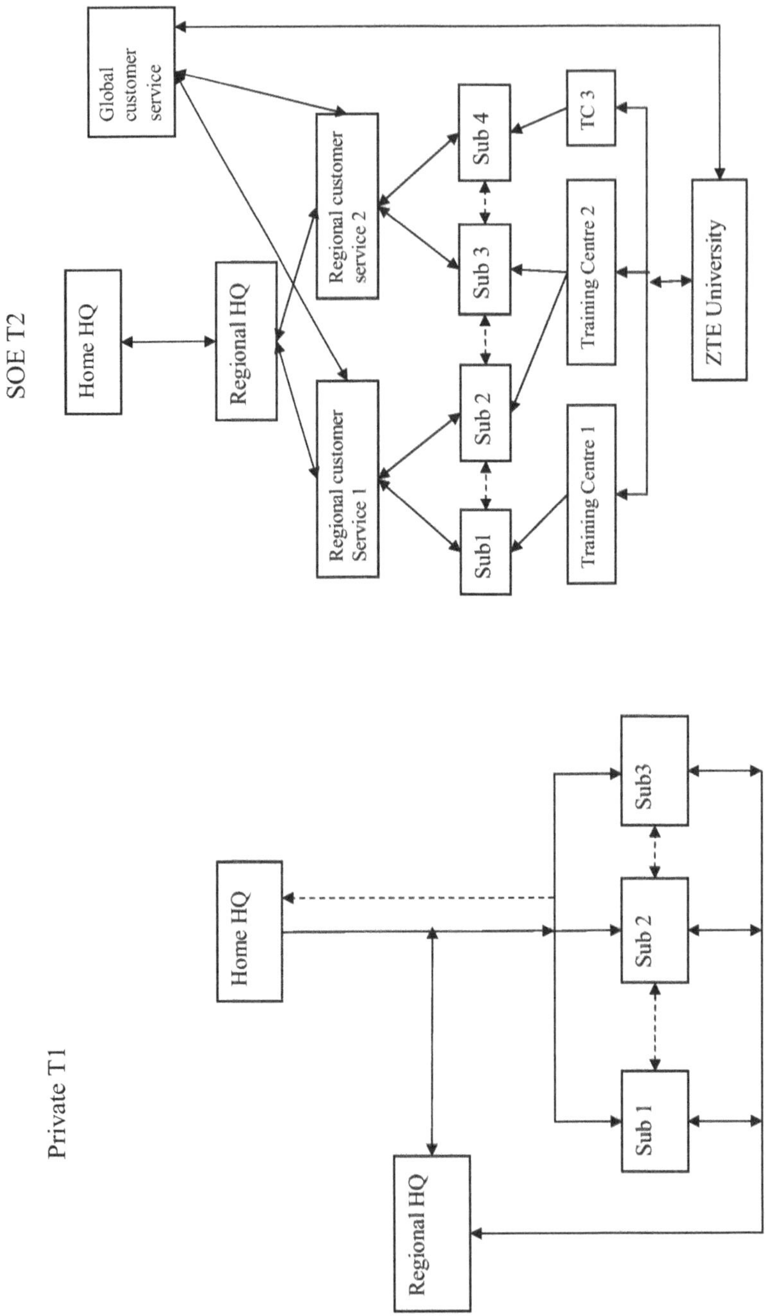

Fig. 7.3 The Comparison of Hierarchy of ICT MNEs in Africa

ZTE Corporation is dedicated to constant improvement of its capacity of global customer services, and around the world it has gradually built eight regional customer service centres (RCSC), 45 local customer service centres (LCSC), and has set up technical support service systems consisting of local, regional and head offices and steady localised field support service teams for the overall implementation of customer support service standardisation management. Differently, this company provides a more systematic structural hierarchy in technology transfers and highly specialised function of departments.

Local Innovation

Two different types of laboratories applied to Chinese telecommunication MNEs: fundamental R&D and Training Centre.

Since its establishment in 2008, the Huawei SA Training Centre has trained their partners from Vodacom, MTN, Telkom and Cell C and local staff. For local engineers, Huawei has launched its Training & Certification Solution, based on years of experience in developing ICT talents and deep insight into industry developments. The technical certification programme, that includes several levels, is created to match the career development life cycle of the ICT industry. For channel partners, Huawei also provides specialist certification for three types of positions.

As the announcement of the first R&D Centre established in South Africa in 2009, this new development of subsidiary function seeks to position itself in both assisting South Africa's telecom technology innovation and in the global innovation strategy of the group. South Africa's R&D centre is Huawei's 16th and the second in Africa following a recent launch in Nigeria.

Beyond the training centre on one way technology transfer, collaborating with mobile and fixed line operators (local and other foreign telecom investors) and third research parties to generate marketing analysis; ensuring service innovation and solution design; and dealing with telecom challenges[33] in South Africa and the region are addressed as the main functions of the R&D unit.

---

[33] Source: Huawei "Huawei establish SA's first telecoms Research & Development (R&D) Facility".

The facility aims to bring global telecommunications technology innovations to South Africa and will further engage with the global experts team of Huawei headquarters to meet the local requirements of the telecoms market and discover new ways of providing services to local operators.

South Africa's Minister of Communications says, 'The establishment of the first telecommunications Research and Development facility in South Africa marks an important milestone to the rapid advancement of the telecommunications technology in this country.'[34] (Huawei, 2009). Mediating development is stepped up in IMNE from physical provision of telecommunication infrastructure projects to bringing the company's international expertise of technology innovation to pioneer locally for soft telecom developments.

With slight differences, the innovation and knowledge system is set up in an independent position rather than involving in all functions. In Africa, ZTE setup four training centres in Egypt, Algeria, Ghana and Ethiopia, respectively, and an R&D centre (ZTE University Branch)[35] in Ethiopia. All technical issues and innovative activities are undertaken by a special team (ZTE University). ZTE trains staff and customers in different training centres all over the world depending on the level of technology and management.

On laboratory perspective, the performance of training centres of both Huawei and ZTE are clearly considered as a traditional support laboratory (SL1), aiming to assist associated production subsidiaries to assimilate and optimise the effectiveness and transfer of existing group-level technology. The core technology of both companies are generally enough to adapt to the production and solution in host countries. There are seldom local innovative activities but support the subsidiaries to learn core technology.

[34] The quote is taken from the Huawei's press releases on their official website.

[35] The ZTE University was founded in July 2003 as a corporate university initiated by ZTE Corporation. The purpose is to provide customers and employees with professional training, consulting services and technology solution. It consists of 4 overseas branches and 14 training centres around the world, and the headquarters located in Shenzhen, China.

Difficulties

The inflexible structure of Chinese companies also causes the information lag between HQ and Subsidiaries. '*Perception*' (Private T1)—inefficiency of the management: complicated structure. '*Multiple doing function*' (Private T1) overlaps in the involvement of the departments and brings inefficiency in dealing with an issue, i.e. different departments deal with one customer.[36] On one hand, it is good for getting the company fully involved in the programme and cooperating and ensures different departments of the company understand the whole operation of the unit. On the other hand, it causes trouble in understanding to the particular customers who they work with.

The highly concentrated structure seldom contributes to main technology improvement and real managerial autonomy. Decisions must go through an elaborate process of being examined and approved by higher layers. Due to the government requirement in projects, higher layers offer all 'YES' to satisfied the customer and secure their relational FSAs. However, the over-ambitious promises under delivery can cause both the internal and external conflicts.

The Impact of Chinese Telecommunication Investment

Contribution to the Group

Market-seeking is main purpose of Huawei and ZTEs expansion in Africa and therefore their income becomes the most important contribution to the group, for example, the annual revenue from African markets account for 20% of total overseas revenue. The African market as a whole is still too young for firm benefits from proper knowledge-seeking, due to limitations of education and other technology developments. However, '*For basic information feedback and technical solution, some high-level subsidiaries become more functional in recent years*' (Private T1).

[36] The ideas come from the summary of interviewee response.

Contribution to Local Economy

Technology Spillover

By setting up different levels of functional subsidiaries in technology transfer and adaptation, approximately 12,000 candidates finished training course with Huawei certificates in different level and become engaged in telecom industry. For ZTE, in another story, the North Africa Training Centre[37] cooperated with NPTIC (Algerian Post and Communication University) and has given customer training for more than 50 times, and undertaken more than 20 times of social training with the number of trainees exceeding 1800 people.

Research from Frontier Advisory[38] argued that it is difficult to understand how to manage products by African local operators alone, because of inadequate technical, managerial power and outlook on industry development. Local telecom construction firms may lack capacities to maintain projects in the long term due to financial problems, maintaining technology. Unlike much previous infrastructure investment, Huawei and ZTE are embedded in Africa and therefore can fit local firms telecom industry effectively into their value chain.

Local Recruitment

To discuss the local recruitment, it is important to understand the local labour situation. As has been introduced, large quantity of labour is hard to get employed into technology areas since they are mainly unskilled and untrained. Two third of the labour supply are involved in agriculture in long term and live outside of the urban areas. The accommodation and unskilled problems cause instability of the labour market which brings risks to foreign employers.

[37] The first pan-network integrative training centre of ZTE Corporation in Africa provides a complete set of training in products such as GSM, CDMA, DSL, SDH, power supply, etc.

[38] Frontier Advisory is a research, strategy and investment advisory company in South Africa. The firm involves in assisting clients to improve their competitiveness in emerging market economies and research cooperation with many MNEs from Emerging markets.

Huawei has more than 4000 staff in Africa, and local staffs are over 60%, though the levels of local staff are different according to local education situation. In its Mozambique subsidiary, over 70% are local staff (including employees from other African countries). Cooperating with 1200 subcontractors creates 11,000 more employment indirectly. ZTE University with the four training centres in Africa also creates training opportunities and get young people into skilled education.

Improvement of Local Industry

Over last 10 years, Huawei has reached 1.5 billion dollars in total stock of assets investment in Africa and spent more than 0.8 billion dollars local purchasing every year. By 2008, Huawei has founded 200 solar stations for wireless system. More than 4200 green stations that allow utilising local resources advantages for solutions.[39]

Case 2 Traditional Infrastructure in Construction

To consider infrastructure investment in the construction sector, the allocation and complexity of contracts in the market are not only involved with firms in the markets but come after government project awards. Markets representing firms in construction industry are representative of either monopolistic competition or oligopoly. Traditionally thinking, a high percentage of Chinese MNEs role in infrastructure in Africa, especially the state-owned construction companies, undertake ODA programmes to strengthen the diplomatic ties between home and host country, although ultimate ownership patterns are heterogeneous. 'State investment' ensures the status of oligopolistic advantages in construction investment. The interviews are mainly applied to Chinese companies which are related to infrastructure contributions in Mozambique. According to the interviews, the motivation, organisation structure, leveraging and strategies of Chinese infrastructure investment in construction does vary significantly regarding to the ownership structures.[40]

[39] For instance, Hawei provided solution to Safaricom on building up a telecom station with combination use of solar, wind energy and oil to reduce the consumption of oil in Kenya.

[40] The analysis of construction sector is given in next section respectively by ownership structure.

General Analysis of Chinese Construction Sector

Dunning (1988a, 1993) explains that investment is motivated by a firm's ownership-specific advantages which allow it to exploit economies of scale and to develop monopoly power based on its size and established position. According to internalisation advantages, a firm has an incentive to claim hierarchical control over cross-border production and its value-added activities when risks of large-scale production are high. The exploitation of these advantages is affected by the competition-oriented regulation in the host country.

At the early age of the investment in Africa only a few Chinese investors entered for the entire market. The firms' control over price means less competitive bidding for the programmes. Chinese first movers in Africa were SOEs which were obtaining distinctive ownership advantages deriving from both home-country supports (developmental CSAs and relational FSAs) and firm specific competitiveness (asset FSAs) over a long period of experience within the industry. It is unlikely that Chinese Multinationals as a whole entered into price competition with other home-country infrastructure projects rivals. Although the firms are competing at the home-end, the movements to African markets individually were under some joint arrangements by home country government. For the groups working in the industry, 'collusion' is practice in contractual agreements across the whole programme offered by host governments. The collusive behaviour explained how the allocation of Chinese SOEs in infrastructure investment overspread the African continent. This collusion is big business participants from home country operating underneath the organising by Chinese governments. *'Each group has their focusing area'* said one interviewee (SOE C1). The group entry strategy applied to the early age of investment in large construction projects. On the other hand, the construction infrastructure investment required large amounts of financial support access to which is highly associated with parent company competitiveness. The first movement to African construction industry for large projects was initiated by a very few large firms that understand each other well and adapt similar technology and experiences. Small and other new-home entrants then face relative barriers to entry because of insufficient finance and limited foreign investment experience. In other words, the construction industry for Chinese infrastructure investors becomes an oligopolistic market. To rephrase Lipsey and Crystal (1995), firms in an oligopolistic industry will make more profits if they agree to cooperate as a group. The oligopolistic features of an industry implies that decisions of one firm are directly influenced by and influence that of other firms in the industry, so that firms in their own strategies explicitly or implicitly take into account the strategies of other firms in the industry. Firms' strategic interaction can take many forms from competitive (non-cooperative) to collaborative (cooperative) strategies (Brandenburger & Nalebuff, 1995). The common characteristic is that firms' actions under oligopolistic industry structure are determined by actual or expected behaviour of rivals given the mutual interdependence of players in the industry. Taking this view into FDI, FDI is seen as a result of mutual interdependence between the major players in an industry and becomes manifest when 'a firm's decision to engage in FDI hinges on the behaviour or expected behaviour of its rivals' (Hennart & Park, 1994). This, in fact, explains the early non-competitive arrangement of Chinese MNEs in the construction sector. It was argued before as the policy arrangement by Chinese government, however, in the cases of firm-level responses, at a very high level of national industry concentration, the rival firms stop adopting defensive competitive strategies and instead of use collusion to remove risk from their environment (Flowers, 1976). In other words, the firms decide to expand as part of their international strategies but they may do this in non-competitive ways.

Competition in Infrastructure Investment

Because the MNEs' strong OAs provided the capability to behave aggressively, MNEs are located in concentrated industries. Firms in such oligopoly industry structures in a particular country observe the behaviour of their rivals and consider the strategy of expansion in certain countries. Knickerbocker and Flowers (1976) conclude that the in highly concentrated industries where such oligopoly behaviour is prominent other firms will set up operations in the country soon after the first firm, so there will be a bunching of moves of firms in the industry following the first firms. Infrastructure industry is highly concentrated owing to the requirement of technology, finance and production scale as well as 'natural monopoly' characteristic. At the initial age, few proper scale construction firms located and competed for the infrastructure projects; for instance, '*it used to be roughly two firms competing for one programme eight years ago*' said an interviewee (Private C). So the first mover could gain big advantages from its new operation in the host country, and then this is likely to affect very adversely the long-term competitive position that remained left-behind in home country or in other investment host countries.

Such oligopolistic behaviour can bring other firms into international expansion. The expansion process into the host country by a leading player influences other firms which may be the rivals within home country to respond competitively by matching the entry. With access to such substantial liquidity, therefore it is unsurprised that Chinese SOEs are at the forefront of China's engagement with Africa. Thus, while the size and capacity of private companies is growing rapidly, SOEs still dominate China's construction market and continue to win the majority of these international contracts. Construction related industry is characterised by a large number of small firms, which very few barriers to entry and a relative low level of fixed costs. The contractors, subcontractors and material suppliers all possess relatively competitive advantages distinguished from their rivals. Consequently, the opportunity to secure excessive or supernormal profit is limited in the sector once those subcontractors are embedding in African markets. African markets in construction sector provide more access to global competitors year by year; the market is getting less concentrated. Therefore, '*bidding for infrastructure projects is increasingly difficult as the numbers of competitors rise*' (Private C, SOE C1). The new-coming Chinese firms as subcontractors or material suppliers, or unrelated industry but involving infrastructure contributions achieve better quality / reliability overspread the host country. Generally, these firms obtained the monopoly advantages in the industry in a short term, but it returned to a competitive market due to producing similar products and services in the long term. The subcontractors are introduced by China (home country), local emerging firms and other foreign construction investors. The markets are still far from perfect competition, in the long term their small and new entrants will respond with similar products from different ends. That keeps the market very competitive and constrains the profits from non-competitive 'collusion'.

Differences between SOEs and POEs in Construction Provision: Outputs vs. Outcomes

Unlike the telecommunications sector, the performance of Chinese firms related to construction provision is more complicated between different bodies because of the initial motivations of overseas investment in Africa. Generally speaking, construction provision is not the major outputs of POE. For further expansion of the company and reducing the transaction cost in the weak host environment, POEs invest in infrastructure related projects which become the part of the outcomes of the investment. By contrast, construction SOEs are the historical providers in infrastructure deriving from earlier age ODA. They continue to target new infrastructure and maintaining projects over the continent as their major production.

Expansion in Africa

POE[41]

The surveyed company was founded for steel investment in Mozambique in 2007, but simultaneously, water supply, electronic support and roads became its parallel investments.

SOEs

The subsidiary was founded in Mozambique in 2002. The group had started its international expansion in Southeast African market with first entry dated back to the early age cooperation with Tanzania, and then geographically expanding to Congo and Mozambique. By 2012, the company has locally registered wholly-owned subsidiaries in 10 African countries.[42]

---

[41] POE and SOE are based on interviews of Private C and SOE C1/C2.

[42] Tanzania, Mozambique, Namibia, Zambia, Rwanda, Liberia, Guinea, Senegal, Congo (Dem).

Motivation of Overseas Investment in Africa

Most private owned enterprises in Africa are driven by market potentials. African markets allow them to find a wide range of product varieties at low price, *'offering projects provision in low price and globalised recruiting project managers'* claimed by the participant (Private C). The competitiveness of the firm is attributed to the construction project skills and constructional experience, through being a domestic subcontractor in home-country infrastructure industry. African countries are considered as the first step of expansion into global markets due to the low barriers of entry to the industry. Cost–effective production motivates the POE involved in infrastructure provision to reduce cost of overcoming weak infrastructure in a host location. Maximising the use of local goods moves the POE towards efficiency-seeking, and extends the outcomes of POE investment in a host country into infrastructure provision.

The motivation of more hierarchical controlled SOE are established on MS in order to usefully adapt products and process to better embed in local market and respond to local needs. *'Increasing the revenue for the group' 'Overseas experience for further internationalisation of the group'* (SOE C1) The operations of subsidiary represent the attempt to contribute to extension of group-wide competitiveness (Pearce & Papanastassiou, 2009).

Lengthen of Investment

To build up reputation, POEs are more likely to diversify the investment in long term; therefore, POEs may diversify investments into different industries. With continuous input over time, POE involves in both small and large scale projects. On the contrary, SOEs (especially Central SOEs) focus on short-term programme with low profit and fast accomplishment. These projects usually require large inputs at single time.

Bidding and Leverage Process

Bidding processes have slight differences between POE and SOE depending on where the company bids for the projects (Fig. 7.4). After firms have located in the host country, the process is more commercialised through

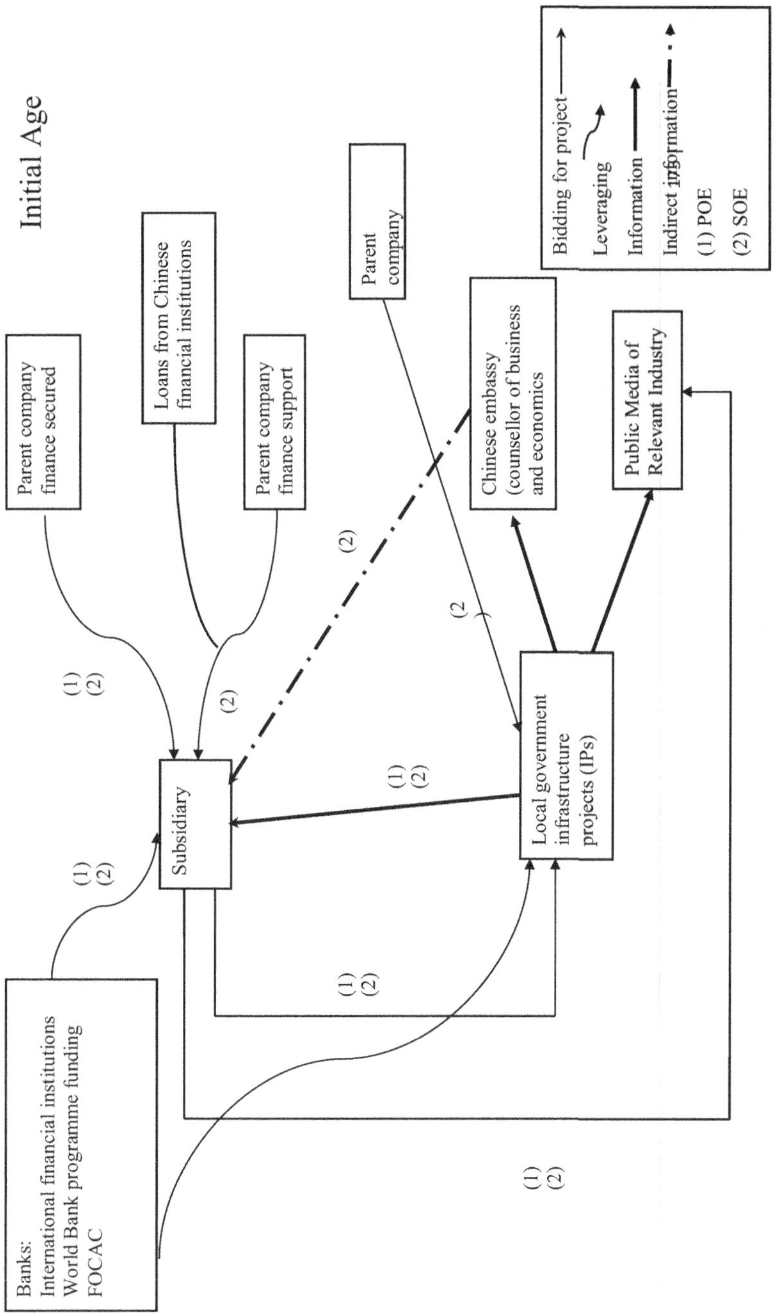

Fig. 7.4 Processes of Bidding and Funding Flows

two main approaches, i.e. media information in relevant industry and governmental published projects. This usually happens between the subsidiaries and local governments. Local construction projects are described as an extension business for POE. They focus on the infrastructure that their own business can benefit from and also meet local government requirement.[43] SOE seek to invest in government released infrastructure construction projects. With more powerful support in bidding and leverage process, besides bidding for local government released projects, SOE are able to become involved in international bidding projects that are created by international institutions. At the commercial bidding stage, the FSA-Rs of the company enable a SOE to obtain more information. For some projects, parent company organises a particular working team domestically and sends it to the target country after obtaining the projects.

At the initial stage, parent company financial support in pre-payment of investment is considered as a guarantee of competitiveness in local markets. Infrastructure projects were not target investments in the initial stages partially due to the lack of capital access in home country and regulation restrictions from the home government. Private firms have low power level of entry into the market. Funding here is mainly from loans from home-country commercial banks and internationally. POE subsidiaries are less reliant on parent company financial support after they are embedded in a local market. SOE enjoy the purposeful effort of home governments in the leverage process. Multi-channels of leveraging ensure the bargaining power of a company during the bidding process. Inefficient banking systems may make soft loans to potential outward investors, either as policy or through inefficiency (Warner et al., 2004; Child & Rodrigues, 2005). Owing to the strong relational FSAs, SOEs have capital made available to them at such soft constraints on loans.

The Structure of Company: Organisation Hierarchy

With similar structure of companies (Fig. 7.5), construction firms possess the most decisive hierarchical control where parent companies provide the potential sources of competitiveness to subsidiaries. Thereby, a

[43] The company is also required by local government for provision on school and hospital.

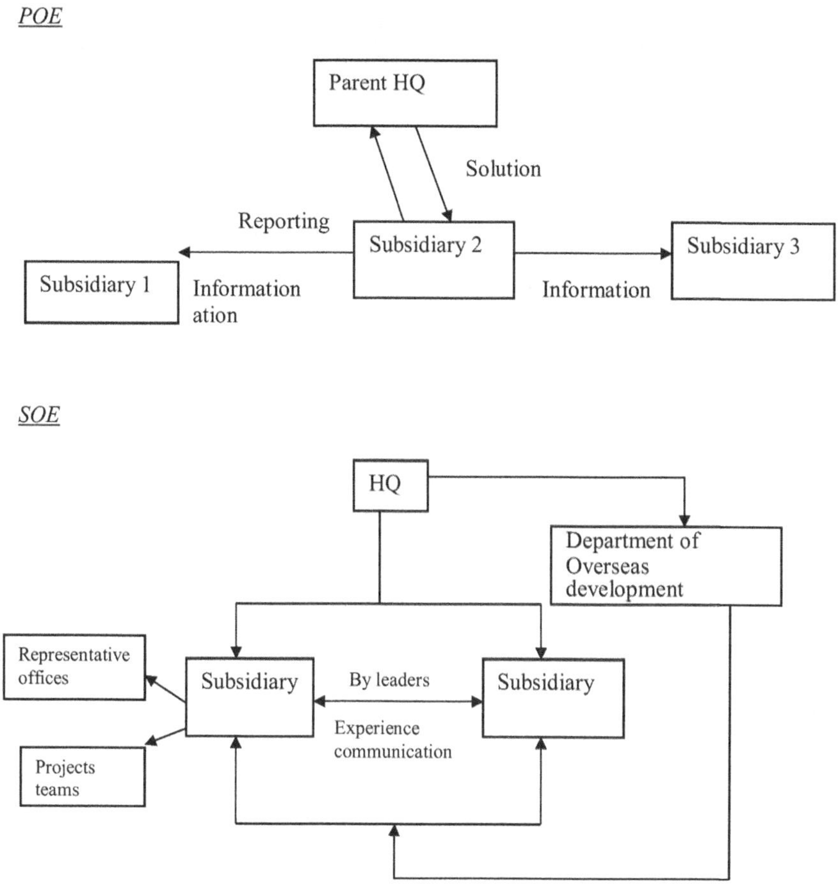

Fig. 7.5 the structure of companies

degree of subsidiary-level individualisation represents the motivation and performance of firms in one location. Both firms' subsidiaries are independent of each other but controlled by HQ. Regarding to host country characteristics, none of the participants in construction sector engaged in innovation-oriented activities. *'Whole-owned subsidiary in different country with independent accounting system'* (Private C, SOE C1). The parent company sets up a special working group for coordination. A comparatively large subsidiary works as regional headquarter. Several working teams are controlled and organised by one subsidiary.[44] The structure and management is simple and less intrusive. Parent company is responsible for financial arrangement and transfers of personnel.

Difficulties

Local governments make increasing programmes for meeting the needs of local people and raising the quality requirement because of competition. The local government and industry have more choices of contractors on bidding for local programmes because of the increasing entries of foreign firms. Qualities become more concerned issues in evaluation of investment. Low quality with low price was tagged on investment in Africa at the initial stage. It was the advantage of Chinese firms on getting into such programmes. Offering a low price for bidding projects is less attractive for host government in assessment of bidding companies. Chinese firms' early strategy cannot properly apply to secure winning the programme and to expanding investment. *'With increasing of infrastructure related investment, local government have been increasing the knowledge on the process of investment and MNEs operation'* (Private C). As the competitive investors[45] in one infrastructure project increases, more opportunities are provided but with higher requirements.

'The group reduces the subsidies' (SOE C1) after the subsidiary has embedded for marketisation. Companies have to rely on outside capital in local programmes. Low cost is no longer the advantage for further investment as it become *'difficult to ensure the quality'* (SOE C1). The local requirement of investment increase: Salary requirement: the salary increase 7% for local staff.

[44] Six teams in Malawi company; 10 teams in south African company; 8 teams in Mozambique.

[45] For instance, it used to be roughly two firms competing for one programme eight years ago while now nearly 20 competitors (said by the interviewee).

Supply Chain

POE

Efficiency seeking becomes a part in the strategy of private firms in construction provision as firms aim to maximise the profits from their established mature goods. POE, although still dependent on the stock of centrally–created technology, considers adjusting this to increase the proportion of this that is input from host factors. '*We firstly consider of local purchasing, then the regional countries, last choice is import from China.... to reduce the cost...contribute to other local industry and get access to local supply chain*' (Private C)

SOE

Internal Integration

Differently from the private firm where the first consideration was local purchasing, '*Our company is inclined to spur exporting of domestic manufacturing [from China]*' said by a participant (SOE C1). As most respondents mentioned, Chinese construction companies import materials from a domestic supplier instead of building up the backward linkages with the local market. Sourcing from China is not a systematic global value chain. The purposes of SOEs are not only developing their own capabilities but also building internal integration capabilities which indirectly help to build the market and increase China's exports. Intermediate goods, here varies the role of market seeking. A participant explained that '*to secure the quality and familiarity of inputs materials, subsidiary is engaged mainly in domestic purchase including steel reinforcement and pipes and brings equipment from home*' (SOE C1). The second layer of material sourcing is importing from other developed countries to secure the quality of input materials, followed by local materials.

Thus a long established relationship with a domestic supplier guarantees the low cost. The firm itself accumulates the network well with these suppliers which contribute to the firms FSA-A. Increasing the export records indirect benefits to the home government which enhance their FSA-R.

Thus it was said *'Building up our own value chain and spur the construction materials export'* (SOE C1). A major motivation for promoting infrastructure projects was the expectation that they or their correlated firms from home country could sell a range of products and services to the infrastructure project (Ramamurti & Doh, 2004).

Contribution to Local Economy

POE

Local cooperation

Due to cost of dealing with difference of culture, language, familiarity of local law and regulation, POE usually chooses to operate on its own. Thus limited skill/knowledge spills over to local enterprises.

Local recruitment

Local recruitment reaches 70–80%,[46] that is approximately 10% higher than other interviewees in local recruiting, due to two reasons: for one thing, recruiting unskilled local workers for small enterprises is an efficient way to reduce the production cost at the beginning, i.e. the salary for local staff is normally lower than completely bringing Chinese workers from home country. This also helps the firm getting into business quickly (efficiency). For the second thing, to meet the local government requirement and to build up reputation in host country, high rate of local recruitment accelerates localisation of SME. Training is repeatedly mentioned by the company.[47] Accordingly, 100 Mozambican workers are funded and sent for training in China. Thus POE can contribute to the skills transfer to local labour.

Improvement of purchasing power

By diversification of its business in Mozambique, the company gets involved in different industries locally that lower the local price for local

[46] For instance, 100 Chinese workers in Mozambique company and 5000 local staff. Other interviewees claimed 60–70% local recruitment.

[47] Local staffs are taking the training for three to five years and gradually being localised company.

customers (mentioned by the company); for example, in long term, foreign investment in local real estate reduces the price of house

Improvement of technology

Local technology is far behind the average level in the industry. The government is also lacking in the regulation of quality on technology. The company provides technology reports to local government, and offers chances for training in getting to be familiar with the techniques and visiting the parent company for further communication on understanding of technology which spreads skills locally.

SOE

Local cooperation

Limited partnership and subcontracting opportunities with local construction firms as the low skills of the local firms cannot reach the quality demanded. More often, Chinese private firms will become the SOE's choice as subcontractors. Additionally, as mentioned above, the SOE focuses on building up its own supply chain with home country and, therefore, it reduces the possibility of linkages with local enterprises.

Contribution to the group

The group has less expectation of profitability[48] because the Mozambique market becomes more competitive. The first target of each subsidiary is to ensure the amount of contracts so ultimately expanding the scale of projects. The subsidiary has to take advantage of leveraging for exploring the new fields and regional markets and increasing the future revenues of programmes. However, as the interviewee explained, the African market as a whole is major source of overseas revenue for the group.

Local recruitment

The employees are not able to start similar business on their own since the skills that the local workers learnt and trained from the home staffs

[48] The profit expectation reduced by 20–30%.

are based on the certain equipment which are not affordable by local private enterprises. Training the unskilled workers for using basic equipment and engineering ability is the main CSR of the company.

Localisation

Stability is one of the most important factors of location choice for the parent company. Owing to the whole circumstances of African market, the company mainly focuses on political stability and social stability. The IMNEs face hazards in marketised investment in the infrastructure sector that originate directly from the variations and unpredictability in political and institution systems rather than as the entities of ODA programme between countries. The infrastructure projects are inherently characterised by host-country government (see Chap. 5) that plagued many risks including exchange rate, stability of government (political actions of interest groups, changes in governments) and the risk of governments' reneging on their commitment (Ramamurti, 2003). Vernon's study (1971) introduced the notion that investors' bargaining power in host countries would 'obsolesce', over time, especially in industries such as infrastructure that are characterised by high fixed costs and the inability to transfer capital investment to the home country or another host.[49] The local governments have greater leverage over foreign firms in these sectors once firms have committed investment to the market. This makes changes in host government behaviour especially problematic because of the absence of alternative uses for the investment projects. Therefore, large SOE concerns with stability of local environment.

Longer term investment

The infrastructure industries functioned best as natural monopolies, with huge sunk cost of projects, are more likely be formulated for long-term investment declining the average cost. The early stage of Chinese ODA in infrastructure provision concentrated on short term and large input projects.

---

[49] Vernon (1971); Doz and S. Prahalad (1980); N. Fagre and L. T. Wells (1982); S. Kobrin (1987); Murtha and Lenway (1994) and Wells and Gleason(1995) all had studies on how government and institutions affect MNEs from different perspectives.

Proposition 5a *Telecommunication firms are more commercially driven in their internationalisation.*

Proposition 5b *Construction firms have stronger backward linkage to home country needs and support.*

7.5.2 Ownership structure of IMNEs issues

Ownership Structure Comparison—Three Major Types of Chinese IMNEs in Africa

The second case study is motivated to focus on the specific motivations and strategic performance of Chinese IMNEs based on the differentiation of company ownership.

In line with internalisation theory, firms tend to utilise their own assets and capabilities in expanding into foreign markets (Buckley & Casson, 1976; Rugman, 1981; Dunning, 1991; Pearce & Papanastassiou, 2009). In most cases, Chinese firms related to infrastructure investment in Africa are considered to be responding to home-country economic and political objectives. With the visible hand of government involvement driving Chinese outward investment, the expanding on firms' FSA-As is enhanced by relationship with home countries authorities. The relationships with government and government agents yield inevitable effects on firms' competitive advantages which influence their location decisions and motivations (Wang et al., 2012). Chinese firms develop unique capabilities which depend strongly on how firms transform the nature of China's Developmental CSAs into their inherent FSA-A. This special capability of Chinese MNEs is defined as Relational FSAs (FSA-R). This set of factors all come together to determine the competitiveness of Chinese MNEs. FSA-Rs, building on interaction with government involvement, reflect the capabilities to benefit from non-market relationships. The relationship with home government guarantees the trustworthiness of a firm in competing for large projects. Looking beyond the generalised government involvement, the influences are distinguished through the various levels of relationship with different types of government involvement.

Measuring from firm dimension, variations of FSA-Rs requires ability to establish working relationship that is constrained by ownership structures.

Summarily, Chinese firms related to infrastructure investment in Africa have diversified and gradually contain most types of ownership structures: firms with the central government or the local government as the controlling stakeholder are generally categorised as SOEs; second, firms with large scale of production and highly affiliated with government and privatised former SOEs; third, private firms in manufacturing industry and involved in infrastructure projects to supplement their local production.

Home government intervenes with building up a firm's specific advantages for internationalising by institutional force, but not all types of government involvements have equal benefit to MNEs (Wang et al., 2012), and not all firms related to infrastructure investment have the same abilities to internalise such government ties and respond to African markets. On the government dimension, the special treatments underline the 'go global' policies set by Chinese central government for MNEs and provide the general framework on obtaining the benefits from major institutions of the state on investing in Africa. Many rules and procedures are differentiated when the policies are decentralised to lower level governments and agencies. Furthermore, the central policies mix economic and political orders. But they never have clear written and announced willingness on making use of the international expansion of particular Chinese companies to achieve national needs in host countries. These mixed eco-political policies differ depending on the influence of institutional forces and government preferences towards firms undertaking the specific projects and strategic expansion. Government's informal influence, or formal authorities over the way in which the firms adapt resources and internationalise, depends on the degree of state ownership in a given firm (Wang et al., 2012). Internally, the Chinese government directly controls international trajectories of SOEs through ownership arrangements and associates with managers of non-SOEs by semi-official titles (FSA-R). Associated with external mechanisms, home government establish outsider participation relationships (e.g. partnership in particular series of investment or government organised association) in which government and firms interact within a more marketised system, rather than formalised arrangement.

From firm dimension, the leverage of competitive advantages (FSA-Rs) derives from the hierarchies of institutional embeddedness, i.e. the level of political competences (Boddewyn & Brewer, 1994). Firms with a higher degree of state ownership need to balance political acceptability and market requirements, and ensure that decision-making is aligned with the objectives of their own State, including global strategy of the country. Government involvements in relational FSAs through ownerships are more likely to affect the use of resources and willingness of internationalisation. Central SOEs internationalisation decisions depend largely on the goals of government and accommodate political objectives (Ramamurti, 2001). Their expansions in Africa are recognised as success with government support and less concerned with economic returns at the initial stage and with optimisation of resources. Hence, the SOEs are more likely to partly sacrifice firms' performance for political goals. Chinese SOEs undertake large infrastructure projects with low bidding price in Africa or are responsible to ODA projects. By contrast, the MNEs with lower degree of state-ownership depend less on governments as resource providers. These firms are likely to commercially spread over the market with FSA-As (traditional FSAs).

To secure the benefits from government ties, firms require strategic options to maximise the benefits of reciprocal relationships (Sun et al., 2010); these enable access to factors in home-country environment. Firms with higher level government affiliation have a greater status to access, and leverage, home-country factors that raise the competitive advantages in trustworthiness (Table 7.3). On one hand, the higher the level of connection with governments, the more the firms are encouraged to invest in the countries although the location may not be their priorities. This is viewed as part of the implicit requirements of appropriate goals on integration of home country into the host economy (Child & Rodrigues, 2005; Wang et al., 2012). On the other hand, in order to obtain government support in investment, firms enhance their ties with their home country by taking part of the responsibility of looking after home government encouragement. On the contrary, interests of lower-level governments are often more concerned with maintaining local financial stability that is partially attributes to provincial or municipal

Table 7.3 ownership structure of Top 50 Chinese companies

Rank	Names	Ownerships	City	Assets ($ millions)	Industry	Africa investment
1	Sinopec Group	State/Central	Beijing	225,388.20	oil	√
2	China National Petroleum	State/Central	Beijing	399,101.10	oil	√
3	State Grid	State/Central	Beijing	315,268.30	Utilities	√
4	China Mobile Communications	State/Central	Beijing	160,728.60	Telecommunication	√
5	China Railway Group	State/Central	Beijing	59,078.00	Railway	√
6	China Railway Construction	State/Central	Beijing	53,142.60	Railway	√
7	China Life Insurance	State/Central	Beijing	269,514.60	Insurance	
8	Nobel Group		HK	17,337.50		
9	Dongfeng Motor	State/Provincial	Wuhan	33,046.10	Automobile	√
10	China State Construction Engineering	State/Central	Beijing	60,327.30		√
11	China Southern Power Grid	State/Central	Guangzhou	74,475.80	Utilities	√
12	Shanghai Automotive	State/Provincial	Shanghai	44,390.50	Automobile	√
13	China National Offshore Oil	State/Central	Beijing	93,661.30	oil	√
14	Sinochem Group	State/Central	Beijing	32,088.80	Various Sectors	√
15	China FAW Group	State/Central	Changchun	26,184.80	Automobile	
16	China Communications Construction	State/Central	Beijing	47,205.00	Transportation	
17	Baosteel Group	State/Central	Shanghai	65,576.60	Steel	
18	CITIC Group	State/Central	Beijing	385,307.00	Financial Services	√
19	China Telecom	State/Central	Beijing	98,280.70	Telecommunications	√
20	China South Industries Group	State/Central	Beijing	33,282.50		
21	China Minmetals	State/Central	Beijing	30,166.00	Mining	√
22	China North Industries Group	State/Central	Beijing	34,655.20		
23	China Huaneng Group	State/Central	Beijing	100,520.40		
24	HeBei Iron & Steel Group	State/Provincial	Shijiazhuang	42,806.60	Steel	√
25	People's Insurance Co. of China	State/Central	Beijing	66,860.30	Insurance	
26	Shenhua Group	State/Central	Beijing	83,604.20		
27	China Metallurgical Group	State/Central	Beijing	48,266.70		

28	Aviation Industry Corp. of China	State/Central	Beijing	71,214.50		
29	Jardine Matheson		Hong Kong	48,076.00	Various Sectors	
30	Shougang Group	State/Central	Beijing	47,062.60	Steel	
31	Ping An Insurance	State/Central	Shenzhen	117,796.70	Insurance	
32	Aluminum Corp. of China	State/Central	Beijing	56,788.40	Aluminum	√
33	Wuhan Iron & Steel	State/Central	Wuhang	30,931.20	Steel	
34	China Post Group	State/Central	Beijing	534,267.40	Post	
35	China Resources	State/Central	Hong Kong	69,656.70		
36	Huawei Technologies	Private	Shenzhen	24,407.90	Technology	√
37	Sinosteel	State/Central	Beijing	19,095.80		
38	Hutchison Whampoa		HK	92,776.20		
39	COFCO		Beijing	35,298.60		
40	Jiangsu Shagang Group	private	Zhangjiagang	24,242.00	Steel	
41	China United Network Communications	State/Central	Shanghai	67,296.90	Telecommunication	√
42	China Datang	State/Central	Beijing	78,999.40	Utilities (Electricity)	√
43	China Ocean Shipping	State/Central	Beijing	48,497.60	Shipping	√
44	China Godian	State/Central	Beijing	81,314.40	electric	√
45	China Electronics	State/Central	Beijing	18,727.90		
46	China Railway Materials Commercial	State/Central	Beijing	7549.70	energy/ trading	√
47	China National Aviation Fuel Group	State/Central	Beijing	4567.80		
48	Sinomach	State/Central	Beijing	19,933.40	engineering / trading	√
49	Henan Coal & Chemical	State/Provincial	Zhengzhou	21,330.20	energy	
50	Lenovo Group	Private/ state-holding	Beijing	10,705.90	Technology	√

Source: CNN Fortune 2011—Global 500 listing

SOEs and large private firms. Companies are only encouraged to expand internationally when they can reallocate labour and assets of the province or cities.

The FSA-Rs are affected by the hierarchy of governments where the privileged information and resources provided would help the firm to accumulate and manage knowledge. Central SOEs, or those large firms associated with higher level governmental authorities, have greater international capabilities to secure market power and more opportunities to influence institutions to assist their international strategy (Wang et al., 2012; Cantwell et al., 2010). The stronger political connection creates strong relational FSAs. Ownership structure also influences on the obligation of adapting resource use and willingness to internationalise. Coercive pressures and normative expectation usually appear in its internationalisation process where state control persists over the use of firms' assets and managerial personnel, for instance, where the managers are former government officials or where government officials are on the boards. With strong authority relationship, FSA-Rs are more likely to be the key influence to how the organisation can expand to internationalise the FSA-As, i.e. the firm departs from its established strategic plans to fit with the demands of state. In most cases, Chinese large construction SOEs investing and undertaking infrastructure projects in Africa indicated that the push of higher government is required to list SOEs in the stock market internationally, so increasing the channel of leveraging. FSA-Rs exist in Chinese firms where the business-government interdependence is applied in Chinese MNEs investment. However, the relational FSAs are of limited value when firms possess strong assets FSAs including financial background. The relationship with government is then less effective to integrate the state's internationalisation plans into firms' own routines and overseas operations.

The stronger the FSA-Rs Chinese firms possess, the more tolerant they can be to economic risks and political instability. Capital market failure in the banking system of China distorts the leverage for internationalisation. Infrastructure investment requires large amount of capital in initial inputs that intensify uncertainty of returns. However, Chinese firms are being successful in infrastructure investment in Africa since government ties enable the firms to get access to capital through lobbying government or enjoying preferential treatment of being state-ownerships. Relational FSAs reduce the constraints of obtaining bank loans for overseas investment, especially those projects and investments that contain political objectives. The fact that firms with high relational FSAs have less pressure in high-risk investment and long-term performance is due to the sufficient supply of capital from home country, i.e. the SOEs. Those lower government connected firms tend to be more cautious in consideration of risks and resources in African market. As a result, Chinese SOEs in infrastructure investment lead to different attitudes toward the host-country environment rather than more conventional expansion strategies.

Private Firms in Infrastructure

POE is not mainly motivated in infrastructure investment at the initial stage of investment due to the large amount input of infrastructure creation. Thanks to the degree of link with Chinese government, these companies can be perceived as effectively differentiated in utilising CSAs in building up international competitiveness.

Private C[50] one of the interviewees in this case, provides a clear example of Chinese private investment involving in construction creation. Different from some infrastructure related SOEs in Africa, private firms pursue maximised profit and lower the cost in their major business wherever they located. The firms have to face to the lack of infrastructure in water supply, electrics and road construction. Therefore, infrastructure provision becomes the important parenthesis of the investment which is called 'group systematisation' by the CEO[51] (Private C) of the company. Self-provision on basic infrastructure is the efficient way to reduce the transaction costs. This private company in construction claims that it obtains less direct benefit from building up competitiveness from CSA-Is

[50] A Chinese private medium size multinational enterprise centrally locates in Maputo, Mozambique in 2007 and expands in Botswana, Zimbabwe, Malawi, South Africa and Ethiopia. Diversifying business operation in Steel and Iron industry, construction materials and real estate.

[51] The CEO of the company explained the reason of diversification of investment.

because of its rare links with home government. However, the expansion derives from taking advantages of local low-cost resources, multi-channel leveraging are built on utilising CSA-D.

Huawei, is another case of private investment involved in telecommunication creation, established privately with complicated ownership structure including the founder, their subsidiaries, provincial telecom operators and employees collectively and individually. Although it is named as a private firm, it is associated closely to a provincial government because of the production scale and large contribution to domestic finance. Huawei relies more on its own research potentials (FSA-A) deriving from the early-age support of technology development from China and the recruitment and development of local talents, for example, 40% of its 16,000 staff is occupied in R&D. To compete and seek profit at home, Huawei is also following a very proactive invention patent strategy to enhance competitive advantages and to accomplish a global innovation system through into the long term. The evolution of China's new innovation system provides a favourable home-country specific advantage to boost Chinese telecom MNEs to quickly formulate their firm specific advantages over the 20 years through strong government support, sophisticated networks with technology-based research institutions and well-trained researchers and engineers. The firms can therefore embed their first step abroad into emerging markets attributable to similar market experience, in house R&D capabilities and a financing system for price competitiveness.

Provincial State-Owned Enterprises

According to the study of Luo and Tung (2007) on categorising emerging market MNEs, provincial State-owned MNEs are presented as 'transnational agents' that have invested abroad for their international expansion while the large scale of investment and sufficient financial support is still being subjected to home government (provincial governments) influences and instructions. The international competitiveness comes from the long term relations with domestic government and institutions that enable them to lower technology barriers. The provincial SOE may obtain privileged access to financial capital that has been given the comparative advantages due to the relatively strong FSA-R.

These companies generally operate in vital sectors that are of strategic importance to their respective countries. As such, their governments are usually their largest shareholders. They are going global to grasp opportunities to boost overall business growth while supporting economic development at home.

ZTE, another model of ownership, with 31.8%[52] state-holding share, which is less than the standard 50%, yet the state is still the largest shareholder and de facto controller. It is more dependent on the financial market but also more likely to benefit from national research funding in their R&D investment. In this study, ZTE is considered as state-controlled in ownership that enables it to take advantages of financial support of national policy to ensure the funding for scale of production and technology investment.

In the construction firm on the other hand, FSA-As determine the unique capability of proprietary advantages of an organisation that contributes to further internationally expansion. Sufficient financial background of the group also secured the long-term investment in large programme bidding. Accordingly, the group has been developing for 20 year before the entry into Mozambique. It also benefits from using similar experience of working in undeveloped situation over last a few decades of China's development (CSA-D). The group is interested in long term projects for lowering cost on equipment and accumulating experiences. Rugman (2007) states that home-country CSAs are not essentially applied to firms' long run expansion as the firms have generated strong FSA-As in marketing and customisation for certain markets. Therefore, strong FSA-R of provincial SOEs enables the use of CSAs from home country.

Owing to variation in international diversification and world-stage aspirants, SOEs may be more competitive in getting projects from host country and have more opportunities in high returns at the beginning than private companies. This is attributed to home CSA-Is of the firm.

[52] ZTE Annual Report, 2011, https://www.zte.com.cn/mi_imgs/global/investor_relations/348956/P020120917397063693372.pdf

Strong governmental background and competitive organisation of resources incorporate the nature of ownership, a dimension typically absent in CSAs of private firms, which explains the significantly varying strengths, risk-assessing behaviours, investment strategies, subsidiaries' governance and parent-subsidiary relations. Being a 'transnational agent' of the home government it receives greater institutional support and government underwriting but higher bureaucratic and political interferences. Under government influence, the group may have less discretionary power of location choice in international expansion (Luo & Tung, 2007).

Proposition 6a *Chinese IMNEs ability to expand on FSA-A in African markets arises from variation of ownership structures.*

Proposition 6b *SOEs concentrated in construction sector for traditional construction programmes are more likely to build up value chain to domestic industries.*

7.6 Bilateral Development

Turning from the initial ODA entities to private investors in market bidding for basic infrastructure projects, Chinese construction SOEs access and move to market-based pricing of infrastructure.

These projects reduce the burden on traditional public financing by increasing role of private sector as an important financers and long-term operators (Ramamurti, 2000). The fact that, given the capital intensity associated with infrastructure, in most African countries, host governments are short of resources to undertake the needed investment. The introduction of competition in infrastructure investment has an effective catalyst on accelerating overall growth.

> *The provincial SOEs and other SMEs in construction are more interested in long term programme…both small and large projects and normally more than 0.5billion as the additional inputting during the programme.* (Private C)

Appendix

Table 7.4 Leveraging system for Outward Investment

Thresholds for verification and approval of overseas investments
Overseas investment for exploration and development of natural resources:
≥ US$ 30 million: verification and approval by the NDRC
≥ US $ 200 million: verification and approval by the NDRC; report to the State Council
< US$ 30 million: verification and approval by Development and Reform Dept. on provincial level
Overseas investment non-resources sector:
≥ US $ 10 million: verification and approval by the NDRC
≥ US $ 50 million: verification and approval by the NDRC; report to the State Council
< US$ 10 million: verification and approval by Development and Reform Dept. on provincial level
Regulation for overseas investment for SOEs
< US$ 30 million, resource development: independent decision by enterprises
< US$ 10 million, other investment: independent decision by enterprises
Outward investments encouraged and promoted
Promotion in the manufacturing sector:
textile, garment and footwear, production of chemical fibers and polyester, processing of wood production/products of paper, chemical fertilizers/ pharmaceuticals, smelting and processing of cooper and aluminium, production and installation of large-scale telecommunications satellites, consumer electronics.
Support in the service sector:
transport of goods on sea-lanes, operation of telecommunication networks, software development, product research in high-end technology, road and rail, transport of goods.
The key investments encouraged and supported by institutions:
natural resources and raw materials, constructions and infra-structure, export sectors in which China has a global competitive advantage, sectors which raise China's technology R&D capabilities and capacities, sectors which enable China to obtain advanced technology and management skills and capabilities.

Source: Ministry of Commerce; adapting from Berger and Berkofsky (2008)

Bibliography

Alden, C. (2005). China in Africa. *Survival: Global Politics and Strategy, 47*(3), 147.

Alden, C., & Alves, A. C. (2009). *China and Africa's natural resources: The challenges and implications for development and governance*. Braamfontein: South African Institute of International Affairs.

Alden, C., & Davies, M. (2006, Summer/Autumn). A profile of the operations of Chinese Multinationals in Africa. *South African Journal of International Affairs, 13*(1). (original version: Chinese Multinational Corporations in Africa, Offshore Oil, Issue: 3–4, 1–11, Africa Institute of South Africa).

Baker, M., Foley, C., & Wurgler, J. (2009). Multinationals as arbitrageurs: The effect of stock market valuations on foreign direct investment. *Review of Financial Studies, 22*(1), 337–369.

Berger, B., & Berkofsky, A. (2008). *Chinese outward investments: Agencies, motives and decision-making*. CASCC Briefing Paper, 172.

Boddewyn, J., & Brewer, T. (1994). International business political behaviour: New theoretical directions. *Academy of Management Review, 19*(1), 119–143.

Brandenburger, A. M., & Nalebuff, B. J. (1995). *The right game: Use game theory to shape strategy* (Vol. 76, pp. 57–71). Chicago: Harvard Business Review.

Broadman, H. G. (2007). Chinese-African trade and investment: The vanguard of south-south commerce in the twenty-first century. In R. I. Rotberg (Ed.), *China into Africa—Trade, aid and influence*. Brookings Institution Press.

Buckley, J. P., & Casson, M. C. (1976). *The future of multinational enterprises*. Macmillan.

Buckley, P., Clegg, J., Cross, A., Liu, X., Voss, H., & Zheng, P. (2007). The determinants of Chinese outward foreign direct investment. *Journal of International Business Studies, 38*(4), 499–518.

Cantwell, J., Dunning, J. H., & Lundan, S. M. (2010). An evolutionary approach to understanding international business activity: The co-evolution of MNEs and the institutional environment. *Journal of International Business Studies, 41*(4), 567–586.

Centre for Chinese Studies. (2006). *China's interest and activity in Africa's construction and infrastructure sectors*. Stellenbosch University.

Child, J., & Rodrigues, S. B. (2005). The internationalization of Chinese firms: A case for theoretical extension? *Management and Organization Review, 1*(3), 381–410.

Child, J., & Tsai, T. (2005). The dynamic between firms' environmental strategies and institutional constraints in emerging economies: Evidence from China and Taiwan. *Journal of Management Studies, 42*(1), 0022–2380.

Corkin, L., Burke, C., & Davies, M. (2008). *China's role in the development of Africa's infrastructure.* SAIS Working papers in African Studies, 04–08.

DiMaggio, P. J., & Powell, W. W. (1983). The Iron cage revisited: Institutional isomorphism and collective rationality in organizational fields. *American Sociological Review, 48*(2), 147–160.

Doh, J. P., & Ramamurti, R. (2003). Reassessing risk in developing country infrastructure. *Long Range Planning, 36*, 337–353.

Doz, Y., & Prahalad, S. (1980, March–April). How MNCs cope with host government intervention. Harvard Business Review, 149–157.

Duanmu, J. (2012). Firm heterogeneity and location choice of Chinese multinational enterprises. *Journal of World Business, 47*, 64–72.

Dunning, J. H. (1988a). The theory of international production. *The International Trade Journal, 3*, 21–66.

Dunning, J. H. (1991). Governments and multinational enterprises: from confrontation to co-operation? *Millennium, 20*(2), 225–244.

Dunning, J. H. (1993). Internationalizing Porter's diamond. *MIR: Management International Review*, 7–15.

Dunning, J. H. (2006a). Comment on dragon multinationals: New players in 21st century globalisation. *Asia Pacific Journal of Management, 25*(2), 139–141.

Dunning, J. H., & Lundan, S. M. (2008). Institutions and the OLI paradigm of the multinational enterprise. *Asia Pacific Journal of Management, 25*, 573–593.

Eden, L., Lenway, S., & Schuler, D. A. (2004). *From the obsolescing bargain to the political bargaining model.* Bush School Working Paper 403.

eLearning Africa. (2011). 6th international conference on ICT for development, education and training the key networking event for developing eLearning capacities in Africa, Available from https://www.elearning-africa.com/conference/ressources/pdfs/report/postreport_eLA2011_small.pdf

Estache, A. (2004). *PPI partnerships vs. PPI divorces in LDCs.* World Bank and ECARES.

Fagre, N., & Wells, L. T. (1982). Bargaining power of multinationals and host governments. *Journal of International Business Studies, 13*, 9–23.

Flowers, E. B. (1976). Oligopolistic reactions in European and Canadian direct investment in the United States. *Journal of International Business Studies, 7*(2), 43–55.

Flyvbjerg, B., Holm, M. S., & Buhl, S. (2002). Underestimating costs in public works projects: Error or lie? *Journal of the American Planning Association, 68*(3), 279–295.

Flyvbjerg, B., Skamris Holm, M. K., & Buhl, S. L. (2003). How common and how large are cost overruns in transport infrastructure projects? *Transport Reviews, 23*(1), 71–88.

Gould, D. M., & Ruffin, R. J. (1993). What determines economic growth. *Economic Review, 2*, 25–40.

Grosse, R., & Behrman, J. N. (1992). Theory in international business. *Transnational Corporations, 1*(1), 93–126.

He, W., & Lyles, M. A. (2008). China's outward foreign direct investment. *Business Horizons, 51*, 485–491.

Hennart, J. F., & Park, Y. R. (1994). Location, governance, and strategic determinants of Japanese manufacturing investment in the United States. *Strategic Management Journal, 15*(6), 419–436.

Herzer, D. (2008). The long-run relationship between outward FDI and domestic output: Evidence from panel data. *Economics Letters, 100*(1), 146–149.

Huawei. (2009). *Huawei establish SA's first telecoms Research & Development (R&D) Facility*, Johannesburg. Retrieved September 30, 2009.

Huawei. (2010). *Africa fact sheet*. www.huawei.com/ucmf/groups/public/documents/…/hw_090307.pdf

Khanna, T., & Palepu, K. G. (2010). *Winning in emerging markets: A road map for strategy and execution*. Harvard Business Press.

Kobrin, S. (1987). Testing the bargaining hypothesis in the manufacturing sector in developing countries. *International Organization, 41*, 609–638.

Kolstad, I., & Wiig, A. (2012). What determines Chinese outward FDI? *Journal of World Business, 47*(1), 26–34.

Kragelund, P. (2010). *The potential role of non-traditional donors' aid in Africa*. Issue Paper No. 11. ICTSD Programme on Competitiveness and Sustainable Development.

Larçon, J. P., & Barré, G. (2009). Technology-based competition and Chinese multinationals. *Chinese Multinationals*, 127–149.

Li, J., Newenham-Kahindi, A. M., Shapiro, D. M., & Chen, V. Z. (2013). The two-tier bargaining model revisited: Theory and evidence from China's natural resource investments in Africa. *Global Strategy Journal, 3*(4), 300–321, forthcoming.

Lipsey and Crystal. (1995). *An introduction to positive economics, 8th edition*. Oxford University Press.

Luo, Y., & Tung, R. L. (2007). International expansion of emerging market enterprises: A springboard perspective. *Journal of International Business Studies, 38*(4), 481–498.

Manolopoulos, D., Papanastassiou, M., & Pearce, R. (2009). Technology sourcing in multinational enterprises and the roles of subsidiaries: An empirical investigation. In *The strategic development of multinationals* (pp. 57–77). Palgrave Macmillan: London.

Mathews, J. A. (2002). Competitive advantages of the latecomer firm: A resource-based account of industrial catch-up strategies. *Asia Pacific Journal of Management, 19*, 467–488.

Mathews, J. A. (2006). Catch-up strategies and the latecomer effect in industrial development. *New Political Economy, 11*(3), 313–335.

Morck, R., Yeung, B., & Zhao, M. (2008). Perspectives on China's outward foreign direct investment. *Journal of International Business Studies, 39*, 337–350.

North, D. (1990). *Institutions, institutional change and economic performance*. Cambridge University Press.

North, D. C. (1996). Institutions, organizations and market competition. In *Keynote address to the sixth conference of the international Joseph Schumpeter society* (pp. 2–5). Stockholm.

Oliver, C. (1997). Sustainable competitive advantage: Combining institutional and resource based view. *Strategic Management Journal, 18*(9), 697–713.

Papanastassiou, M., & Pearce, R. (1997). Firm strategies and the research intensity of US MNEs 'overseas operations: An analysis of host-country determinants'. In R. Pearce (Ed.), *Global competition and technology: Essays in the creation and application of knowledge by multinationals*. The Macmillan Press Ltd..

Pearce, R., & Papanastassiou, M. (2009). Creative transition and the role of MNE subsidiaries in host-country industrialisation. In M. Papanastassiou & R. Pearce (Eds.), *The strategic development of multinationals: Subsidiaries and innovation*. Palgrave Macmillan.

Peng, M. W., Wang, D. Y., & Jiang, Y. (2008). An institution-based view of international business strategy: A focus on emerging economies. *Journal of International Business Studies, 39*, 920–936.

Perkins, D. H. (2005). China's economic growth in historical and international perspective. *China Economic Quarterly-being, 4*(4), p. 891.

Ramamurti, R. (2001). The obsolescing 'bargaining model'? MNC-host developing country relations revisited. *Journal of International Business Studies, 32*(1), 23–39.

Ramamurti, R. (2003). Can governments make credible promises? Insights from infrastructure projects in emerging economies. *Journal of International Management, 9*(3), 253–269.
Ramamurti, R., & Doh, J. P. (2004). Rethinking foreign infrastructure investment in developing countries. *Journal of World Business., 39*(2004), 151–167.
Rock, M. T., & Bonnett, H. (2004). The comparative politics of corruption: accounting for the East Asian paradox in empirical studies of corruption, growth and investment. *World Development, 32*(6), 999–1017.
Rugman, A. M. (1981). *Inside the multinationals: The economics of internal markets*. Columbia Press.
Rugman, A. M. (2007). Theoretical aspects of multinational enterprises from emerging economies, with particular reference to China.
Sally, R. (1994). Multinational enterprises, political economy and institutional theory: Domestic embeddedness in the context of internationalization. *Review of International Political Economy, 1*(1), 161–192.
Stopford, J. M., Strange, S., Henley, J. S., & Henley, J. S. (1991). *Rival states, rival firms: Competition for world market shares* (No. 18). Cambridge University Press.
Sun, P., Mellahi, K., & Thun, E. (2010). The dynamic value of MNE political embeddedness: The case of the Chinese automobile industry. *Journal of International Business Studies, 41*(7), 1161–1182.
Vernon, R. (1971). *Sovereignty at bay* (pp. 44–59). Pelican.
Wang, C., Hong, J., Kafouros, M., & Wright, M. (2012). Exploring the role of government involvement in outward FDI from emerging economies. *Journal of International Business Studies, 43*, 655–676.
Warner, M., Hong, N. S., & Xu, X. (2004). 'Late development' experience and the evolution of transnational firms in the People's republic of China. *Asia Pacific Business Review, 10*(3–4), 324–345.
Wells, L. T., & Gleason, E. S. (1995, September/October). Is foreign infrastructure investment still risky? *Harvard Business Review*, 44–53.
World Investment Report. (2008). *Transnational corporations and the infrastructure challenge*. UNCTAD.
Xi. (2013). *The statement of President Xi Jinping in his foreign debut tour after visiting three African countries: Tanzania, South Africa and the Republic of Congo.*

8

Conclusion

The research is concerned with Chinese infrastructure MNEs' operations in Africa over recent decades. The study mainly aims to conceptualise Infrastructure Multinational Enterprises (IMNEs) in terms of their nature (capabilities), motivations (MS, ES and KS) and performance, and to examine the determinants of such firms' location decisions. It begins with an attempt to formalise the broad parameters of infrastructure MNEs (derived within established modes of IB analysis) and applies aspects of this to discussion of Chinese FDI in the Construction and ICT sectors in Africa. From the macro-level background of China in Africa it is suggested that Chinese IMNEs that expand into Africa are serving to mediate between the needs and potentials of two differently-based and differently-phased processes of economic development.

This study utilises mixed methods in order to give a comprehensive overview and empirical profile of Chinese IMNEs. Therefore, the main findings provide a prelude in understanding the infrastructure multinationals from a range of different aspects that validates both the value of established theories and their upgraded adjustment to important differentiated contexts. It also covered the perspectives from the partners and related participants of these IMNEs in Africa.

Y. Tang, *The Operations of Chinese Infrastructure Multinationals in Africa*,
https://doi.org/10.1007/978-981-16-2562-6_8

8.1 Background Review of China in Africa

A decade's explosion of commerce between China and African countries reflects a remarkable trend in the global economy. China has been targeting Africa by turning exchange in needed resources for bilateral development into particular commercial interests. Like trade, China's FDI in Africa is growing rapidly with the acceleration of bilateral cooperation agreements, such as setting up FOCAC, establishing CADF for investment. The investments have diversified into different industries which bring a broader strategic context to China's global strategy. Therefore, what is noteworthy about is Chinese outward investment in Africa is not the quantity of investment, but its rate of growth (see Figs. 2.1 and 2.3).

The major developmental complementarities between China and Africa are natural resources and infrastructure. From the supply side, Chinese MNEs accumulate appropriate competences to expand in Africa. Earlier Chinese development has progressed to the point where it possesses the capacity to provide both the appropriate competences for infrastructure provision and also investable capital. This alleviates the existing constraints of African development which are the shortage of capital and the lack of relevant types of knowledge and expertise on infrastructural creation. Meantime, the leverageable advantages create commercial opportunities for Chinese firms. From the demand side, China's high domestic growth rates increasingly emphasise the needs to secure from external sources supplies of energy and primary resources from Africa—a major natural resource exporter, while African countries' long-term needs on enhanced infrastructure provision to unlock their endogenous weakness and accelerate economic development in the region.

8.2 Conceptualisation of IMNEs

From reviewing the general trend and features of China's investment Africa in Chap. 2, the study in Chap. 5 then focuses on one of the most remarkable of these investments, i.e. infrastructure sector. Because of the distinctive features of the investments in infrastructure sectors, it started from conceptualising the term of infrastructure MNEs. As such, the conceptualisation chapter (Chap. 5) developed an analytical framework that addresses the notable phenomenon of infrastructure FDI from China. Here it reviews issues raised by the participation and internationalisation of Chinese MNEs in infrastructure provision and creation in Africa. To find out *how* and *why* infrastructure MNEs have emerged, this framework investigates the nature of the firms and how they work.

Firstly, the study defines the centre of activity—an attractive infrastructure project (IP) outlined by a host government depending on conventional LAs (see Sect. 5.4.1). Secondly, it specified the participants of infrastructure investment by categorising them into the host-country government, and IMNEsp and IMNEsu (see Sect. 5.4.2). This brought a triangular bargaining system that sees IMNEsp initially bargaining with the host-country government (or agency) to define the nature of projects and expected contribution and rewards, and then lowering the transaction cost and securing the project's achievement by IMNEsu bargaining on particular terms of their participation and contracted involvement (see Sect. 5.4.3). This specification of investment participants gave a better idea of defining the operationalised process and the responsibilities on different levels of Chinese IMNEs.

FDI in Infrastructure provision implicates the competence of local governments in designing and contracting IPs and also the capabilities of multinationals which derive from both FSAs and CSAs. The capacities of the Chinese IMNEs are thus seen to reflect their position in the achieved developments of the Chinese economy. Firstly, one facet of this can certainly reflect imperfections in the Chinese capital market, in the form of country-specific advantages that are the access to capital and foreign exchange. Secondly, the Chinese MNEs may indeed possess very particular technologies and practices that are distinctively appropriate to initiation of infrastructure capacities in emergent economies, since their firm-specific advantages (technologies and skills) are learnt in playing a role in infrastructure creation in China. This framework then defined four concepts on the nature of Chinese Infrastructure firms (see Sect. 5.5). *Developmental* country-specific advantages (CSA-D) can specify development roles that emergent MNEs may play (e.g. resource seeking) and provide support (e.g. capital and/or foreign exchange) to enable them to expand overseas. Then *institutional* country-specific advantages (CSA-I) are the policy defining and implementing institutions that can determine these roles and then allocate resources and responsibilities to the potential MNEs. At the micro-level, the abilities of particular firms then become vehicles for these development-supporting aspects of internationalisation. Here *asset* firm-specific advantages (FSA-A) are the unique capacities of a firm that allow it to carry out particular value-adding operations competitively. But in emerging economies these FSA-As are still unlikely to be well established and, therefore, may need the support of CSA-D to achieve an operative basis for internationalisation. Therefore, the relevance of *relationship* firm-specific advantages (FSA-R) is defined in the form of an ability to operate within the network of CSA-I to secure the support from CSA-D. This ability reflects the status of particular firm within the internationalisation of elements of development processes.

8.3 Key Results

8.3.1 Determinants and Motivations of Location Choice

The first key result is produced from traditional theory of location choice and institutional theory in building a discussion on how these IMNEs react to host countries' economic and institutional environments, respectively. The empirical study (Chap. 6) shows that Chinese infrastructure investment, particular in the telecommunication sector, is not only based on political ties and the ODA between China and African governments, but also on the ambition of firms themselves. Seeking new markets and broader processes of internationalisation are more likely to motivate Chinese telecommunication investment in Africa. On the national-level perspective, China's role in infrastructure investment in the region can be understood by looking at the evident economic complementarities (Chap. 2). The intersection points towards the bilateral development that can be mediated by Chinese IMNEs. On the strategic firm-level context, in terms of sectors that can feed positively into early stages of telecommunication industrialisation and development, such enterprise-level competences can be significant elements of potentials of China's African involvement and be applied in their international expansion.

Macroeconomic and institutional environments of African countries have different effects on the two telecommunication companies owing to the differences of their ownership advantage and MNEs' motivations that were generated in China. The two Chinese telecommunication companies are considered as the token of emerging Chinese large enterprises that possess both inherent features of being distinctive Chinese MNEs and but increasingly globalised companies. Location advantage of a host country in this case can be considered as both economic and institutional environments, which it remains necessary to take into account for Chinese infrastructure MNEs. Chinese enterprises have learnt, from their involvement within China's earlier development, types of expertise and competence that can underpin logically their extension into African infrastructure creation (i.e. FSA-A). Here, at the more micro-level analysis, these Chinese firms have tended to support the presence of Chinese capital by carrying out significant infrastructure projects. This becomes the push factors that motivated Chinese ICT firms investing in the countries with comparatively weak environment under the policy-driven forces.

The primary context of the study is the resource-seeking/infrastructure-creation nexus of China's operations in Africa, but the first key findings in this empirical work can realistically be applied to the issues of international business, which are likely inter alia to motivated by firm-level measurement of the sustainability and augmentation of their international expansion. As traditional consideration of MNEs, the macroeconomic environment and institutions generally determine the location decision of the companies, but the results show that influential components are often differentiated by ownership structures. Chapter 6 applies two sets of tests in the case of two Chinese telecommunication MNEs and provides comparison analysis on the both the determinants and motivations of location decision in 40 African countries:

The first set of models (M1-M8) measured the determinants of location choice by dividing the pull- and push factors into two groups

1. Pull factors

For the same macroeconomic environments of host countries, the likelihood of investments are driven differently by the determinants owing to the differentiated ownership structures of companies, i.e. the company with state-ownership appears unlikely to be driven by basic location advantages; conversely, the private one emphasises need for positive location advantages. The national attractiveness influences the investments of both firms differently. Only FDI stock brought a consistently positive consideration to Chinese IMNEs' location choice. Both companies are unlikely to consider investment because the country is an oil exporter. This explains that the telecommunication investments are hardly related to China's natural resources strategy.

2. Push factors

Location choice of firms with state ownership is more likely to be impacted by bilateral governmental cooperation agreements of host country. Historical diplomatic ties have limited influence on the two companies' location choice. But Chinese telecommunication firms are more like to invest in host countries where China has already experienced a large amount of total outward FDI.

3. Institutional factors

Chinese IMNEs generally continue to consider quality of institutions and to invest in better ranked institution system countries, while the Chinese telecommunication MNEs individually had different considerations. ZTE emerges as more likely to locate in countries with higher political stability because its state ownership would have to measure the political instability of each country. Huawei is more likely to choose these low-risk countries of government effectiveness in order to reduce the cost of dealing with the frequent changes of local policies.

The second group of tests (M9-12) demonstrate that both companies are undoubtedly seeking the potentials of particular markets, perhaps as well as efficiency or potential knowledge seeking. Here they are influenced by the viability of their commitment beyond the 'confidence building' step of creation of preliminary infrastructure.

Indeed, neither of the companies is inherently motivated to fill the gap of host country telecommunication infrastructure. 'Filling gap' is one of the strategies to locate in the market (explained in Chap. 7 too). On the contrary, the better the manufacturing potentials in telecommunication the host country has, the more likely is to such the investment.

The result also shows a very implicit fact which is that Chinese telecommunication companies are more likely to invest in countries with higher-level human capital. The higher education level with the rapid population growth rate, provides human capital of host countries which can improve the probability of embedding there. Telecommunication infrastructure provides a high technology basis that can bring potential knowledge seeking through technology adaption and skills transfer.

8.3.2 Mediating Development and Internationalisation Performance

The second key result derives from case-specific studies to seek extension of existing frameworks and understanding of real-world issues. It also generally evaluates the significance of participation of Chinese IMNEs in African development. In Chap. 7, we provided a diagram to illustrate the comprehensive structure of China's IMNEs in Africa from both national and firm level. This group of results are based on the comparisons between two main infrastructure sectors and two different African countries. At the macro-level the economics of the finance/resource interaction and the content of governmental level cooperation explains Chinese commitment to participation in African IP. The participation of Chinese IMNEs in the creation and provision of infrastructure in Africa can be seen to be mediating between the two differently phased processes of economic development. At a more micro-level, Chinese IMNEs are positioning themselves in the implementation of many of the IP. The precise forms of Chinese IMNEs' participation in African IPs can help alleviate the second constraint noted above, by providing access to the most relevant and competent sources of necessary knowledge and expertise, particularly in

Mozambique and in the construction sector. Bilateral national development at demands are realised eventually by firm-level performance. However, specifically from the Chinese side the study discerns several factors innate to the process of development that have proved to have a crucial influence on the involvement in infrastructure creation in Africa. At the more micro-level the processes of securing, and widening the sustainable scope of, economic development in China have led to the generation of forms of knowledge and expertise specific to particular enterprises that can then provide them with the capacity to play distinctive roles in such Chinese international economic expansion. Such enterprise-level competences can be significant elements of China's African involvement, from construction of very basic infrastructure through to creation of ICT networks which laid the foundation of future expansion in the ICT market. According the results from Chap. 6, the ICT firms emerge as more commercially by driven in their African expansion. The field work results prove that the organisational hierarchy within the companies effectively connects their African operators strategies. However, the construction firms are more likely to operate backward linkages to home-country development from their status of SOE. Notably, some private construction firms are seeking the potential market in Mozambique as a result of the gap and opportunities of provision of infrastructure. Infrastructure provision becomes the outcome of localised production from investment in other industries. Construction IMNEs with the initial motivation of infrastructure support for African countries are less active in South Africa.

The key findings are built on the propositions on two levels:

1. National level

Bilateral developmental demands determine the bargaining processes of infrastructure investment. The roles of host governments in infrastructure investment derive from their goals and initial definition of the projects; while the role of home government is how to secure their bargaining power for both tier1 and tier 2 bargaining.

The primary motivations expanding Chinese infrastructure MNEs in African market are due to exogenous sources of home country (1) developmental CSAs (2) institutional CSAs, and then host countries' CSA-I can impact on Chinese IMNEs' location choice and strategies in African markets.

2. Firm-level

The performances are differentiated on sector. Telecommunication firms are more commercially driven in their internationalisation whilst construction firms have stronger backward linkage to home country. To complement the analysis in Chap. 6, Chinese IMNEs' ability to expand on FSA-A in African markets arises from variation of ownership structures. SOE concentrated in construction sector for traditional construction programmes are more likely to build up value chain to domestic industries.

8.4 Areas for Further Study

A most important extension work to this study would be applying this framework to the wider scope of the emergence of MNEs from China and developing countries. At this stage of study, the limited sample size of investigated companies would not comprehensively perform in econometric estimations. But this concept of IMNEs would be effectively to applied to more detailed estimation and investigation of Chinese firms. The origins and nature of the particular competitive advantages now possessed by Chinese IMNEs may also apply to other Chinese firms. This framework can approach an evaluation of implications of firm-level competences to Chinese outward investment.

Additionally, as this framework is based on adoption and adaption of the existing analytical work in other sectors, it would be interesting to generalise the components of capacity of Chinese firms in their internationalisation.

Another improvement can be following up the progress of the case studies. There are many useful points from the interviews which can be analysed in different dimensions. It would help in further understanding of the dynamics of Chinese IMNEs.

Bibliography

Acemoglu, D., & Johnson, S. (2005). Unbinding institutions. *Journal of Political Economy, 113*(5), 949–995.

African Development Bank. (2008). *African Development Report 2007*. Abidjan, Côte d'Ivoire: African Development Bank.

African Statistical Yearbook. (2009). African Development Bank. Retrieved January 15, 2010 from https://www.afdb.org/en/documents/document/african-statistical-yearbook-2009-16546

Aizenman, J. (2003). Volatility, employment and the patterns of FDI in emerging markets. *Journal of Development Economics, 72*(2), 585–601.

Alden, C. (2007). Emerging countries as new ODA players in LDCs: The case of China and Africa. Paris, IDDRI, Idées pour le débat, 1, 2007.

Alden, C., & Davies, M. (2006, Summer/Autumn). A profile of the operations of Chinese Multinationals in Africa. *South African Journal of International Affairs, 13*(1). (original version: Chinese Multinational Corporations in Africa, Offshore Oil, Issue: 3–4, 1–11, Africa Institute of South Africa).

Alden, C., & Alves, A. C. (2009). *China and Africa's natural resources: The challenges and implications for development and governance*. Braamfontein: South African Institute of International Affairs.

Alon, T. M. (2010). Institutional analysis and the determinants of Chinese FDI. *The Multinational Business Review, 18*(3), 1–24.

Y. Tang, *The Operations of Chinese Infrastructure Multinationals in Africa*,
https://doi.org/10.1007/978-981-16-2562-6

Asiedu, E. (2002). On the determinants of foreign direct investment to developing countries: Is Africa different? *World Development, 30*(1), 107–119.
Asiedu, E. (2006). Foreign direct Investment in Africa: The role of government policy, institutions and political instability. *The World Economy, 29*(1), 63–77.
Asiedu, E., & Nandwa, B. (2007). On the impact of foreign aid in education on growth: How relevant is the heterogeneity of aid flows and the heterogeneity of aid recipients? *Review of World Economics, 143*(4), 631–649.
Aykut, A. D., & Ratha, D. (2004). South-south FDI flows: How big are they? *Transnational Corporations, 13*(1), 149–176.
Baker, M., Foley, C., & Wurgler, J. (2009). Multinationals as arbitrageurs: The effect of stock market valuations on foreign direct investment. *Review of Financial Studies, 22*(1), 337–369.
Balaam, D., & Veseth, M. (2008). *Introduction to international political economy* (4th ed.). Pearson Education.
Baltagi, B. H. (2005). *Econometric analysis of panel data—Third edition*. John Wiley & Sons.
Bartels, F. L., Buckley, P., & Mariano, G. (2009). *Multinational enterprises' foreign direct investment location decisions within The Global Factory*. UNIDO. Research and Statistics Branch Working Paper 04/2009. Beijing Declaration on the Establishment of a Comprehensive Strategic Partnership between The Republic of South Africa and The People's Republic of China.
Bartlett, C., & Ghoshal, S. (1986). Tap your subsidiaries for global reach. *Harvard Business Review, 64*, 87–94.
Bartlett, C. A., & Ghoshal, S. (1991). Global strategic management: Impact on the new frontiers of strategy research. *Strategic Management Journal*, 5–16.
Bellak, C., Leibrecht, M., & Damijan, J. P. (2007). *Infrastructure endowment and corporate income taxes as determinants of Foreign Direct Investment in Central- and Eastern European Countries*. LICOS Discussion Paper, No. 193.
Berger, B., & Berkofsky, A. (2008). *Chinese outward investments: Agencies, motives and decision-making*. CASCC Briefing Paper, 172.
Bevan, A., Estrin, S., & Meyer, K. (2004). Foreign investment location and institutional development in transition economics. *International Business Review, 13*, 43–64.
Blonigen, B. A. (2005). A review of the empirical literature on FDI determinants. *Atlantic Economic Journal, 33*, 383–403.
Boddewyn, J., & Brewer, T. (1994). International business political behaviour: New theoretical directions. *Academy of Management Review, 19*(1), 119–143.

Boisot, M. (2004). Notes on the internationalization of Chinese firms. Unpublished paper, Open University of Catalonia, Barcelona, Spain.

Bosshard, P. (2007). China and the West in Africa: Shared interests? *The China Monitor, 19*, 8–10.

Brandenburger, A. M., & Nalebuff, B. J. (1995). *The right game: Use game theory to shape strategy* (Vol. 76, pp. 57–71). Chicago: Harvard Business Review.

Brautigam, D. (2011). *The dragon's gift: The real story of China in Africa*. OUP Oxford.

Brink, C. H. (2004). *Measuring political risk: Risks to foreign investment*. Ashgate Publishing.

Broadman, H. G. (2006). *Africa's silk road: China and India's new economic frontier*. World Bank Publications.

Broadman, H. G. (2007). Chinese-African trade and investment: The vanguard of south-south commerce in the twenty-first century. In R. I. Rotberg (Ed.), *China into Africa—Trade, aid and influence*. Brookings Institution Press.

Brunetti, A., & Weder, B. (1998). *Investment and institutional uncertainty: A comparative study of different uncertainty measures. Weltwirtschaftliches Archiv, 134*(3), 513–533.

Buck, T. (2011). Case selection informed by theory. In R. Piekkari & C. Welch (Eds.), *Rethinking the case study in international business and management research* (pp. 192–209). Edward Elgar.

Buckley, J. P. (1983). New theories of international business: Some unresolved issues. In M. Casson (Ed.), *The growth of international business* (pp. 34–50). Allen & Unwin.

Buckley, J. P., & Casson, M. C. (1976). *The future of multinational enterprises*. Macmillan.

Buckley, J. P., Voss, H., Cross, A., & Clegg, L. J. (2011). The emergence of Chinese firms as multinationals: The influence of the home institutional environment. In R. Pearce (Ed.), *China and the multinationals: International business and the entry of China into the global economy*. Edward Elgar.

Buckley, P., Clegg, J., Cross, A., Liu, X., Voss, H., & Zheng, P. (2007). The determinants of Chinese outward foreign direct investment. *Journal of International Business Studies, 38*(4), 499–518.

Buckley, P. J., Clegg, J. L., Cross, A. R., Voss, H., Rhodes, M., & Zheng, P. (2008). Explaining China's outward FDI: An institutional perspective. *The Rise of Transnational Corporations from Emerging Markets: Threat or Opportunity*, 107–157.

Buckley, P. J. (2009). The impact of the global factory on economic development. *Journal of World Business, 44*, 131–143.
Buckley, P. J., & Casson, M. C. (2009). The internalisation theory of the multinational enterprise: A review of the progress of a research agenda after 30 years. *Journal of International Business Studies, 40*, 1563–1580.
Bulter, K. C., & Joaquin, D. C. (1998). A note on political risk and return on foreign direct investment. *Journal of International Business Studies, 29*(3), 599–607.
Burke, C. (2007). China's entry into construction Industries in Africa: Tanzania and Zambia as case studies. *China Report, 43*(3), 323–336.
Busse, M., & Hefeker, C. (2007). Political risk, institutions and foreign direct investment. *European Journal of Political Economy, 23*(2), 397–415.
Cantwell, J. (1989). *Technological innovation and multinational corporations.* B. Blackwell.
Cantwell, J., Dunning, J. H., & Lundan, S. M. (2010). An evolutionary approach to understanding international business activity: The co-evolution of MNEs and the institutional environment. *Journal of International Business Studies, 41*(4), 567–586.
Cappellari, L., & Jenkins, S. P. (2003). Multivariate probity regression using simulated maximum likelihood. *The Stata Journal, 3*(3), 278–294.
Casson, M., & Pearce, R. (1987). Multinational enterprises in LDCs. In N. Gemmell (Ed.), *Surveys in development economics*. Blackwell.
Caves, R. (1971). The industrial economics of foreign investment. *Economica, 38*(149), 1–27.
Caves, R. E. (1982). *Multinational enterprises and economic analysis*. Cambridge University Press.
Caves, R. E. (1996). *Multinational enterprises and economic analysis* (2nd ed.). Cambridge University Press.
Centre for Chinese Studies. (2006). *China's interest and activity in Africa's construction and infrastructure sectors*. Stellenbosch University.
Chan, S. (2006). Scramble for China. Prospect 126, http://www.prospect-magazine.co.uk/article_details.php?id=7712
Chen, A. Y. (2009). China's role in infrastructure development in Botswana. China in Africa Project, Occasional Paper No. 44, September.
Chen, C., Goldenstein, A., Chiu, P., & Orr, R. (2009). An Empirical Analysis of Chinese construction firms' entry into Africa. *International Symposium on Advancement of Construction Management and Real estate*, 8–13 August, Publish, Sydney.

Chen, C., Goldenstein, A., & Orr, R. (2009). Local operation of Chinese construction firms in Africa. *The International Journal of Construction Management, 9*, 75–89.

Chen, C., & Orr, R. J. (2009). Chinese contractors in Africa: Home government support, coordination mechanisms, and market entry strategies. *Journal of Construction Engineering and Management, ASCE/Nov, 2009*, 1201–1210.

Cheng, S., & Liang, G. (2011). Social responsibility of Chinese investment in Africa: What does it mean for EU-China Cooperation on development policy towards Africa? *Trade Negotiations Insights, 10*(3), Access from International Centre for Trade and Sustainable Development (ICTSD).

Cheng, S., & Stough, R. R. (2007, April). The pattern and magnitude of China's outward FDI in Asia. *ICRIER Project on Intra-Asian FDI Flows in New Delhi*, 25–26.

Cheung, Y.-W., & Qian, X. (2009). Empirics of China's outward direct investment. *Pacific Economic Review, 14*(3), 312–341.

Cheung, Y. W., De Haan, J., Qian, X., & Yu, S. (2012). China's outward direct investment in Africa. *Review of International Economics, 20*(2), 201–220.

Chichava, S. (2008). *Mozambique and China: From politics to business?* IESE Instituto de Estudos Sociaies e Economicos.

Child, J., & Rodrigues, S. B. (2005). The internationalization of Chinese firms: A case for theoretical extension? *Management and Organization Review, 1*(3), 381–410.

Child, J., & Tsai, T. (2005). The dynamic between firms' environmental strategies and institutional constraints in emerging economies: Evidence from China and Taiwan. *Journal of Management Studies, 42*(1), 0022–2380.

China in Africa: A strategic overview. (2009). Prepared by: Executive Research Associates (Pty) Ltd.

China Mobile Mulls Investments in Asia, Africa to Fuel Growth. (n.d.).

China-Africa Development Fund. (n.d.). Accessed January 15, 2010, from http://www.cadfund.com

China-Africa Trade and Economic Relationship Annual Report. (2010).

Chinese Government's Official Web Portal. (2010). *Full text: China-Africa Economic and Trade Cooperation*. www.english.gov.cn/official/2010-12/23/content_1771603_4.htm

Clark, T., & Pugh, D. S. (2001). Foreign country priorities in the internationalization process: A measure and an exploratory test on British firms. *International Business Review, 10*(3), 285–303.

CNN Fortune. (n.d.). http://money.cnn.com/magazines/fortune/global500/2011/countries/China.html

Cohn, T. (2005). *Global political economy: Theory and practice* (3rd ed.). Pearson Education, Inc.

Corkin, L., Burke, C., & Davies, M. (2008). *China's role in the development of Africa's infrastructure*. SAIS Working papers in African Studies, 04–08.

Coyne, I. T. (1997). Sampling in qualitative research. Purposeful and theoretical sampling; Merging or clear boundaries? *Journal of Advanced Nursing, 26*, 623–630.

Cross, A., Buckley, P., Clegg, J., Voss, H., Rhodes, M., Zheng, P., & Liu, X. (2007). An econometric investigation of Chinese outward direct investment. In J. H. Dunning & T. M. Lin (Eds.), *Multinational enterprises and emerging challenge of the 21st century* (pp. 55–86). Edward Elgar.

Cuervo-Cazurra, A. (2017). *State-owned multinationals: Governments in global business*. Palgrave Macmillan.

Cui, L., & Jiang, F. (2009). FDI entry mode choice of Chinese firms: A strategic behavior perspective. *Journal of World Business, 44*, 434–444.

Cui, L., & Jiang, F. (2012). State ownership effect on firms' FDI ownership decisions under institutional pressure: A study of Chinese outward-investing firms. *Journal of International Business Studies, 43*(3), 264–284.

Davies, M., Edinger, H., Tay, N., & Naidu, S. (2008). *How China delivers development assistance to Africa*. Centre for Chinese Studies, University of Stellenbosch.

Deng, P. (2004, May–June). Outward investment by Chinese MNCs: Motivations and implications. *Business Horizons, 47*(3), 8–16.

Deng, P. (2007). Investing for strategic resources and its rationale: The case of outward FDI from Chinese companies. *Business Horizons, 50*, 71–81.

Deng, P. (2009). Why do Chinese firms tend to acquire strategic assets in international expansion? *Journal of World Business, 44*, 74–84.

Desta, A. (2009). China's south-south cooperative investments and co-development modalities in Africa. *International Journal of Business Research, 9*(6), 19–33.

DiMaggio, P. J., & Powell, W. W. (1983). The Iron cage revisited: Institutional isomorphism and collective rationality in organizational fields. *American Sociological Review, 48*(2), 147–160.

Dimitropoulou, D., Pearce, R., & Papanastassiou, M. (2009). Strategic heterogeneity in MNEs and the integrating European economy. In M. Papanastassiou

& R. Pearce (Eds.), *The strategic development of multinationals: Subsidiaries and innovation*. Palgrave Macmillan.

Doh, J., Rodrigues, S., Saka-Helmhout, A., & Makhija, M. (2017). International business responses to institutional voids. *Journal of International Business Studies, 48*(3), 293–307.

Doh, J. P., & Ramamurti, R. (2003). Reassessing risk in developing country infrastructure. *Long Range Planning, 36*, 337–353.

Downs, E. S. (2007). The fact and fiction of Sino-African energy relations. *China Security, 3*(3), 42–68.

Doz, Y., & Prahalad, S. (1980, March–April). How MNCs cope with host government intervention. Harvard Business Review, 149–157.

Duanmu, J. (2012). Firm heterogeneity and location choice of Chinese multinational enterprises. *Journal of World Business, 47*, 64–72.

Duanmu, J., & Guney, Y. (2009). A panel data analysis of locational determinants of Chinese and Indian outward foreign direct investment. Journal of Asia Business Studies, 3(2), 1–15. ISSN 1558-7894.

Dunning, J. H. (1977). Trade, location of economic activity and the MNE: A search for an eclectic approach. In B. Ohlin, P. Hesselborn, & P. M. Wijkman (Eds.), *The international allocation of economic activity*. Macmillan.

Dunning, J. H. (1980, Spring/Summer). Toward an eclectic theory of international production: Some empirical tests. Journal of International Business Studies, 11(1), 9–31.

Dunning, J. H. (1981). Explaining the international direct investment position of countries: Towards a dynamic or developmental approach. *Weltwirtschaftliches Archiv, 117*(1), 30–64.

Dunning, J. H. (1988a). The theory of international production. *The International Trade Journal, 3*, 21–66.

Dunning, J. H. (1988b). The eclectic paradigm of international production: A restatement and some possible extension. *Journal of International Business Studies, 19*(1), 1–31.

Dunning, J. H. (1991). Governments and multinational enterprises: from confrontation to co-operation? *Millennium, 20*(2), 225–244.

Dunning, J. H. (1993). Internationalizing Porter's diamond. *MIR: Management International Review*, 7–15.

Dunning, J. H. (1995). *Multinational enterprises and the global economy*. Addison-Wesley Publishing Company.

Dunning, J. H. (1998). Location and the multinational enterprise: A neglected factor. *Journal of International Business Studies, 29*(1), 45–66.

Dunning, J. H. (2000). The eclectic paradigm as an envelope for economic and business theories of MNE activities. *International Business Review, 9*, 163–190.

Dunning, J. H. (2002). *Global capitalism, FDI and competitiveness* (Vol. 2). Edward Elgar Publishing.

Dunning, J. H. (2001). The eclectic (OLI) paradigm of international production: Past, present and future. *International Journal of the Economics of Business, 8*(2), 173–190.

Dunning, J. H. (2003). Some antecedents of internalization theory. *Journal of International Business Studies, 34*(2), 108–115.

Dunning, J. H. (2006a). Comment on dragon multinationals: New players in 21st century globalisation. *Asia Pacific Journal of Management, 25*(2), 139–141.

Dunning, J. H., & Lundan, S. (2009). *Multinational enterprises and the global economy* (2nd ed.). Edward Elgar.

Dunning, J. H., & Lundan, S. M. (2008). Institutions and the OLI paradigm of the multinational enterprise. *Asia Pacific Journal of Management, 25*, 573–593.

Dunning, J. H., & Pitelis, C. N. (2009). The political economy of globalization—Revisiting Stephen Hymer 50 Years On. *Munich Personal RePEc Archive*, ID. 23184.

Dunning, J. H., & Rugman, A. M. (1985). The influence of Hymer's dissertation on the theory of foreign direct investment. *American Economic Review: Papers and Proceedings, 75*(2), 228–260.

Dupasquier, C., & Osakwe, P. N. (2005). *Foreign direct investment in Africa: Performance, challenges and responsibilities*. ATPC Work in Progress No. 21, September.

Economic Development in Africa Report. (2010). *South-South Cooperation: Africa and the New Forms of Development Partnership*.

Eden, L., & Dai, L. (2010). Rethinking the O in Dunning's OLI/eclectic paradigm. *Multinational Business Review, 18*(2), 13–34.

Eden, L., Lenway, S., & Schuler, D. A. (2004). *From the obsolescing bargain to the political bargaining model*. Bush School Working Paper 403.

Eden, L., & Miller, S. (2004). Distance matters: Liability of foreignness, institutional distance and ownership strategy, forthcoming. In M. A. Hitt & J. L. C. Cheng (Eds.), *The evolving theory of the multinational firm: Advances in international management* (Vol. 16). Elsevier.

Eden, L., & Molot, M. A. (2002). Insiders, outsiders and host country bargains. *Journal of International Management, 8*, 359–388.

eLearning Africa. (2011). 6th international conference on ICT for development, education and training the key networking event for developing eLearning capacities in Africa, Available from https://www.elearning-africa.com/conference/ressources/pdfs/report/postreport_eLA2011_small.pdf

Eisenhardt, K. M., & Graebner, M. E. (2007). Theory building from cases: Opportunities and challenges. *Academy of Management Journal, 50*(1), 25–32.

Estache, A. (2004). *PPI partnerships vs. PPI divorces in LDCs*. World Bank and ECARES.

Estache, A. (2006). *Africa's infrastructure: Challenges and opportunities*. World Bank and ECARES.

Evans, C. L. (2007). National Border Effects: Location, not nationality, matters. *Review of International Economics, 15*(2), 347–369.

Fagre, N., & Wells, L. T. (1982). Bargaining power of multinationals and host governments. *Journal of International Business Studies, 13*, 9–23.

Fan, D., Nyland, C., & Zhu, C. J. (2010). Strategic implications of global integration and local responsiveness for Chinese multinationals: An area for future study. *Management Research News, 32*(12), 922–940.

Fenwick, M., Edwards, R., & Buckley, P. J. (2003). Is cultural similarity misleading? The experience of Australian manufacturers in Britain. *International Business Review, 12*(3), 297–309.

Ferrari, F., & Rolfini, R. (2008, May). Investing in a dangerous world: A new political risk index. SACE Group Working Paper No. 06.

FIAS/MIGA. (2006). *Firm survey—Chinese outward foreign direct investment*. Presented by Battat, J. http://rru.worldbank.org/Documents/PSDForum/2006/joe_battat.pdf

Fletcher, M., & Plakoyiannaki, E. (2011). Case selection in international business: Key issues and common misconceptions. In R. Marschan-Pierkkari & C. Welch (Eds.), *Rethinking the case study in international business and management research*. Edward Elgar.

Flowers, E. B. (1976). Oligopolistic reactions in European and Canadian direct investment in the United States. *Journal of International Business Studies, 7*(2), 43–55.

Flyvbjerg, B., Holm, M. S., & Buhl, S. (2002). Underestimating costs in public works projects: Error or lie? *Journal of the American Planning Association, 68*(3), 279–295.

Flyvbjerg, B., Skamris Holm, M. K., & Buhl, S. L. (2003). How common and how large are cost overruns in transport infrastructure projects? *Transport Reviews, 23*(1), 71–88.

FOCAC. (2018). http://www.focac.org/

Foster, V., & Briceno-Garmendia, C. (2010). *Africa's infrastructure—A time for transformation*. The International Bank for Reconstruction and Development, The World Bank.

Foster, V., Butterfield, W., Chen, C., & Pushak, N. (2008). *Building bridges: China's growing role as infrastructure financier in Africa*. Public Private Infrastructure Advisory Facility, Trends and Policy Options, No. 5. World Bank, Washington.

Franco, C., Rentocchini, F., & Vittucci Marzetti, G. (2008). *Why do firms invest abroad? An analysis of the motives underlying foreign direct investments*.

Gao, L., Liu, X., & Lioliu, E. (2015). A double-edged sword: The impact of institutions and political relations on the international market expansion of Chinese state-owned enterprises. *Journal of Chinese Economic and Business Studies, 13*(2), 105–125.

Gelb, S. (2005). *South-South investment: The case of Africa*. Africa in the World Economy—The National, Regional and International Challenges Fondad. www.fondad.org

Gelb, S. (2010). *Foreign direct investment links between South Africa & China*. The Edge Institute.

Ghauri, P. (2004). Designing and conducting case studies in international business research. In R. Piekkari & C. Welch (Eds.), *Handbook of qualitative research methods for international business*. Edward Elgar.

Ghauri, P., & Holstius, K. (1996). The role of matching in the foreign market entry process in the Baltic States. *European Journal of Marketing, 30*, 75–88.

Gholami, R., Lee, S., & Heshmati, A. (2005). The Causal relationship between ICT and FDI. Research Paper No. 205/26. UNU-Wider, Helshinki.

Ghoshal, S., & Nohria, N. (1989). Internal differentiation within multinational corporations. *Strategic Management Journal, 10*(4), 323–337.

Gill, B., Huang, C., & Morrison, J. S. (2007). Assessing China's growing influence in Africa. *China Security, 3*(3), 3–21.

Gill, B., & Reilly, J. (2007, Summer). The tenuous hold of China Inc. in Africa. *The Washington Quarterly*, pp. 37–52.

Goldstein, A., Pinaud, N., Reisen, H., & Chen, X. (2006). *The rise of China and India: What's in it for Africa?* OECD Development Centre.

Gould, D. M., & Ruffin, R. J. (1993). What determines economic growth. *Economic Review, 2*, 25–40.

Graham, E. M. (1978). Transatlantic investment by multinational firms: A rivalistic phenomenon? *Journal of Post Keynesian Economics, 1*(1), 82–99.

Grosse, R., & Behrman, J. N. (1992). Theory in international business. *Transnational Corporations, 1*(1), 93–126.

Greene, W. (2004). Convenient estimators for the panel Probit model: Further results. *Empirical Economics, 29*(1), 21–47.

Gu, J. (2009). China's private Enterprises in Africa and the implications for African development. *European Journal of Development Research Special Issue, 24*(1), 570–587.

Gu, J., Humphrey, J., & Messner, D. (2008). Global governance and developing countries: The implications of the rise of China. *Journal of World Development, 36*(2), 274–292.

Gugler, P., & Boie, B. (2008). *The Chinese international investments: Corporate and government strategies. NCCR Trade regulation.* Working paper No. 2008/25.

Guillén, M., & Garcia-Canal, E. (2012). *Emerging markets rule: Growth strategies of the new global giants.* McGrawHill Education.

He, W. (2007). The balancing act of China's Africa policy. *China Security, 3*(3), 23–41.

He, W., & Lyles, M. A. (2008). China's outward foreign direct investment. *Business Horizons, 51*, 485–491.

Hennart, J. F., & Park, Y. R. (1994). Location, governance, and strategic determinants of Japanese manufacturing investment in the United States. *Strategic Management Journal, 15*(6), 419–436.

Henisz, W. J. (1998). The institutional environment for international investment: Safeguarding against state sector opportunism and opportunistic use of the state. University of California.

Henisz, W. J. (2000). The institutional environment for multinational investment. *Journal of Law, Economics and Organisation, 16*(2), 224–364.

Henisz, W. J. (2003). The power of the Buckley and Casson thesis: The ability to manage institutional idiosyncrasies. *Journal of International Business Studies, 34*, 173–184.

Henisz, W., & Swaminathan, A. (2008). Institutions and international business.

Henisz, W. J., & Williamson, O. E. (1999). Comparative economic organization- within and between countries. *Business and Politics, 1*, 261–277.

Hennart, J. F. (1982). *A theory of multinational enterprise.* University of Michigan Press.

Hennart, J. F. (2009). Down with MNE-centric theories! Market entry and expansion as the bundling of MNE and local assets. *Journal of International Business Studies, 40*, 1432–1454.

Herzer, D. (2008). The long-run relationship between outward FDI and domestic output: Evidence from panel data. *Economics Letters, 100*(1), 146–149.

Hillebrand, G. G., Miyamoto, K., Schnell, B., Ichihashi, M., Shinkura, R., & Akiba, S. (2001). Quantitative evaluation of skin condition in an epidemiological survey of females living in northern versus southern Japan. *Journal of Dermatological Science, 27*, 42–52.

Hodel, M. (2008, Springer). The scramble for energy: China's oil investment in Africa. Edited by C. Pacheco. *The Journal of International Policy Solution,* Vol. 9.

Hong, E., & Sun, L. (2006). Dynamics of internationalization and outward investment: Chinese corporations' strategies. *The China Quarterly, 187*, 610–634.

Hsiao, C. (2003). *Analysis of panel data* (2nd ed.). Cambridge University Press.

Huawei. (2009). *Huawei establish SA's first telecoms Research & Development (R&D) Facility*, Johannesburg. Retrieved September 30, 2009.

Huawei. (2010). *Africa fact sheet*. www.huawei.com/ucmf/groups/public/documents/…/hw_090307.pdf

Huawei. (2012). *Annual report*. Huawei Investment & Holding, Ltd.

'Huawei in Africa'. (n.d.). Retrieved June 19, 2010, from http://www.huawei.com/africa/en/catalog.do?id=521

Hung, S.-C., & Tseng, Y.-C. (2017, Springer). Extending the LLL framework through an institution based view: Acer as a dragon multinational. Asia Pacific Journal of Management, 34(4), 799–821.

Hurmerinta, L., & Nummela, N. (2011). Mixed-method case studies in international business research. In R. Piekkari & C. Welch (Eds.), *Rethinking the case study in international business and management research* (pp. 210–225). Edward Elgar.

Hurst, C. (2006). *China's oil rush in Africa*. IAGS Energy Security.

Hymer, S. H. (1970). The efficiency (contradictions) of multinational corporations. *American Economic Review. Papers and Proceedings of the Eighty-second Annual Meeting of the American Economic Association, 60*(2), 441–448.

Hymer, S. H. (1976 [1960]). The international operations of national firms, a study of direct foreign investment (Doctoral dissertation, Massachusetts Institute of Technology, only published in 1976).

ICRG. (2012). *International country risk guide methodology*. Accessed March 12, 2012, from https://www.prsgroup.com/wp-content/uploads/2012/11/icrgmethodology.pdf

ICT in Africa: Boosting Economic Growth and Poverty Reduction, Tokyo: 10th Meeting of the Africa Partnership Forum, April 7–8, 2008.

Jiang, K. W. (2005). Globalization strategies of Chinese companies: A study of China's largest telecommunications equipment companies.
Johanson, J., & Vahlne, J. E. (1977). The internationalization process of the firm: A model of knowledge development and increasing foreign market commitments. *Journal of International Business Studies, 29*(1), 45–66.
Johanson, J., & Vahlne, J. E. (1990). The mechanism of internationalization. *International Marketing Review, 7*(4), 11–24.
Johanson, J., & Wiedersheim-Paul, F. (1975). The internationalization of the firm—Four Swedish cases. *Journal of Management Studies, 12*(3), 305–322.
Kang, Y., & Jiang, F. (2012). FDI location choice of Chinese multinationals in east and Southeast Asia: Traditional economic factors and institutional perspective. *Journal of World Business, 47*, 45–53.
Kaplinsky, R., McCormick, D., & Morris, M. (2006). *The Impact of China in Sub-Saharan Africa*. IDS Working Paper 291.
Kaplinsky, R., & Morris, M. (2009). Chinese FDI in sub Saharan Africa: Engaging with large dragons. *European Journal of Development Research, 24*(1). https://doi.org/10.1057/ejdr.2009.24
Kaufnman, D., Kraay, A., & Zoido-Lobaton, P. (1999). *Governance matters*. Policy Research Working Paper, Vol. 2196. The World Bank, Washington, DC.
Khadaroo, J., & Seetanah, B. (2006). *Transport infrastructure and FDI: Lessons from Sub-Saharan African economies*.
Khanna, T., & Palepu, K. G. (2010). *Winning in emerging markets: A road map for strategy and execution*. Harvard Business Press.
Kinoshita, Y., & Campos, N. F. (2006, February). *A re-examination of determinants of foreign direct investment in transition economies*. IMF.
Kindleberger, C. P. (1969). *American business abroad: six lectures on direct investment*. New Haven: Yale University Press.
Knickerbocker, F. T. (1973). Oligopolistic reaction and multinational enterprise. *The International Executive, 15*(2), 7–9.
Kobrin, S. J. (1984). Expropriation as an attempt to control foreign firms in LDCs: Trends from 1960 to 1979. *International Studies Quarterly, 28*(3), 329–348.
Kobrin, S. (1987). Testing the bargaining hypothesis in the manufacturing sector in developing countries. *International Organization, 41*, 609–638.
Kolstad, I., & Wiig, A. (2009). Is transparency the key to reducing corruption in resource-rich countries? *World Development, 37*(3), 521–532.
Kolstad, I., & Wiig, A. (2012). What determines Chinese outward FDI? *Journal of World Business, 47*(1), 26–34.
Kragelund, P. (2009). Knocking on a wide open door: Chinese investments in Africa. *Review of African Political Economy, 36*(122), 479–497.

Kragelund, P. (2010). *The potential role of non-traditional donors' aid in Africa.* Issue Paper No. 11. ICTSD Programme on Competitiveness and Sustainable Development.

Kravis, I. B., & Lipsey, R. E. (1982). The location of overseas production for exports by U.S. multinational firms. *Journal of International Economics, 12*, 201–223.

Kroeber, A. (2005). China's century is still a long march away. *Financial Times*, 22.

Kwok, C. C. Y., & Tadesse, S. (2006). The MNC as an agent of change for host-country institutions: FDI and corruption. *Journal of International Business Studies, 37*(6), 767–785. Three Lenses on the Multinational Enterprise: Politics, Corruption and Corporate Social Responsibility.

Larçon, J. P., & Barré, G. (2009). Technology-based competition and Chinese multinationals. *Chinese Multinationals*, 127–149.

Laschinger, K. (2006, May 4). In the red: South Africa will have to smarten up or zip it. *Finweek*, 62.

Lattemann, C., & Alon, I. (2015). The rise of Chinese multinationals: A strategic threat or an economic opportunity? *Georgetown Journal of International Affairs, 16*(1), 172–179.

Lenway, S. A., & Murtha, T. P. (1994). The state as strategist in international business research. *Journal of International Business Studies, 25*(3), 513–535.

Li, J., Newenham-Kahindi, A. M., Shapiro, D. M., & Chen, V. Z. (2013). The two-tier bargaining model revisited: Theory and evidence from China's natural resource investments in Africa. *Global Strategy Journal, 3*(4), 300–321, forthcoming.

Li, Q., & Resnick, A. (2003). Reversal of fortunes: Democratic institutions and foreign direct investment inflows to developing countries. *International Organization, 57*(1), 175–211.

Lin, X., & Farrell, C. (2013). The internationalization strategies of Chinese state and private sector enterprises in Africa. *Journal of African Business, 14*(2), 85–95.

Lipsey and Crystal. (1995). *An introduction to positive economics, 8th edition.* Oxford University Press.

Lipsey, R., & Sjoholm, F. (2005). The impact of inward FDI on host countries: Why such different answers? *Does foreign direct investment promote development?*

Lorenzo, M. D. (2008). China and Africa: A new scramble? In A. Waldron (Ed.), *China in Africa.* The Jamestown Foundation.

Lundan, S. M. (2010). *What are ownership advantages?* Multinational Business Review.

Luo, Y., & Tung, R. L. (2007). International expansion of emerging market enterprises: A springboard perspective. *Journal of International Business Studies, 38*(4), 481–498.

Luo, Y., Xue, Q., & Han, B. (2010). How emerging market governments promote outward FDI: Experience from China. *Journal of World Business, 45*, 68–79.

MacDougall, G. D. A. (1960). The benefits and costs of private investment from abroad: A theoretical approach 1. *Bulletin of the Oxford University Institute of Economics & Statistics, 22*(3), 189–211.

Manolopoulos, D., Papanastassiou, M., & Pearce, R. (2007). Knowledge-related competitiveness and the roles of multinationals R&D in a peripheral European economy: Survey analysis of Greece. *Management International Review, l47*(5), 661–681.

Manolopoulos, D., Papanastassiou, M., & Pearce, R. (2009). Technology sourcing in multinational enterprises and the roles of subsidiaries: An empirical investigation. In *The strategic development of multinationals* (pp. 57–77). Palgrave Macmillan: London.

Mathews, J. A. (2002). Competitive advantages of the latecomer firm: A resource-based account of industrial catch-up strategies. *Asia Pacific Journal of Management, 19*, 467–488.

Mathews, J. A. (2006a). Catch-up strategies and the latecomer effect in industrial development. *New Political Economy, 11*(3), 313–335.

Mathews, J. A. (2006b). Dragon multinationals: New player in 21st century globalisation. *Asia Pacific Journal of Management, 23*, 5–27.

Mathews, J. A. (2017). Dragon multinationals powered by linkage, leverage and learning: A review and development. *Asia Pacific Journal of Management, 34*(4), 769–775.

Mathews, J. A. (2006). Dragon multinationals: New player in 21st century globalisation. *Asia Pacific Journal of Management, 23*, 5–27.

Menea, J., & Pearce, R. (2004). *Multinationals and transition.* Palgrave Macmillan.

Meniago, C., & Asongu, S. A. (2019). *Harnessing FDI spillovers on TFP and economic growth in Sub-Saharan Africa: The relevance of value chains across economic sectors.* African Governance and Development Institute Working Paper.

Meyer, K. E. (2018). Catch-up and leapfrogging: Emerging economy multinational enterprises on the global stage. *International Journal of the Economics of Business, 25*(1), 19–30.

Meyer, K., Estrin, S., Bhaumik, S. K., & Peng, M. W. (2009). Institutions, resources, and entry strategies in emerging economies. *Strategic Management Journal, 30*, 61–80.

Milhaupt, C. J., & Zheng, W. (2014). Beyond ownership: State capitalism and the Chinese firm. *Georgetown Law Journal, 103*, p. 665.

MOFCOM. (2008). *Statistical bulletin of China's outward foreign direct investment.*

MOFCOM. (2018). *Statistical Bulletin of Chinese Outward Foreign Direct Investment.* Available from (mofcom.gov.cn) http://hzs.mofcom.gov.cn/article/date/201512/20151201223578.shtml

MOFCOM. (2019). *2019 Statistical Bulletin of Chinese Outward Foreign Direct Investment.* Available on www.fdi.gov.cn

Morck, R., Yeung, B., & Zhao, M. (2008). Perspectives on China's outward foreign direct investment. *Journal of International Business Studies, 39*, 337–350.

Moyo, D. (2012). *Winner take all: China's race for resources and what it means for world.* Basic Books.

Murtha, T. P., & Lenway, S. A. (1994). Country capabilities and the strategic state: How national political institutions affect multinational corporations' strategies. *Strategic Management Journal, 15*, 113–130.

Mwanawina, I. (2008). *China-Africa economic relations: The case of Zambia.* A Study Commissioned by the African Economic Research Consortium.

Nachum, L., & Wymbs, C. (2002). Firm-specific attributes and MNE location choices: Financial and professional service FDI to New York and London.

Naidu, S., & Mbazima, D. (2008). China–African relations: A new impulse in a changing continental landscape Futures. *ScienceDirect, 40*, 748–761. Elsevier Ltd.

Nel, P. (2003). Income inequality, economic growth, and political instability in sub-Saharan Africa. *The Journal of Modern African Studies, 41*(4), 611–639.

Niosi, J. (1999). *The internationalization of industrial R&D: From technology transfer to the learning organization.* Research Policy.

Nolan, P. (2012). Is China buying the world? *Challenge, 55*(2), 108–118.

Nolan, P., & Zhang, J. (2002). The challenge of globalization for large Chinese firms. *World Development, 30*(12), 2089–2107.

North, D. (1990). *Institutions, institutional change and economic performance.* Cambridge University Press.

North, D. C. (1996). Institutions, organizations and market competition. In *Keynote address to the sixth conference of the international Joseph Schumpeter society* (pp. 2–5). Stockholm.

OECD. (2006). Africa and China, Atlas on Regional Integration in West Africa economy series.

OECD. (2008). China's FDI Statistics, *OECD Investment Policy Review* 'Africa 2006' Huawei in Africa. http://market.huawei.com/hwgg/focac/local.html

OECD Investment Policy Review: China. (2008). Chapter 2: China's FDI Statistics. ISBN 978–92–64-05366-3.

Okafor, G., Piesse, J., & Webster, A. (2017). FDI determinants in least recipient regions: The case of sub-Saharan Africa and MENA. *African Development Review, 29*(4), 589–600.

Oliver, C. (1997). Sustainable competitive advantage: Combining institutional and resource based view. *Strategic Management Journal, 18*(9), 697–713.

Orr, R. J., & Kennedy, J. R. (2008). Highlights of recent trends in global infrastructure: New players and revised game rules. *Transnational Corporations, 17*(1), 99–133.

Papanastassiou, M., & Pearce, R. (1997). Firm strategies and the research intensity of US MNEs 'overseas operations: An analysis of host-country determinants'. In R. Pearce (Ed.), *Global competition and technology: Essays in the creation and application of knowledge by multinationals*. The Macmillan Press Ltd..

Pearce, R. (1997). Global interdependence, MNE strategy and technology. In *Global competition and technology* (pp. 3–12). Palgrave Macmillan, London.

Pearce, R. (2001). Multinationals and industrialisation: The bases of 'inward investment' policy. *International Journal of the Economics of Business, 8*(1), 51–73.

Pearce, R. (2006a). Globalisation and development: An international business strategy approach. *Transactional Corporations, 15*(1), 39–74.

Pearce, R. (2006b). Technology strategy in the competitive evolution of multinationals. *European International Business Academy conference.*

Pearce, R. D. (1999). Decentralised R&D and strategic competitiveness: Globalised approaches to generation and use of technology in multinational enterprises (MNEs). *Research Policy, 28*(2–3), 157–178.

Pearce, R., & Papanastassiou, M. (2006). To 'almost see the world': Hierarchy and strategy in Hymer's view of the multinational. *International Business Review, 15*(2), 151–165.

Pearce, R., & Papanastassiou, M. (2009). Creative transition and the role of MNE subsidiaries in host-country industrialisation. In M. Papanastassiou &

R. Pearce (Eds.), *The strategic development of multinationals: Subsidiaries and innovation*. Palgrave Macmillan.

Perkins, D. H. (2005). China's economic growth in historical and international perspective. *China Economic Quarterly-being, 4*(4), p. 891.

Piekkari, R. (2009). International management. *The Handbook of Business Discourse*, 269–278.

Piekkari, R., Welch, C., & Paavilainen, E. (2009). The case study as disciplinary convention: Evidence from international business journals. *Organizational Research Methods, 12*, 567–589.

Peng, M., & Khoury, T. A. (2009). Unbundling the institution based view of international business strategy. In A. Rugman (Ed.), *The Oxford handbook of international business* (pp. 256–268, 2nd ed.). New York: Oxford University Press.

Peng, M. W. (2003). Institutional transitions and strategic choice. *The Academy of Management Review, 28*(2), 275–296.

Peng, M. W. (2006). *Global strategy*. Thomason South-Western.

Peng, M. W., Lee, S., & Wang, D. Y. L. (2005). What determines the scope of the firm over time? A focus on institutional relatedness. *Academy of Management Review, 30*(3), 622–633.

Peng, M. W., Wang, D. Y., & Jiang, Y. (2008). An institution-based view of international business strategy: A focus on emerging economies. *Journal of International Business Studies, 39*, 920–936.

Pigato, M. A. (2001). *The Foreign Direct Investment Environment in Africa*. Africa Region Working Paper Series No. 15.

Pitelis, C. N. (2002). *Stephen Hymer, the multinational firm and 'multinational corporate capital.* University of Athens and Cambridge University.

Power, M., & Mohan, G. (2008). The geopolitics of China's engagement with African development. PDF online: https://www.open.ac.uk/socialsciences/bisa-africa/workshop/mohan_and_%20power.pdf

PPIAF. (2010). Annual Report.

Ramamurti, R. (2000). A multilevel model of privatization in emerging economies. *Academy of Management Review, 25*(3), 525–550.

Ramamurti, R. (2001). The obsolescing 'bargaining model'? MNC-host developing country relations revisited. *Journal of International Business Studies, 32*(1), 23–39.

Ramamurti, R. (2003). Can governments make credible promises? Insights from infrastructure projects in emerging economies. *Journal of International Management, 9*(3), 253–269.

Ramamurti, R. (2004). Developing countries and MNEs: Extending and enriching the research agenda. *Journal of International Business Studies, 35*, 277–283.

Ramamurti, R. (2009). 13 What have we learned about emerging—market MNEs? *Emerging multinationals in emerging markets*, 399.

Ramamurti, R. (2012). Competing with emerging market multinationals. *Business Horizons, 55*(3), 241–249.

Ramamurti, R., & Doh, J. P. (2004). Rethinking foreign infrastructure investment in developing countries. *Journal of World Business., 39*(2), 151–167.

Ramamurti, R., & Singh, J. V. (2009). *Emerging multinationals in emerging markets*. Cambridge University Press.

Rock, M. T., & Bonnett, H. (2004). The comparative politics of corruption: accounting for the East Asian paradox in empirical studies of corruption, growth and investment. *World Development, 32*(6), 999–1017.

Rodriguez, P., Siegel, D. S., Hillman, A., & Eden, L. (2006). Three lenses on the multinational enterprise: Politics, corruption, and corporate social responsibility. *Journal of International Business Studies, 37*, 733–746.

Rugman, A., & Li, J. (2007). Will China's multinationals succeed globally or regionally? *European Management Journal, 25*(5), 333–343.

Rugman, A. M. (1981). *Inside the multinationals: The economics of internal markets*. Columbia Press.

Rugman, A. M. (2007). Theoretical aspects of multinational enterprises from emerging economies, with particular reference to China.

Rugman, A. M. (2010). Reconciling internalization theory and the eclectic paradigm. *Multinational Business Review, 18*(2), 1–12.

Rugman, A. M., & Verbeke, A. (1998). Corporate strategies and environmental regulations: An organizing framework. *Strategic Management Journal, 19*(4), 363–375.

Rugman, A. M., & Verbeke, A. (2002). Edith Penrose's contribution to the resource-based view of strategic management. *Strategic Management Journal, 23*(8), 769–780.

Rugman, A. M., & Verbeke, A. (2003). Extending the theory of the multinational enterprise: Internalization and strategic management perspectives. *Journal of International Business Studies, 34*(2), 125–137.

Rugman, A. M., Verbeke, A., & Nguyen, Q. T. K. (2011). Fifty years of international business theory and beyond. *Management International Review, 51*, 755–786.

Rui, H., & Yip, G. S. (2008). Foreign acquisitions by Chinese firms: A strategic intent perspective. *Journal of world business, 43*(2), 213–226.

Sader, F. (2000). *Attracting foreign direct investment into infrastructure: Why is it so difficult?* (Vol. 12). World Bank Publications.
Sally, R. (1994). Multinational enterprises, political economy and institutional theory: Domestic embeddedness in the context of internationalization. *Review of International Political Economy, 1*(1), 161–192.
Sally, R. (2013). Multinational enterprises, political economy and institutional theory: Domestic embeddedness in the context of internationalisation. *Review of International Political Economy, 1*(1), 161–192.
Sawant, R. (2009). The economics of large-scale infrastructure FDI: The case of project finance. *Journal of International Business Studies, 41*, 1036–1055.
Schmitt, G. (2007). Is Africa Turning East? China's new engagement in Africa and its implications for Africa's development perspectives. *Africa Regional Consultative Conference of the Donor Committee for Enterprise Development.*
Sebastian, R. (2008, September 17). China-Africa Investments: An Analysis of China's Investments in Africa. *China Vest*, 1–7.
Sinkovics, R., Penz, E., & Ghauri, P. (2008). Enhancing the trustworthiness of qualitative research in international business. *Management International Review, 6*, 689–714.
Stellenbosch University Centre for Chinese Studies. (2006). *China's interest and activity in Africa's construction and infrastructure sector.* Stellenbosch University Press.
Stopford, J. M., Strange, S., Henley, J. S., & Henley, J. S. (1991). *Rival states, rival firms: Competition for world market shares* (No. 18). Cambridge University Press.
Structural Vulnerability, Imperfect Contracts, and "Political Risk" in Natural-Resource and Private-Infrastructure Projects. Institute for International Economics, pp. 141–150. http://www.iie.com
Sun, P., Mellahi, K., & Thun, E. (2010). The dynamic value of MNE political embeddedness: The case of the Chinese automobile industry. *Journal of International Business Studies, 41*(7), 1161–1182.
Sun, J., Wang, S. L., & Luo, Y. (2018). Strategic entry or strategic exit? International presence by emerging economies enterprises. *International Business Review, 27*(2), 418–430.
Tang, Y., & Pearce, R. D. (2011). The political economy of infrastructure multinationals: The case of Chinese investment in Africa. In R. Pearce (Ed.), *China and the multinationals—International business and the entry of China into the global economy.* Edward Elgar.

Taylor, I. (2006). China's oil diplomacy in Africa. *International Affairs, 82*(5), 937–959.
Taylor, R. (2002). Globalization strategies of Chinese companies: Current developments and future prospects. *Asian Business& Management, 1*, 209–225.
Tchamyou, V. S., Erreygers, G., & Cassimon, D. (2019). Inequality, ICT and financial access in Africa. *Technological Forecasting and Social Change, 139*, 169–184.
Tolentino, P. E. (2008). Explaining the competitiveness of Multinational Companies from developing economies: A critical review of the academic literature. *International Journal of Technology and Globalisation, 4*(1), 23–38.
Tulder, R. V. (2010). Toward a renewed stages theory for BRIC multinational enterprises? A home country bargaining approach. Chapter 4.
Tull, D. M. (2006). China's engagement in Africa: Scope, significance and consequences. *The Journal of Modern African Studies, 44*(3), 459–479.
UNCTAD. (2006). *World investment report: FDI from developing and transition economies: Implications for development.*
UNCTAD. (2008). *World investment report 2008: Transnational corporations, and the infrastructure challenge.*
UNCTAD. (2008). Measuring the Impacts of ICT for Development, avalible from https://unctad.org/system/files/official-document/dtlstict2011d1_en.pdf
UNCTAD. (2018). *World Investment Report: Investment and New Industrial Policies.*
Velde, D. W. T. (2010, March 17). *China in Africa: The new role of BRICs in LICs.* Overseas Development Institute.
Verbeek, M. (2004). *A Guide to Modern Econometrics* (2nd ed.). John Wiley & Son Ltd.
Vernon, R. (1971). *Sovereignty at bay* (pp. 44–59). Pelican.
Vernon, R. (1966). International investment and international trade in the product life cycle. *The Quarterly Journal of Economics, 80*(2), 190–207.
Voss, H., Buckley, P. J., & Cross, A. R. (2010). *The impact of home country institutional effects on the internationalization strategy of Chinese firms.* Multinational Business Review.
Wang, C., Hong, J., Kafouros, M., & Wright, M. (2012). Exploring the role of government involvement in outward FDI from emerging economies. *Journal of International Business Studies, 43*, 655–676.
Wang, J.Y. (2007). *What drives China's growing role in Africa?* IMF Working paper 211.

Wang, M. (2010). Empirical study on African energy resources and China's outflow foreign direct investment. *Allied Academies International Internet Conference, 12*, 148–153.
Wang, M. Y. (2002). The motivations behind China's government-initiated industrial investments overseas. *Pacific Affairs, 75*(2), 187–206.
Wang, Q., & Boateng, A. (2007). Cross-Border M&as by Chinese firms: An analysis of strategic motivation and performance. *International Management Review, 3*(4), 19–31.
Warner, M., Hong, N. S., & Xu, X. (2004). 'Late development' experience and the evolution of transnational firms in the People's republic of China. *Asia Pacific Business Review, 10*(3–4), 324–345.
Wei, G. (2007). Ownership structure, corporate governance and company performance in China. *Asia Pacific Business Review, 13*(4), 519–545.
Wei, Z. (2010). The literature on Chinese outward FDI. *Multinational Business Review, 18*(3), 73–112.
Wells, L. T., & Gleason, E. S. (1995, September/October). Is foreign infrastructure investment still risky? *Harvard Business Review*, 44–53.
Wheeler, D., & Mody, A. (1992). International investment location decision: The case of U.S. firms. *Journal of International Economics, 33*(1–2), 57–76.
Wild, L., & Mepham, D. (2006). The new Sinosphere: China in Africa. *The China Quarterly, 190*, 478–480.
Williamson, O. E. (1975). *Markets and hierarchies: Analysis and antitrust implications: A study of the economics of internal organizations*. Free Press.
Williamson, O. E. (1981). The economics of organization: The transaction cost approach. *The American Journal of Sociology, 87*, 548–577.
Williamson, P. J., Ramamurti, R., Fleury, A., & Fleury, M. T. L. (Eds.). (2013). *The competitive advantage of emerging market multinationals*. Cambridge University Press.
Wooldridge, J. M. (2010 [2002]). *Econometric analysis of cross section and panel data*. Cambridge, Mass: MIT Press.
World Bank. (2011). *World Bank Strategy Sector Information & Communication Technologies Approach Paper*, available from https://www.unapcict.org/resources/ictd-infobank/2011-world-bank-strategy-sector-information-communication-technologies-approach-paper
World Investment Report. (2006). *FDI from developing and transition economies: Implications for development*. UNCTAD.
World Investment Report. (2008). *Transnational corporations and the infrastructure challenge*. UNCTAD.

Wright, M., Filatotchev, I., Hoskisson, R., & Peng, M. W. (2005). Strategy research in emerging economies: Challenging the conventional wisdom. *Journal of Management Studies, 42*, 1–33.

Xi. (2013). *The statement of President Xi Jinping in his foreign debut tour after visiting three African countries: Tanzania, South Africa and the Republic of Congo.*

Yamin, M., & Sinkovics, R. R. (2009). Infrastructure or foreign direct investment? An examination of the implications of MNE strategy for economic development. *Journal of World Business, 44*, 144–157.

Yin, R. (1994/2009). *Case study research: Design and methods*. Sage Publications.

Yin, R. K. (1994). *Case study research design and methods: Applied social research and methods series* (2nd Ed.), Thousand Oaks, CA: Sage Publications.

Yin, R. K. (2009). *Case study research: Design and methods* (4th Ed.), Thousand Oaks, CA: Sage Publications.

Zaheer, S. (1995). Overcoming the liability of foreignness. *Academy of Management Journal, 38*(2), 341–363.

Zanfei, A. (2000). Transnational firms and the changing organisation of innovative activities. *Cambridge Journal of Economics, 24*(5), 515–542.

Zhan, J. X. (2009). *World investment report 2009: Transnational corporations, agricultural production and development*. Trade and Development Board.

Zhang, M., & Edwards, C. (2007). Diffusing 'best practice' in Chinese multinationals: The motivation, facilitation and limitations. *International Journal of Human Resource Management, 18*(12), 2147–2165.

Zhang, Z. (2011). Developing a mindset of corporate consciousness. *China Report*, 3. Access from China Africa. http://www.chinafrica.cn/english/china_report/txt/2011-01/02/content_322394.htm

Zheng, N., Wei, Y., Zhang, Y., & Yang, J. (2016). In search of strategic assets through cross-border merger and acquisitions: Evidence from Chinese multinational enterprises in developed economies. *International Business Review, 25*(1), 177–186.

Zhou, J., Xiao, S. Y., Cui, S. C., & Fang, G. (2010). Study on the impact of institutional environment in host countries on the outward FDI of China. *Melbourne: 2010 International Conference on Management Science & Engineering* (17th), 24–26 November.

Zhu, Y., Lynch, R., & Jin, Z. (2011). Playing the game of catching-up: Global strategybuilding in a Chinese company. *Asia Pacific Business Review, 17*(4), 511–533.

ZTE aims to be African Telecom market leader. (n.d.). 30/08/2006. Retrieved June 19, 2010, from http://wwwen.zte.com.cn/en/press_center/news/200405/t20040506_156176.html

Index[1]

[1] Note: Page numbers followed by 'n' refer to notes.

Y. Tang, *The Operations of Chinese Infrastructure Multinationals in Africa*,
https://doi.org/10.1007/978-981-16-2562-6

The manufacturer's authorised representative in the EU is Springer Nature Customer Service Centre GmbH, Europaplatz 3, 69115 Heidelberg, Germany. If you have any concerns regarding our products, please contact ProductSafety@springernature.com

Printed and bound by CPI Group (UK) Ltd, Croydon, CR0 4YY

30/09/2026

02225326-0009